ARIZONA'S
DARK
AND
BLOODY
GROUND

A band of sheep driven over the rim
of the Mogollons started the trouble.

Arizona's Dark and Bloody Ground

Earle R. Forrest

Introduction by William MacLeod Raine

THE UNIVERSITY OF ARIZONA PRESS
Tucson, Arizona

ABOUT THE AUTHOR

Earle R. Forrest (1883–1969) was an Arizona range-rider in the early 1900s and later worked on cattle spreads in Colorado and Montana. Forrest later worked as a photographer in Arizona and New Mexico, and he was the first to photograph the Shiprock Navajo. In 1914 he turned his attention to writing, producing newspaper and magazine columns and several books on American history.

Copyright © 1950 and 1979
The Caxton Printers, Ltd.
All Rights Reserved

THE UNIVERSITY OF ARIZONA PRESS
First Printing 1984
Manufactured in the U.S.A.

Published by arrangement with
The Caxton Printers, Ltd., Caldwell, Idaho.

Library of Congress Cataloging in Publication Data

Forrest, Earle Robert, 1883–
Arizona's dark and bloody ground.

Reprint. Originally published: Caldwell, Idaho:
Caxton Printers, 1950.
Bibliography: p.
Includes index.
1. Graham-Tewksbury Feud.   I. Title.
HV6452.A7G7   1984   979.1   84-124

ISBN 0-8165-0853-4

To
MY OLD COMRADES
of the Arizona cattle range
of long ago.

PREFACE

BY EARLE R.
FORREST THE PLEASANT VALLEY
vendetta t h a t swept
through the Tonto Ba-
sin country in central Arizona during the latter
1880's was one of the most sanguinary and
bitter range feuds the old West ever knew.
Its ferocity and hatreds were rivaled only by
the bloody battles and assassinations of the
Lincoln County war in New Mexico ten years
before, but it is doubtful, even with all its
terrorism, if the number of killed there equaled
the casualties in Pleasant Valley. Both were
born of blood feuds, and both were fought
in defiance of the law of the land until they
burned themselves out after most of the participants had either been killed or had grown weary
of strife. Even the well-known Hatfield-McCoy
feud that held the West Virginia and Kentucky
mountains under a reign of terror for almost
twenty years did not surpass the lifelong
hatreds born of the Pleasant Valley war.

It is a singular fact that in all three of these
vendettas, in such widely separated localities,
officers of the law were unable to stop bloodshed.
Echoes of the fighting in Lincoln County reached
President Hayes at Washington, but, in spite of
the fact that he appointed General Lew Wallace

Governor of New Mexico for the special purpose of restoring order, the law was powerless. Even after a personal interview with Billy the Kid and a promise of pardon, Governor Wallace failed. Sheriff William Mulvenon, of Yavapai County, assisted by Sheriff Commodore Owens, of Apache County, invaded Pleasant Valley on two occasions, but he, too, failed, and the fighting went on until peace was brought about only after the blood feud had burned itself out to the last man. The hatreds were too bitter for any other course.

The principal actors in the tragedy of Pleasant Valley have all gone over the last trail. Jim Roberts, the last fighting man of either side, died January 8, 1934, at Clarkdale, Arizona, hale and hearty and active to the very last in spite of his seventy-five years. John W. Weatherford, the last survivor of Sheriff Mulvenon's posses, was sick and bedfast in Phoenix when last I heard from him in 1932; and still living at Crown King, Arizona, is Walter Tewksbury,[1] younger half brother of the fighting Tewksburys, but he was only a child in 1887 and took no active part in the feuding.

Authentic information has been very difficult to obtain, for the dreaded hand of the feud still

---

[1]Died May 21, 1945, at the Pioneer's Home at Prescott, Arizona, at the age of sixty-five years.

reaches down across nearly half a century and seals the lips of most of those who might tell its bitter, sanguinary story. To this day it is an unpardonable sin in central Arizona to "talk too much," even more so than a quarter of a century ago; and many persons who took no part but are acquainted with the facts and gave me valuable information requested that their names be withheld, for personal and business reasons. The complete story of Pleasant Valley will never be told. Two writers have heretofore attempted short accounts, but they were only able to give fragmentary versions, pieced together from range legends.

I have made careful investigations as far as possible of every incident related here, and I am satisfied that each has some basis of truth at least. It has been very difficult to verify every story of the vendetta, impossible in some cases, and this work has required years of patient effort. Although all who took active part are dead, there are among the old-timers still living in Arizona some who recall vividly those days when men rode the trails of the Pleasant Valley country with a watchful eye and hands on their guns, expecting any instant to feel the venomous sting of lead in their vitals; and this account of those sanguinary days will undoubtly be subjected to many criticisms from those same old-

timers. The truth of many of my statements
will be honestly questioned; but that I fully expect. It has been very hard to sift out truth
from fiction, for very few of those engaged in
this feud could forget its bitterness and hatreds, even with the passing of years. For most
of the important incidents I have documentary
evidence in the form of old court records and
newspaper accounts published during the war,
and in letters from old friends and others who
lived during those times. Other versions related
are based on personal interviews.

PREFACE

Since the first edition
was published, in 1936,
I have received many
letters from residents
of Arizona and other
states who had knowledge of the events related
or who knew the scenes in later years. Therefore, some changes were necessary in the second
edition to make this account as nearly accurate
as possible. With the passing of time some locations where events took place have been lost, and
there is some dispute, even in Arizona today as to
where this or that occurred. However that is not
so very important; but the fact that such an
event did take place is of importance to the
history of the Pleasant Valley war. I have made
corrections as far as possible, but errors will still
be found.

The original narrative has been preserved,
and the reader should remember that what he is
reading is as it was written years ago, and, therefore, refers to that time (at least prior to 1936)
in placing locations, and to persons as still living
as they were, then, when the book was first published. Most of them have since died.

For later information I am indebted to the
following: E. D. Tussy, Phoenix, Arizona; Miss

Ruth Blevins, Phoenix; Alva L. Weaver, Secretary of the Arizona State Prison, Florence, Arizona; Walter Hofman, chairman of the Board of Pardons and Paroles, Phoenix; Mrs. M. I. Gallagher, Sacramento, California; Miss Ola Young, Young, Arizona; Ralph Hubert, Mesa, Arizona; A. L. Ozanne, Phoenix; Arthur H. Burt, Hyde Park, Massachusetts, a cousin of James Stott; E. Arthur Allen, Pasadena, California; Stephen C. Pool, Rochester, New York; James Peterson, Mesa, Arizona; and to my friend of many years, Leslie E. Gregory, old-time newspaper man, who died at Globe, November 29, 1946, I am deeply indebted for many favors and much information over a long period of years.

Earle R. Forrest.

CONTENTS

14 CONTENTS

LIST OF ILLUSTRATIONS

INTRODUCTION

BY WILLIAM
MACLEOD
RAINE

No FEUD in the history of the West has been more dramatic, more ruthless, more tragic than the one known as the Pleasant Valley war. It raged with such savage intensity that almost every principal was killed. No settler could remain in the Tonto Basin during those days without taking sides. A man had to be for the Grahams or against them. He had to be a partisan of the Tewksburys or their enemy. The only other course was to move out swiftly and inconspicuously.

Major Frederick R. Burnham in his *Scouting on Two Continents* tells how he was dragged into the orbit of the feud, though he was only a boy and had nothing to do with it. He hid for many days before he could escape from the valley. So bitter was the feuding that Zane Grey, gathering material for his novel *To the Last Man*, three decades after the events, spent three summers under the rim of the Mogollons before he could unlock the lips of the old-timers.

The stark harsh facts were shrouded in the mists of mystery. Scores of unauthenticated rumors sprang up. Whispered gossip became accepted as truth. About the whole story there has always been a strange sense of unreality. With amazing patience, with tireless research Earle R. Forrest has separated fact from fiction, has made the Graham-Tewksbury feud a documented history. Only those who have investigated this vendetta can realize what a heroic task this must have been.

I speak with some authority, for I wrote more than thirty years ago the first magazine story of this feud that ever appeared in print. Even now I recall the fogs that drifted over the battlefields and obscured certainties. Never have I done a piece of work of which I was less sure. But Mr. Forrest has dug up a thousand facts from a hundred sources. He has found the old court records, read newspapers, consulted survivors, examined contemporary letters, authenticated numberless details. When he had finished his work, the story of the Pleasant Valley war stood on realities.

The story is a fascinating one. Even before Mr. Forrest rescued the truth from a mass of fiction, moments of sharp drama would emerge from the haze. One such I remember. The man who killed poor Billy Graham was telling me the story. He said:

"One day I was coming down from Holbrook and stopped at Hegler's. I says, 'I guess I'll get supper and stop awhile.' He says, 'Get supper but don't stop—the Grahams have been here, and I don't want no fight at the ranch.' I says, 'All right, I'll eat and go on.' I went up on a hill above the trail to the Graham ranch and picketed my horse and slept out till daylight. Then I got down on the trail behind a tree. I knew John Graham would come along, and I had a warrant for him and was going to get him. Instead of John Graham, Bill Graham come, and I didn't have a warrant for him because he was one of the younger ones. I stepped out, and Bill drew a gun on me. I tried to stop him. When I first see it was him, I tried to speak to him, but it was no use. As he pulled his gun I turned loose and shot him. His horse whirled, and I shot two-three times—knew it was the only thing to do, for he was pumping at me fast as he could pull the trigger. He went away and died in two days."

I can still see the cold hard eyes of the man who had killed, set in a leathery brown face. He was chewing tobacco, and he spoke evenly, in the voice of one telling about meeting a neighbor.

Mr. Forrest makes a thousand such moments stand out in his book. Not only is it a valid historical document, but it is an exciting story that will stir your blood.

WILLIAM MacLEOD RAINE

ARIZONA'S
DARK
AND
BLOODY
GROUND

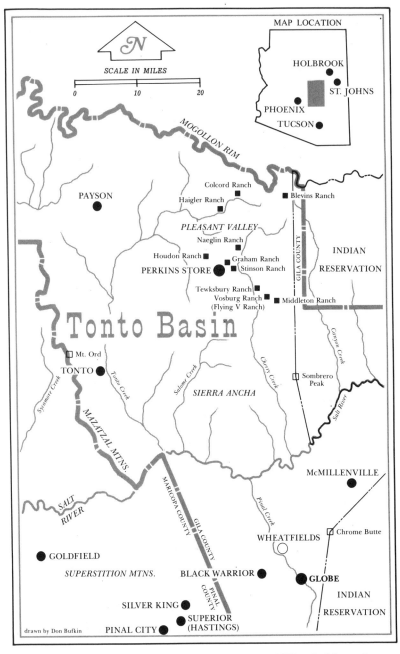

Map reprinted from *Globe, Arizona* by Clara T. Woody and Milton L. Schwartz by permission of the Arizona Historical Society.

CHAPTER I

THE STAGE   "THE TEWKSBURYS are
IS SET   driving sheep over the
rim of the Mogollons."
From mouth to mouth, from ranch to ranch
throughout all Pleasant Valley this message
was carried by dashing young cowboys in Paul
Revere style. The effect was like an electric
shock and more dangerous than a charge of
dynamite. For years the cattlemen of this little
valley in the wilderness of central Arizona had
successfully held their range against the encroachments of sheepmen from the north who
were only too eager to scatter their flocks over
the luxuriant grass of this beautiful land.

Hastily those cattlemen and their cowboys
saddled their horses and rode out to investigate.
Perhaps it was only a rumor after all; but with
their own eyes they could see them in the distance, like a great mass of maggots rolling down
over the trail from the rim and swarming out
over the valley at the foot of the Mogollons: like
a plague of locusts, greedily devouring the
grass, tearing it out by the roots; and already a
cloud of dust drifted up in the lazy morning air
from the desert they left behind.

The die was cast. The Tewksburys wanted
war. Well, they would get it; all they wanted

and more than they had bargained for. Those cattlemen had not wrested this range from the ferocious Apaches only to have it devastated and taken from them by these woolly, squirming, maggot-like creatures that every cattleman, cowboy, and even a rustler held in utmost contempt.

A bitterness that had been smouldering for several years between the Graham brothers and the Tewksburys was the real reason that those sheep were driven over the rim of the Mogollons. Every man in Pleasant Valley had known that some day this hatred would break out in open warfare; but they had never dreamed that the Tewksburys would dare invade the range with woollies. The Tewksburys had made many threats, and an alliance with northern sheep owners had been talked of for months; but the cattlemen of Pleasant Valley rested easy in the belief that this was only a threat to scare the Grahams. Now the menace was a reality. The sheep were here, hundreds of them, and more would follow. The feud had never reached the point of an open rupture; but now settlers who had no quarrel with either the Grahams or the Tewksburys must defend their range. The cattlemen must support the Grahams or desert their ranches. A bloody range war was imminent.

Pleasant Valley was the name given to that

locality by the first settlers who went there in
the early 1880's in defiance of the Apache menace; but around it hangs one of the most
sanguinary tales of the West of other days,
for this was the scene of the Graham-Tewksbury
feud, known as the Pleasant Valley war, which
swept through old Arizona's cattleland in the
latter 1880's until it burned itself out "to the
last man" in five short years, when only one of
the Tewksbury boys was left. Yet of all range
wars this is the least known today. For years
it has been shrouded in mystery. Those who
could relate its bloody incidents always refused
to talk; and it was only after the most persistent
efforts and through friends of the old Arizona
range that I finally secured the story.

Just how many men paid the price of blood
lust will never be definitely known. Old settlers
claim there were between thirty and fifty; but,
like all affairs of this kind, the number has
grown with the years, and it is doubtful if it
actually exceeded twenty-five. I have secured
the names of nineteen persons known to have
been killed, and possibly one or two more will
complete the list.

The Graham family was completely wiped
out, and of the six Blevins', father and five sons,
who fought with the cattlemen, only one survived the feud; but contrary to the general re-

port, John Tewksbury was the only member of that family killed, for Jim died a natural death after the war began, and John D. Tewksbury, Sr., the father, who took no part in the conflict, lived for several years after hostilities ceased. Edwin Tewksbury was the sole survivor of the three brothers and the "last man" of either the Graham or the Tewksbury families. This gave rise to the story that all were killed except him.

Five victims of the feud are buried in the little boot hill cemetery on the old Graham ranch, and the graves of two others, the only members of the Tewksbury faction known to have been killed, are near the site of the John D. Tewksbury house.

It is a strange coincidence that this land, which became soaked in the blood of its pioneers, should have been called Pleasant Valley; and stranger still that the name has stuck all these years. "The Valley of Death" would be more appropriate. Located in Gila County, beginning at the head of Cherry Creek under the rim of the Mogollons, it is entirely surrounded by mountains. Far away to the south the outlines of the historic Sierra Anchas, hiding place and stronghold of hostile Apaches in days long past, loom up high and clear on the skyline. Like a sentinel guarding an empire, McFadden Peak towers high above this mountain world; while other peaks and ranges dot the turquoise blue of the Arizona sky until all merge into one continuous chain around the valley from north to south and east to west.

With its tranquility, its wild, rugged beauty, and its vast, untrammeled distances, covered with that mystic, purple haze peculiar to the Southwest, this land fascinates the wilderness wanderer. Far removed from a railroad or the main lines of overland travel, this is one spot left in Arizona where the old-time life of cattle-land still survives, although greatly modified. Ranches are scattered over the valley, and much of the old range is fenced; but cattle still roam over the mountain slopes and hillsides, and it is still a land of cowboys, a wild land even today after white men have lived there for more than half a century. The hostile Indian has disappeared, but an occasional peaceful Apache from the White Mountain Reservation to the east wanders there as a reminder of the old days, not so very long ago, when he hunted the white man's scalp.

The Arizona of those days was the far frontier, where the last of the gunmen and fighters of the old West were making their stand against the civilization and law that was slowly but surely creeping across the desert lands west of the Pecos. They fought hard and died hard, those men of long ago; but before they passed out they made some history that is remembered to this day.

Pleasant Valley was the most remote section of the wild, lawless Arizona of other days. The nearest white settlement was a hundred miles away; the passes to the valley were few and easily guarded, and the arm of the law had not yet grown long enough to reach across the intervening mountains and deserts. Some of those early settlers were honest cattlemen, but many others went there for another reason, and the valley soon became a haven for cattle rustlers and men "wanted" by some sheriff in more civilized communities where folks had learned to frown upon the practice of branding other people's cows and horses or shooting the citizens without due regard for law and order.

Those first settlers were all cattlemen. Besides Jim Stinson and the Tewksburys there were William Middleton, Tom and John Graham, James F. Roberts, W. H. Bishop, George Blaine, William Richards, Houdon, and Mart Blevins and his five sons, one of whom went by the name of Andy Cooper for reasons that will be explained later. Others drifted in from year to year until the valley was fairly well settled, and several big cow outfits ranged in the surrounding territory when the war broke out in the summer of 1887.

Among those later men were Joseph Boyer, George A. Newton, Jacob Lauffer, George Wagner, William Jacobs, Al and Ed Rose, and the cowboys of the Aztec Land and Cattle Company, known as the Hash Knife, one of the most famous of old Arizona's cow outfits. Some of those Hash Knife punchers became involved in the feud, and found lonely graves in the Arizona wilderness.

According to some of the stories you will still hear in Arizona today, the Grahams and Tewksburys were originally from Texas, where they had been neighbors and friends.[1] This adds a fantastic touch to tales of the feud; but, unfortunately, for the romantic side of the picture, there is not a word of truth in the story. From information furnished by relatives[2] still living in the Middle West I can state positively that the Grahams never saw Texas, and it is very doubtful if any of the Tewksburys were ever in the Lone-Star State.

Tom and John Graham were born on a farm near Boone, Iowa, the sons of Samuel Graham by his first wife. William was their half brother and much younger. Some time in the 1870's the two elder brothers went to California; and John

Graham never saw his old home again, but in 1880 Tom returned for a short visit.

In 1882 they located in Pleasant Valley, Arizona.[3] Tom was the oldest, and because of the personal enmity that later developed between the Grahams and Tewksburys he became the acknowledged leader around whom the cattlemen rallied when sheep invaded the valley.

Tom Graham is pictured in fiction of the vendetta as the leader of the rustlers that swarmed through the mountains, a ruffian and killer of the worst type. Nothing could be further from the truth; for he was a quiet, peaceful man and honest in all his dealings. Even after the invasion of the sheep made war certain he refused to take human life; and his restraining hand held his followers in check until the first blood spilled by Tewksbury forces made further restraint impossible. But he has been held responsible all these years for the acts of others. My investigations have established to my own satisfaction at least that Andy Cooper was the leader in much of the lawlessness committed by the Graham fighters in the first stage of the war; and these acts undoubtedly contributed largely to the vendetta.

John D. Tewksbury, Sr., the father of the three brothers—Edwin, John, and James—was a native of Boston, who went to California at an

early date, probably during one of the gold
rushes of '49 or the early 1850's, and it is
doubtful if he ever saw Texas, for his trail to
the West Coast was by sailing vessel around
the Horn. After wandering about the gold
camps for some time he settled down in Humboldt County. White women were scarce in the
old West, and like many another pioneer of those
early gold rush days he supplied the deficiency
with an Indian squaw from the Eel River district,[4] who became the mother of the three sons
that figured so prominently in the Pleasant Valley war. Whether it was the lure of the squaw
that took John D. Tewksbury to the solitude of
the Humboldt County wilderness or whether it
was the loneliness of that wilderness that drove
him to seek companionship by becoming a squaw
man cannot be said today. Tradition tells us
that he married her, which was more than most
men of that period did in their relations with
Indian women.[5]

I have been unable to learn when or where
John D. Tewksbury's Indian wife died, but the
supposition is that it was in California; for
when he appeared at Globe, Arizona, about 1879
or 1880 with his three grown sons—John,
James, and Edwin[6]—their mother was dead. It
was at Globe[7] that he married his second wife,
a widow named Lydia Crigler Shultes, an Eng-

lishwoman with two husbands already to her credit. By her he had two sons,[8] Walter and Parker Tewksbury, both of whom were children during the trouble in Pleasant Valley in 1887 and who took no part in the war.

John Tewksbury, the only one of the brothers killed in the war and a son of the Indian squaw, married Mary Crigler, his stepmother's daughter by her first husband.

In pioneer times the ranches of Pleasant Valley were not grouped in the form of a settlement. James Stinson, one of the first of the cattlemen who discovered the rich pasture lands of the Tonto Basin country, was in the vanguard of civilization all his life, and from the first to the last he helped to carve trails over the fading frontier for pioneers to follow. He had first located at Snowflake in the Apache country to the east of Pleasant Valley; but about 1880 he sold his holdings there to the Mormons for twelve hundred head of cattle for money in those remote sections of old Arizona was almost unknown and livestock often passed as legal tender.[9]

Cattle must eat, and so this hardy frontiersman set out in search of a range. This was an easy matter in those days, and in a beautiful valley nestled under the rim of the Mogollons he found the virgin bunch grass growing higher than a horse's knees, with only the deer and antelope to graze it off. That was good enough for Jim Stinson, and he established a home ranch on Cherry Creek not far from the spot where Tom and John Graham built their cabin and corrals two years later when they founded the historic Graham ranch of bloody memory.

John D. Tewksbury was himself a pioneer who had lived so many years beyond the edge of civilization in California that he sought a land beyond the border line as soon as he reached Arizona, and it is quite probable that he had located in Pleasant Valley with his three half-breed sons and the prospect of a growing family by his second wife before the dust of Jim Stinson's herd appeared over the mountains from Snowflake. The Apache menace to life and property in old Arizona, ever present and close at hand in Pleasant Valley in those days, held no terrors for old John Tewksbury. For thirty years he had been on intimate terms with sudden death as it came to a man daring enough to wander beyond the protection of the settlements of the early West. His three sons of that Indian mother were wilderness bred; they could smell danger where other men detected nothing, and in the deadly use of both rifle and six-shooter they were without peers. It is little wonder, therefore, that old John Tewksbury felt perfectly able to take care of himself and any wandering Apaches who might dispute his right to a home in Pleasant Valley.

Globe, a booming silver and copper camp of only four years, was the gateway to Pleasant Valley eighty miles away across the most rugged mountains in all central Arizona. The fame of this new camp had lured old John Tewksbury and his three sons, for it was the center of a district rich in precious metals. The "Stonewall Jackson," the mines of the Richmond Basin, the "Silver Nugget," and the "Pioneer" were the big strikes that had attracted mining men from every corner of Arizona, and even California sent its quota of prospectors.

It was in the summer of 1882 that Tom and John Graham arrived in Globe from California, as shown by the first letter received from them by their father back in Iowa. That they did not remain in the new camp long is shown by another letter received from them that same year, telling the folks at home that they had located a ranch in beautiful Pleasant Valley. Whether they went to work there for Jim Stinson, as some claim, cannot be stated definitely; but I am inclined to doubt this, for they built a cabin[10] on Cherry Creek not far from Stinson's ranch, and were probably employed by him afterwards.

On the north side of Cherry Creek, ten miles southeast of the Grahams', was the Tewksbury home, a cabin in the Arizona wilderness, where old John lived with the three sons of that Indian mother and his new wife, at peace with his neighbors and all the world. Once more he was beyond the rim of civilization, where a man had plenty of room to stretch his elbows without punching someone in the ribs. His few head of cattle grazed unmolested over the hills, and when he needed fresh meat he could shoot a deer or an antelope almost from his cabin door. Of bacon and hams he secured a plentiful supply from the half-wild hogs that he had brought into the valley when he first settled there. After all his years of wandering old John Tewksbury wanted nothing more. He was perfectly satisfied with life. What more could any man want? But that was before the grim hand of the vendetta had closed over the land; and today the most grue-some memory of the feud clings around that peaceful wilderness home of sixty-five years gone.

Al and Ed Rose, active Graham partisans, lived near the ranch and within sight of Per-kins' store, where Charley Blevins and John Graham were killed by Sheriff Mulvenon's men. At the Spring Creek crossing of the Jump-off Trail, nine miles southwest of Pleasant Valley, was the Houdon ranch, one of the first in all that section; and it was there that Al Rose was killed from ambush. Ten miles north of Tewksbury's was the old Middleton ranch, the scene of the first pitched battle, and near by was George Newton's place.

Forty miles away on the rim of the Mogollons was the Long Tom ranch of the Esperanza Cattle Company, owned by Will C. Barnes, for many years a deputy forester of the United States Forest Service at Washington, D.C. Mr. Barnes was one of the pioneer cattlemen of the Mogollon Mountains; and while he was personally acquainted with members of both factions, his ranch was so far from the scene of the trouble that neither he nor his men became involved. But at Bear Spring, only a short distance away, was the log cabin of Jim Stott who, with Jim Scott and Billy Wilson, was lynched by a mob believed to have been composed of men friendly to the Tewksbury cause.

George A. Newton, a Tewksbury partisan whose disappearance after the fighting was over created much excitement, was a jeweler at Globe who had embarked in the cattle business in the early days of Pleasant Valley, and, in partnership with a man named Vosberg, owned a ranch below Middleton's. This outfit was known as the Flying V after its brand. When hostilities between the two factions suddenly blazed out in open warfare during the summer of 1887, the

John Graham

The Old Graham Ranch

Middleton ranch was the property of George Wilson,[11] Newton's young brother-in-law.

Mart Blevins and his five sons—John, Charles, Hampton, Sam, and Andy—all cattlemen in a small way, drifted to the Graham standard as a matter of course. It was the disappearance of Mart Blevins that finally brought the vendetta to a head. Others who fought against the Tewksburys were either cowboys on the various ranches in the Tonto Basin country or rustlers, and little is known of them.

Andy Blevins, known on the old Arizona range as Andy Cooper[12] for the very good reason that a sheriff back in Texas was anxious to meet him, was the son of Mart Blevins by a former marriage. In the language of the old Southwest he was known as a "short trigger man." In other words he was a general all-around bad man, and the most dangerous of all the Graham fighters; a man to be feared; for added to his ability to draw quickly and shoot straight was a cruel nature that made him as deadly and treacherous a killer as ever set foot in old Arizona. At an earlier date he had engaged in the profitable but dangerous business of peddling whisky to the red men in Indian Territory until government agents learned of his activities, and the vigilance of troops made this occupation too hazardous for a man's liberty. Finally, when a

Texas sheriff noted for a quick gun hand set out on Andy's trail for a murder committed in the Lone-Star State, he fled to faraway Arizona frontier, which in the 1880's was a haven for killers and outlaws wanted by the law east of the Pecos. At his father's ranch on Canyon Creek he gathered a band of kindred spirits and became the leader of the rustlers operating in Pleasant Valley and the Mogollon Mountains.

Few of the old-timers remember Mart Blevins' given name, for he was known as "Old Man" Blevins shortly after he settled in Arizona, to distinguish him as the father of the younger generation. His ranch on Canyon Creek was well located for any nefarious operations that his sons might attempt; for it was in a wild, remote section near the western boundary of the White Mountain Apache Indian Reservation and some distance below the Ramer place.

The Aztec Land and Cattle Company, better known as the Hash Knife outfit because of the shape of its brand, was organized about 1883 or 1884 and became one of the most famous of the cow outfits of old Arizona. The headquarters were on the Little Colorado River, opposite the Mormon settlement of Saint Joseph, just west of Holbrook; but its sixty thousand head of cattle ranged far south into Tonto Basin. John T. Jones was the first foreman; but J. E. Simpson

held this position during the trouble in Pleasant
Valley in the summer of 1887. Henry Kinsley,
a young man from the East who, in 1936, was
cashier of a Los Angeles bank, was secretary.
This was one of the largest cattle companies that
ever ranged the Southwest; and like many other
big outfits it was not a financial success.[13]

The company did not take an organized part
in the Pleasant Valley war; but its cowboys
were typical of old Arizona, all first-class cowhands who had drifted into that lonely land from
the four corners of the old West, but as wild and
lawless a bunch as ever rode for one brand. Always looking for trouble, they simply could not
keep out of a good fight, and they naturally
espoused the Graham cause against the invading
sheep.

Among the Hash Knife men who fought in the
war were Tom Pickett, Buck Lancaster, George
Smith, Tom Tucker, John Paine, Robert M. Glasspie, McNeal, Roxy, and Peck—all gun fighters who had drifted to the Arizona frontier
because of records in other sections.

An expert with a six-shooter, a two-gun man
and very dangerous, Tom Pickett had been a
member of Billy the Kid's gang of outlaws in
bloody Lincoln County, New Mexico, in 1880
and 1881. After the Kid was killed and his band
scattered, Pickett left New Mexico, and about

1884 or 1885 he appeared in Arizona, where he
worked for the Hash Knife, driving the chuck
wagon much of the time.[14]

The real names of Roxy and Peck, both killers
of the old frontier type, were never known by
their comrades. Where they came from before
they appeared on the Arizona range no one ever
knew; and when they left they vanished in the
land of forgotten men. There were others of
the same caliber in that old Hash Knife outfit,
but their names have been forgotten with the
passing years.

Several theories have been advanced as to the
cause of the Pleasant Valley war. One authority
claims that James Stinson tried to buy the
Tewksbury ranch and when he failed he hired
the Grahams to drive them out; but this is a mistake, for Stinson left the valley before the trouble started.[15] Somewhere back along the years
I was told by an old cowboy that a woman was
at the bottom of the whole affair; but this, like
many other stories, seems to be without foundation, for I am assured by those in a position to
know that no woman ever figured as a motive
of the feud. So many years have passed since I
heard this story that I have forgotten who
told it.

The real cause of the war is generally believed to have been a band of sheep driven over

the rim of the Mogollons by Daggs Brothers, of Flagstaff, and guarded by the Tewksburys. Even many of those drawn into the conflict later did not know the real motive back of all the bitterness which seems to have had its origin several years before. One old resident of the valley once told me that the feud started in a dispute over the division of stolen cattle. It is a well known fact that in the early days of Pleasant Valley the Graham and the Tewksbury boys were close friends, and, according to this man's story, they were engaged in cattle rustling together; but a quarrel over the division of the spoils brought about bitter feeling which grew from year to year. I cannot vouch for the truth of this, but the story is still told in Arizona.

The cattle-stealing charge was verified to some extent by the venerable James Stinson when he returned to the Salt River Valley on a visit in November, 1930, and in an interview which appeared in the *Arizona Republican*, of Phoenix, he made this statement: "It really was my cattle that started the Pleasant Valley feud. Old Man Church, the Tewksbury family, and two Canadians[16] named Graham were about the only whites in that section. My cattle began disappearing and pretty soon the Canadians and Tewksburys were fighting over them."[17]

The Grahams mentioned were undoubtedly

Tom and John, although William, a half brother
and the youngest of the trio, and Louis Parker,
a nephew of about his own age, went to Arizona
shortly after the others settled in Pleasant
Valley.[18]

The claim that rustling was at the bottom of
the personal enmity that years later developed
into a bloody feud is corroborated in a measure
by the territorial court records, which show that
countercharges of cattle stealing were made,
first against the Grahams and then against the
Tewksburys. The old court records at Saint
Johns, Apache County,[19] discloses the interesting
information that in 1882 and 1883 George and
William Graham, of Pleasant Valley, were
charged with larceny. None of the old-time residents of that section today ever heard of George
Graham,[20] and they are inclined to believe that
this was Tom. Witnesses failed to appear
against them when the case was called for trial,
and they were acquitted.

The next year the Grahams retaliated by
charging the Tewksbury brothers and several
of their friends with cattle stealing. This action
was brought in the territorial court at Prescott,
and on July 16, 1884, two indictments of grand
larceny were returned against Edwin, James,
and John Tewksbury, George Blaine, William
Richards, and W. H. Bishop. They were charged

with stealing ten head of cattle, valued at twenty dollars each, from Thomas H. Graham. The case was dismissed, but the bitterness remained.[21]

Prior to this the same defendants, on July 9, 1884, were acquitted at Prescott of stealing one hundred head of cattle from James Stinson.

The story that a woman was at the bottom of the blood feud may have some foundation after all;[22] for the theory that Tom and George Graham were the same person may well be doubted, in spite of the fact that the latter disappeared from the scene of action after he was acquitted in 1883, and no record of him is found during the bitter fighting in Pleasant Valley in 1887; but in 1888 he once more stepped onto the stage at Saint Johns in answer to another felony charged against him. A full account of this incident is given in another chapter. Alfred Ruiz, an attorney now living at Gallup, New Mexico, was clerk of the district court at Saint Johns in 1888, and he informs me that he well remembers George Graham on that occasion. Sam Brown, of Gallup, New Mexico; Hank Closson, of Ramah, New Mexico; and Fred Murray, of Grant, New Mexico, also recall this George Graham.[23] Mr. Closson says that George Graham and a man named Marion Bagley were rustlers. Bagley apparently took no part in the war, for

I have been unable to find any mention of his name elsewhere.

Mr. W. H. Roberts, of Clarkdale, Arizona, son of old Jim Roberts, a member of the Tewksbury faction, informs me that his father knew of this George Graham in Phoenix after the war closed, but he stated that he was not one of the Grahams in the feud.

After an investigation of Tom Graham's character I am satisfied that he was not guilty of rustling. His reputation for honesty among all who knew him intimately was beyond question; but it is probable that this George Graham was associated in some manner with Andy Cooper, or possibly the Tewksburys, in some questionable cattle dealing.

George Graham's disappearance gives some color to the old story that the love of a woman was the primary cause of all the trouble. This man, who made his debut in the Pleasant Valley drama when he appeared in court at Saint Johns and then vanished when he stepped from the stage after his acquittal in 1883, not to reappear until 1888, may have taken a Tewksbury woman with him, for I have learned that a sister of the Tewksbury brothers died in later years in the Salt River Valley. Whether she had any connection with the trouble is not known today. The theory that the court records confused the names

The Original Hash Knife Outfit

The Old Long Tom Ranch

of George and Tom can hardly be accepted as the logical explanation, for there is no similarity between the two. There must have been a George Graham.[24]

According to the Fish manuscript, the Graham and Tewksbury brothers were employed by ·Jim Stinson as cowboys; but instead of taking care of his cattle, they engaged together in rustling and placed their own brand upon their employer's stock. Fish says further that the affair was brought to a climax when one of the Grahams recorded the partnership brand in his individual name, and then refused to acknowledge the Tewksburys' claim to half ownership.[25]

In some support of this statement by Fish the old brand records at Prescott show that on March 25, 1884, Thomas and John Graham recorded the brand JT on the left hip, with a smooth crop off the left ear and a crop and half underbit on the right ear, as the earmark. On this same date Tom Graham also recorded a TE connected, with a smooth crop off the left ear and a crop and a slit in the right ear.[26] The fact that a band of sheep driven over the "dead line" of the Mogollons was only an incident and not a direct cause is also borne out by the statement made to me by George W. Tewksbury.[27] That Andy Cooper was the leader of the Pleasant Valley rustlers there can now be little doubt, but what connection he may have had with the Tewksburys, if any, I have been unable to learn.

For years the northern sheepmen had looked with greedy eyes upon the tall, luxuriant grass in the valley; but the rim of the Mogollons had always been a barrier beyond which sheep were not permitted. Cattlemen had discovered Pleasant Valley, and they were determined to keep its range for cattle. Attempts had been made to invade its sacred precincts with the woolly squirming, maggot-like hordes that they knew from bitter experience would sweep over the range like a plague, eating off the grass, stamping out the roots, and polluting the water until the land would become a barren waste unfit for man or beast; but honest cattlemen and rustlers had always buried their differences when this danger threatened and met their common foe together, shoulder to shoulder. This opposition had always been of such determined nature that no sheepman had ever had the courage to enter the valley by force; and so the rim of the Mogollons had become an established "dead line," south of which sheep were not allowed. With this prologue the stage was set for the bloody drama of Pleasant Valley when a band of sheep driven across the time-honored "dead line" precipitated the crisis.

CHAPTER II

THE ELDER Tewksbury's fiery temper mixed with the blood of his Indian wife was a dangerous heritage to hand down to his three half-breed sons, as later events proved. An Indian never forgets; an eye for an eye is his code of revenge—and honor; and either the charge of cattle stealing against the brothers at Prescott in 1884 or some other grievance not known today made a wound that never healed. Although they were neighbors they had nothing in common with the Grahams except that they were cattlemen, and they spoke only when necessary. They passed on the trail with a curt nod of the head; but they watched each other carefully, and no act of violence was attempted by either side. It was a case of armed neutrality by mutual consent, but the old wound in the Tewksbury pride was a slow, cancerous sore, festering from year to year until it eventually consumed them all.

The first blood was drawn by Ed Tewksbury, but strange to say the affair had nothing to do with the Grahams. One day in 1886, while John Gilliland, range foreman for Jim Stinson, was hunting for some saddle horses mysteriously missing for some time, he met Ed Tewksbury.

Stinson's cattle had been disappearing, and now these horses—this was too much for Gilliland. In relating the incident afterwards Tewksbury stated that they were both on foot; therefore it is safe to say that the meeting must have been near some ranch. The foreman hinted very broadly that Tewksbury knew something of the missing stock; the latter impatiently denied any knowledge of either the lost horses or cows.

Hot words followed until finally Gilliland, beside himself with rage, suddenly whipped out his six-shooter and fired at Tewksbury but missed him clean. A Tewksbury was never slow, and simultaneously with the roar of the gun, fire flashed from Ed's weapon, and a forty-five drilled a neat hole through the foreman's leg. The wound was not serious, for Tewksbury related that both then turned and ran.[1]

Daggs Brothers,[2] of Flagstaff, at that time the largest sheep owners in northern Arizona, had long had their eyes upon the rich bunch grass of Pleasant Valley for a winter range; but the "dead line" of the Mogollons had always been so well guarded that they were unable to break through. The northern range was overstocked with both sheep and cattle. The A One (A 1 Bar) cowboys of the Arizona Cattle Company[3] guarded the San Francisco Mountains and the surrounding range for miles in every direction

Fort Rickerson

Edwin Tewksbury

so jealously that the sheepmen were forced into the more barren locations. This was all right during the summer, but it was hard to winter sheep there on account of the heavy snows, and it was necessary to drive to a lower altitude.

The sheepmen simply had to find more range, especially for winter feeding, or reduce their herds. Pleasant Valley would make a splendid range for both winter and summer, and when Daggs Brothers heard of this old grudge between the Grahams and Tewksburys they decided that they could turn it to very good advantage in breaking the united ranks of the Pleasant Valley cattlemen, and open the country for sheep. Discord among the enemy was just what they desired, and one day in the late summer or early fall of 1886 the three Tewksburys—John, Jim, and Ed—with Bill Jacobs, might have been seen riding into Daggs' sheep camp in answer to a message. During the conference that followed Daggs Brothers offered a proposition that promised to make them all rich if successful, and at the same time the Tewksburys would make the Grahams pay for that old sore.

Daggses agreed to send a band of sheep into Pleasant Valley under the protection of Tewksbury guns, and for their services the three brothers and Bill Jacobs would receive a share of the profits. After the first herd was well established more would be sent in until the rich range would be well stocked with sheep. The promise that they might all be rich in a few years was no idle dream, for that was before the tariff was removed from wool.

It was a dangerous scheme at best, one that might wipe them all out if it failed, and no one knew that better than the Daggs Brothers; but if anyone in Arizona could carry it through to a successful conclusion those three half Indian brothers could turn the trick. Life in a wilderness that was a constant hazard had made them expert shots with both rifle and revolver, and their courage was beyond question; they were past masters of outdoor lore, and knew every trail and hiding place in the Tonto Basin country and the surrounding mountains. However, the hazards of such a plan made the Tewksburys hesitate, for none knew better than they the opposition that would follow an invasion of the valley with sheep; but wounded pride or a personal grievance is a terrible thing, especially among wilderness people, and that old sore still rankled. Finally, they agreed, and thus precipitated the most deadly of all Western feuds.

Having once decided, they were quick to act; but when the news reached Pleasant Valley that a band of sheep was being driven down upon them, the cattlemen could not believe that the "dead line" would actually be crossed, even though the Tewksbury brothers were acting as guards.

"It's only a bluff to scare Tom Graham," was the general opinion.

He had prospered during the few years he had spent in the valley, and the prediction was freely made that some day he would become one of Arizona's cattle kings. Popular with many of his neighbors and endowed with considerable executive ability, he was a natural leader of men, and his ranch was the headquarters of the cattlemen of the entire Tonto Basin country.

Each day brought the locustlike plague a little nearer the "dead line"; and one hot afternoon when a cowboy dashed down to the Graham ranch with the news that the sheep had actually been driven over the rims of the Mogollons that morning and were swarming down the trail into Pleasant Valley, the wrath of the cattlemen boiled over. If the Tewksburys had even dreamed of the terrible war "to the last man" that was to follow this invasion, it is possible that they would have hesitated. Even their friends were aghast, and made no move to aid them until drawn into the conflict by the blood feud that soon followed.

Honest cowmen and hardened rustlers who

preyed upon their herds, forgetting their differences in the face of this common enemy sweeping
down upon their range, rallied to the clan call.
It was a picturesque crowd, typical of the old
Arizona cow country, that gathered at the Graham ranch one day in the fall of 1886,[4] when the
news spread over the valley that the threat of
sheep had become a reality; cattlemen who had
traveled the Texas trails to the Kansas shipping
towns in their younger days—men who had
grown old at the business as they followed the
vanishing frontier westward in search of new
ranges, their faces wrinkled and tanned by long
years of blazing sun and wind and storms;
young cowboys full of the devil and ready for
any lark that promised excitement; and men
who had stepped beyond the rim of the law in
other lands—killers, rustlers, and bad men,
crafty, cruel and dangerous—such was the pop-
ulation found in every section of the old West
when civilization first came its way.

Their attire was picturesque in its simplicity,
yet lacking in the gaudiness of the professional
rodeo riders and movie cowboys of today. They
were dressed for business. Most of the older
men wore blue overalls with the well-known
"Levi Strauss" brand stamped on the waist-
band, some with the legs outside of their boots
and others with them stuffed inside as suited

their fancy. A few had vests or blue jumpers, and their wide-brimmed Stetsons, held on by a string under the chin, were of the rather high, square-crowned style, a relic of the Spaniards of an earlier day. They all wore high-heeled cowboy boots with the big roweled spurs introduced long years ago by the descendants of the conquistadores. Most of the younger riders were attired in well-worn leather chaps without the wide, hand-carved flaps down the outside legs which are so popular in the movies and rodeo; for those men of the long ago needed them for hard service. A flaming red bandanna or silk hankerchief knotted around a neck here and there added a touch of color. Their attire was completed with well-filled cartridge belts and heavy, long-barreled Colt forty-five six-shooters, while some carried Winchester carbines slung on their saddles; but the revolver was the weapon they depended upon for quick work.

It was the proud boast of those men that they could ride anything that "wore hair." They were past masters with the lariat; but it is doubtful if there was one in the crowd who could "spin a rope" or perform other fancy stunts so popular in the Wild West shows of a later period and on the movie screen today. They had no time for the "show stuff" that was of no practical use in range work; but there was not a man in the

crowd who could not "go over the withers" of a
wild steer or drop a loop over his horns at the
first throw, or "pitch" a rope from the ground
over the dodging head of a saddle horse in a
milling *remuda*.

This type of old-time cowboy has vanished
from the range; but such were the men who
gathered that day long ago at the Graham ranch
in Pleasant Valley. They were a wild lot, those
cowboys of old Arizona, quick on the trigger and
ready for any adventurous enterprise; but the
cool counsel of Tom Graham, their acknowledged leader, prevented a bloody battle taking
place immediately. Andy Cooper, the deadliest
killer of them all, insisted on wiping out the
sheep and every man with the band; but Tom
Graham, well knowing that such an act of lawlessness would precipitate a bloody range war,
refused to countenance such methods.

"There must be no killing and no destruction
of property," he ordered. "I want that understood from the start. We will try other methods,
but human life must not be taken."

"Yes, give 'em a hold in the valley, an' there
won't be enough left to feed a grasshopper by
spring," snarled Cooper. "I'm goin' to lead the
boys on a raid that will end it damned sudden."

"You stay right here," thundered Tom Graham. "The first man that leaves without my

permission will get no support from me. I wouldn't, Andy," he snapped as he saw the rustler's hand stealing towards his six-shooter.

Tom Graham was not a gunman; but no man ever questioned his courage, and the menace of his cold gray eyes was too much for the killer, who turned away without another word.

This policy was followed by the Graham leader until events beyond his control forced him into open warfare; but many of the outrages committed by others were charged against him. With a strong hand he held his wild henchmen in check as long as possible. Acting under the belief that a few well-placed bullets in the vicinity of the herders would serve as a sufficient warning to vacate, he tried this kind of moral persuasion. A shot out of the night, a bullet through a coffeepot or frying pan held by a herder over a campfire usually had the desired effect, and he would vanish like a scared rabbit. But in spite of such tactics the sheep remained; for the Daggses were as determined as the cattlemen, and the Tewksburys, held by their hatred for the Grahams, remained true.

When these warning shots failed of their purpose, new methods were adopted. Hash Knife riders, attracted by rumors of fighting, hastened into the valley, and the wilder element could no longer be held in check. Night riders stampeded the sheep over the bluffs into the creek and shot them down.

According to one story still told around camp-fires, three herders camped in a rocky gulch were surrounded and held under siege while a band of cowboys killed their sheep. That was before the first human life had been sacrificed, and when night came the herders were allowed to escape to the Tewksbury ranch with the news.

The cattlemen drew the first blood by killing a Navajo herder early in February, 1887.[5] There is no doubt that this was a deliberate murder, for several bullet wounds were found in his body. A few days before this occurred, a shot was fired at the herder from ambush; but this Indian was the son of a fighting tribe, and he returned the fire with such good effect that his assailant hastily retreated.

The sheep were driven out of the valley during that spring of 1887 without further casualties, and hostilities ceased for the time being; but whether the trouble would have ended there, had other events not occurred, is a matter of grave doubt, for the smouldering fire of vengeance that was bound to break out sooner or later burned beneath the surface. The death of the Indian herder was of little consequence to either side and would not have brought on hostilities after the sheep were driven out, for he was only

an Indian, after all, and could be easily replaced; but the killing of sheep was an entirely
different matter. That meant the loss of hard-
earned dollars for the Daggs Brothers, and the
Tewksburys smarted under something more
serious than the loss of money—the knowledge
that they had been defeated by their old enemies, the Grahams. And so we find a combina-
tion that was bound to bring about trouble in
Pleasant Valley.

The disappearance of Mart Blevins from his
ranch on Canyon Creek brought about a crisis.
It is told in Arizona to this day that Canyon
Creek Ranch was the headquarters of the Pleasant Valley rustlers, with Andy Cooper as the
leader. At any rate, Cooper was under indictment in Apache County at that time for cattle
stealing. As far as I have been able to learn,
Mart Blevins took no part in the sheep raids;
but his sons, as wild and reckless as any punchers on the Arizona range of the 1880's, joined
the cattlemen.

At this time Mrs. Amanda Gladden, who later
witnessed the fight between Sheriff Commodore
Owens and the Blevins boys in Holbrook, was
living on a homestead near Canyon Creek Ranch,
where her husband had left her to support a
large family of children as best she could in that
wilderness. Mart Blevins kept a watchful eye

upon her, and one day, after the sheep driven into Pleasant Valley had precipitated trouble, he moved the entire family to his ranch, explaining to Mrs. Gladden that her homestead was no place for a woman to live alone with children during the range war that threatened the land.

Mart Blevins' fate is one of the mysteries of the Pleasant Valley war that the passing of more than sixty years has failed to solve. Sam Brown claims that he was killed at his ranch one morning just before breakfast by a band of Navajos hunting horses that had been stolen from the tribe near Holbrook. When the Indians found that the trail led directly to Canyon Creek Ranch they attacked the place killing Mart Blevins and a son, and wounding a cowboy named Tucker. But all of the Blevins boys have been accounted for in other affairs, as will appear later on, and Tucker was wounded in the fight at Middleton's.

That old-time Arizona cattleman, Will C. Barnes, informs me that the story of the Navajo raid is a mistake. He stated that "Old Man" Blevins disappeared from his ranch and that his fate was never known. This statement corroborates the facts that are generally accepted today.

The story afterwards told by Mrs. Gladden is undoubtly the correct version. She stated that shortly after she went to the Blevins ranch a number of horses disappeared, and Mart Blevins went in search of them against the advice of his sons, never to be seen again after riding away from Canyon Creek Ranch that morning. As he was well armed it is possible that he was killed in a fight with the thieves. At least that is a logical conclusion.

Three years after his disappearance a skeleton with a spike driven through the skull was found not far from the ranch, and many believe that this was Mart Blevins; but time has never revealed the manner of his death. In 1894, J. F. Ketcherside, foreman of Vosberg's Flying V cattle ranch on Cherry Creek, found a human skull in a hollow tree on one of the upper tributaries of that stream.[6] Leaning against another tree was a rusty rifle that was identified as the property of Mart Blevins; but, although Ketcherside and his cowboys searched diligently, no other bones were found.

Shortly after their father's disappearance, the sons removed their mother, Mrs. Gladden, and Eva Blevins, the wife of one of the boys, to Holbrook, where they rented the small house where the two families were living at the time of the fatal fight on September 4.

CHAPTER III

WHEN NOTHING WAS
heard from Mart Blev-
ins, after the passing of
more than a week, his
friends were convinced that he had either been
murdered or had met with an accident; and on
August 10 four Hash Knife cowboys, with three
from the Graham ranch, started with Hampton
Blevins in search of him. At least that was the
story given out; but in view of later events it is
more than probable that they were also on another mission, and gave this as a reason to
deceive Tom Graham, for the leader of the cattlemen still restrained his men from any acts
of violence that might lead to loss of life. In
the party that accompanied Hampton Blevins
were John Paine, Tom Tucker, and Bob Glasspie, three Hash Knife cowboys, and Robert Carrington. The others joined them in Pleasant
Valley, but their names are not remembered.[1]

In corroboration of the theory that this party
was looking for trouble, Will C. Barnes[2] tells us
that one afternoon early in August, Blevins,
Tucker, Paine, and Glasspie rode into the Hash
Knife camp on Big Dry Lake, thirty miles south
of Holbrook, and announced their intentions of
going to Pleasant Valley in search of Mart Blev-

ins, and to "start a little war of our own." Ed
Rogers, the Hash Knife wagon boss, and Barnes
advised them to give up the scheme as it was
certain to lead to trouble at that time; but those
old-time punchers were always ready for a good
fight—and they got it. However, Rogers must
have been only half-hearted in his desire to prevent trouble; for as their foreman he had the
authority to order his men back to their posts.
Barnes had joined the Hash Knife outfit with
his wagon for the summer roundup.

That John Paine had been brought in by the
Hash Knife for the purpose of driving sheep off
the cattle range there is little doubt. He was a
"fighting Texan," who needed no incentive to
start trouble, and was generally able to take
care of himself. With his wife and three children he was stationed at Four Mile Spring[3] to
guard the water and adjacent range from the
encroachments of the "woollies." How well he
succeeded is shown by the fact that all the herders soon learned to give that locality a wide berth.

Details of the fight at Middleton's have been
gathered from several sources, principally from
versions told me by the survivors and by an old
man still living in Globe, who as a boy was present that day the cowboys stopped at the cabin.

According to the story told by Tucker and his
comrades, they reached the old Middleton ranch

about noon of August 10, and they decided to stop for dinner. The thought that they might not be welcome never entered their minds for an instant; for the unwritten laws of hospitality on the old-time cattle range were very strict in this respect, but had they known of the men concealed in that cabin watching their every movement, their course of action would have been very different. There was an ominous silence about the place as they rode up; but they had no thought of danger on that beautiful summer day when all the world seemed at peace, and they little dreamed that death rode by their side.

The spark that set off the explosion has never been definitely known, as each side placed the blame on the other. Tom Tucker, who seems to have been the leader of the cowboys, declared they were fired upon without the least provocation; but, on the other hand, Jim Tewksbury claimed that John Paine's attempt to draw was the signal for hostilities to begin. "Fighting" Jim Roberts, of the Tewksbury force, stated years later that Hampton Blevins started the fight by reaching for his gun.[4] As the battle lasted less than a minute, it would be impossible for participants or witnesses to relate the details exactly alike; and conflicting stories carried out of Pleasant Valley, which appeared in the various weekly newspapers published in the towns surrounding Tonto Basin, gave rise to varied accounts, some of which were told for years as the truth. But there is an old man still living in Globe who was at the Middleton ranch that day, and his story agrees in the main with the versions told later by some of the survivors after the bitterness of the feud had cooled down to some extent.

According to Tucker, the cowboys rode up to the fence around the cabin, and when Jim Tewksbury appeared in answer to their call they asked if they could get dinner. In view of the events of the past few weeks those punchers certainly must have known that they were taxing the laws of hospitality, even of the cattle range, to the limit to expect a Tewksbury to furnish them with a meal.[5]

"No, sir, we don't keep a hotel here," Jim replied civilly but curtly.

"Is Mr. Belknap here?" Tucker inquired.

"No, sir, he just rode off," Tewksbury replied.

"Well, boys, we'll go on down to Vosberg's and get some dinner," Tucker said to his companions as he wheeled his horse, and the entire party started away.

As soon as their backs were turned, according to Tucker, jets of flame and smoke suddenly spurted from the half-open doorway as a Winchester roared its defiance at the group of startled cowboys. Horses reared and jumped sideways from the shots, colliding with each other in wild confusion, and then galloped away before their riders recovered from the surprise of this unexpected attack.

Hampton Blevins swayed limply in his saddle as a bullet crashed through his brain, and then he pitched headlong to the ground where he lay motionless, a lifeless heap sprawled in the dust—the first white man who lost his life in the bloody Pleasant Valley war. Quick as lightning, John Paine fired at Jim Tewksbury; but the latter dodged behind the door a fraction of a second before the bullet sped through the opening and buried itself harmlessly in the opposite wall. The next instant, Paine's horse crashed down in the agony of death, pinning its rider's leg to the ground before he could throw himself clear of the unexpected fall. As the cowboy struggled to free himself a slug from Jim Robert's rifle, aimed at his brain, clipped off an ear[6] just as he jerked himself from beneath the body of the dying horse. With blood running down the side of his face and neck he started to run for shelter, but before he had taken half a dozen steps another bullet from that deadly rifle in Jim Tewksbury's hands cut him down; and he, too, lay sprawling in the dust beside Hamp-

PHOTOGRAPHER UNKNOWN: COLLECTION OF ARIZONA PIONEERS' HISTORICAL SOCIETY

Tom Tucker and Billy Wilson

A Roundup in Old Arizona

ton Blevins, the second victim of that deadly vendetta.

Tom Tucker was almost knocked from his saddle by a bullet through his lungs, and Glasspie and Carrington escaped with flesh wounds. At the first shots from the cabin two or three of the surprised cowboys drew their revolvers with lightning speed and returned the fire as they galloped away, followed by scattered shots. Those rifles in the cabin had been fired with deadly accuracy, for five of the eight horsemen had been hit.

The shooting was over within ten seconds after the first shot. Everything was in wild confusion; and the survivors, becoming separated in the general melee of plunging horses and falling men, galloped away in different directions. According to one story, Tucker fell from his horse and was dragged to a place of safety by a comrade; but nothing of this kind is told by the Globe man, the only known person now living who witnessed the fight.

With a Winchester bullet through his right lung, the wonder is that Tom Tucker survived the terrible exposure and ordeal through which he passed before reaching aid. The first reports from Pleasant Valley stated that he had died of his wound, and his subsequent recovery was really a miracle; but those men of old Arizona were hard to kill. The fact is that he clung desperately to his galloping horse until he slipped from the saddle, unconscious from loss of blood. How long he lay on the ground he never knew; but some time that night he was revived by a cold rain and hailstorm. Suffering tortures that would have killed a man of less iron nerve, he finally managed to drag himself, after many hours, to the cabin of Robert Sigsby.[7]

He was in a frightful condition. While he had lain unconscious under the hot sun flies had blown the wound, and maggots were already working when he reached help. Sigsby immediately applied such frontier remedies as he had at hand, which probably included axle grease and sheep dip, the cowboy cure for maggots in flyblown sores on cattle; and under his friend's care the wounded man gradually recovered. As soon as he was able to ride he quietly left Pleasant Valley. Tom Tucker had had enough of the feud.

Joe T. McKinney gives a version that he heard from both Bob Glasspie and Ed Tewksbury. The former's story is little different from the generally accepted version; but he declared that Tucker's horse fell with him. Ed Tewksbury corroborated this; but he stated that Tucker's horse fell on his gun, and the cowboy turned the animal over so that he could secure the weapon from the saddle scabbard. And while he was turning a wounded or dead horse over, seven Winchesters were spitting lead at him from the cabin.[8]

Bob Glasspie, with a bullet wound in the hip, remained in hiding until he left the valley with Tucker. This led to the report that he had been killed; but when Tucker later appeared at Big Dry Lake, where the Barnes and Hash Knife wagons were still camped, Glasspie was with him. They had either met at Sigsby's or on the trail out to safety. The next day both men set out for New Mexico. They had lost all interest in the vendetta. Years later Tucker served as an undersheriff at Santa Fe, and died in Texas at a ripe old age. Glasspie was still living in New Mexico when last heard from; but he has probably been dead for some time.

Tucker placed the blame for the shooting upon Jim Tewksbury. His statement that the cowboys were riding away when this unwarranted attack was made is partly corroborated by the man now living in Globe. Among the legends that have come down across more than sixty years of time is the story that Jim Tewksbury did practically all of the shooting; and this may well be true, for old-timers who knew him will tell you that his equal for quick, deadly work with a Winchester never lived, not even in old

Arizona where fast trigger fingers were the order of the day. This ability with a rifle, together
with his quick temper, made him a dangerous
man.

The Globe man was only a boy at the time,
but the tragedy was burned so vividly upon his
memory that the events are still clear to him
as they were that August day of 1887. This man,
a brother-in-law of one of the Tewksbury partisans, tells a story that gives an entirely different reason for the visit of Tucker and his men
to the Middleton ranch. According to his version, the cattlemen had previously ordered the
ranchers in that section of the valley, which was
Tewksbury territory, to leave the country by a
certain date, and the cowboys had gone to Middleton's that day for the purpose of driving out
those who had refused to obey the mandate.
This is the most logical explanation for the trouble. Cattlemen came and went, and were sometimes gone for days at a time; and Mart Blevins had not really been absent at that time long
enough to create any great uneasiness. Neither
is it reasonable to believe that Jim Tewksbury
would have fired upon such a large party without good cause. Therefore, the explanation that
Tucker and his men were there for the purpose
of driving the Tewksbury partisans out of the
valley is logical.

The Tewksburys were not made of the stuff

that caused them to run from any man, and events happened quickly when the cowboys went there to drive them out. The Globe man gives a vivid description of what followed:

"I'll say Tucker, Glasspie, and Carrington were getting out of there after Paine and Hank Blevins were killed. Tucker wheeled his horse when Blevins went to the ground with a bullet between his eyes. A second bullet from the same gun that got Blevins caught Tucker under an armpit, went through both lungs and out through the other armpit. That's how fast things happened. I happened to be there on the day they came to run everybody off, after giving the ranchers a certain time to leave the country. It was not my fight. I was speechless and could not move my feet while it was going on."

Thus the first white blood was spilled in the bitterest factional war the old West ever knew —a war marked by the intensity of its personal hatreds. Time has never revealed the names of all the men at the Middleton cabin that day; but when the story was told around chuck wagon campfires the credit for the most of the shooting was given to Jim and Ed Tewksbury. Years later, Jim Roberts stated that he and Joseph Boyer were there.[9]

The following account of the fight, taken from the Saint Johns, Arizona, *Herald* of August 18,

1887, contains several variations from the Globe man's story, and from the account now generally accepted as correct. No mention is made of either Jim Tewksbury or of any other man about the ranch, and the site of the fight is given as Newton's and then Tewksbury's. It is evident that this version came from the Graham side:

About a week since several cow boys, who had been in the employ of the Aztec Land and Cattle Company, left Holbrook, where the headquarters of the company are, and went south towards Tonto Basin to a place called Newton's ranch. While there they heard that an old ranchman named Blevans, living on Cañon Creek, had been missing for two or three weeks and the residents of the neighborhood suspected foul play. The boys went over to a ranchman named Graham and being joined by four men from that place, making eight in all, they went in search of the missing man. The next day they reached the residence of one of the Tewksbury's in Tonto Basin, and went up to the place to make some inquiries regarding the man they were in search of. A woman came to the door and stated that none of the men were in, and after a few words had passed, the eight horsemen turned to leave the place. They had scarcely begun to move away, when a volley was fired from the windows of the house. Two men fell dead from their saddles, John Paine and R. M. Gillespie, and a third, G. T. Tucker was shot through the body, the ball entering his left side. Three horses were also killed by the same volley. The men could not tell who their assailants were, and, as the enemy were completely protected the remaining six of the party could do nothing but ride away out of range of the deadly weapons, leaving the dead men and horses on the ground. They made their way to Graham's as rapidly as they could with the wounded man Tucker, but he died before they reached the ranch.

From information brought by a man who left Graham's ranch on Wednesday, a party had started from there to recover the dead bodies of Paine and Glasspie. To do so they would have to go within thirty yards of the house. No information of this expedition has been heard, but it is feared that further bloodshed may have ensued.

There are several errors in this account. In the first place, the fight was at the Middleton ranch; and Hampton Blevins was the other man killed instead of Glasspie, while Tucker survived his wounds many years. This account is given to show how many of the erroneous stories of the feud originated.

The Globe man is silent on the events that occurred at the Middleton ranch after the fight; but I have learned some of the details from Jim Roberts. After they were certain that the cowboys had retreated, Roberts and Joe Boyer went out to remove the bodies, but just as they reached the corral a party of between thirty and forty horsemen suddenly appeared on top of a hill. The distance was so great that the two men could not identify them; but they immediately came to the conclusion that they must be Graham fighters. The Tewksburys had not counted on this danger, and Roberts and Boyer ran for the cabin. An attack by such an overwhelming force would mean their ultimate destruction.

Anxiously the little group of men watched

from the shelter of the log walls as the unknown horsemen descended upon the ranch, well knowing that their lives hung in the balance; but as the strangers drew nearer, the anxious watchers recognized a band of Apache Indians stripped and painted for war. Every man gave an exclamation of relief, for they could repel Indians much easier than whites. With guns trained upon the advancing horsemen they waited with nerves tensed and trigger fingers ready, determined to give them such a warm reception at the first hostile action that they would leave as fast as their horses could carry them. Those men had fought Indians before, and they knew the value of such a surprise. Slowly the Apaches came on with no thought of danger until they beheld the two dead men. Instantly they halted to reconnoiter; and when they saw the threatening Winchesters protruding from between the logs and windows they wheeled their horses and fled swiftly back up the hill. And to quote Jim Roberts, "all you could see were G strings and horse tails." Well knowing that they now faced two dangers, one from the Apaches who would undoubtedly return as soon as they recovered from their panic, and the other from the Grahams when they learned of the fight, the Tewksbury men quickly saddled their horses and fled to the hills.

When a burial party under Charles Perkins and John Meadows reached the Middleton ranch a day or two later they found that the cabin and barn had been burned. The reason for this destruction of the buildings has never been known before; but the appearance of these Apaches undoubtedly explains it. The Indians evidently returned to attack the place, and when they found it deserted they applied the torch. Thus a mystery of more than forty years was solved by Jim Roberts.

Some people in Arizona will tell you that this fight took place at George Newton's ranch, sixty-five miles north of Globe. There is some reason for this story, for all of the old newspaper accounts published this statement. The old Middleton ranch was owned at that time by a young brother-in-law of George Newton, whose main ranch was not far distant, and in 1887 it was run by the latter in connection with his own place. That is the reason the Tewksbury men stopped there that day, as Newton, a cattleman, had been drawn into the feud for some unknown reason as a Tewksbury sympathizer.[10]

The Middleton ranch, one of the very first in Pleasant Valley, was settled in the latter 1870's by William Middleton,[11] who brought in the first herd of blooded cattle ever seen in that section of Arizona; and during the Apache wars his cabin was the scene of another bloody fight. On September 2, 1881, following the battle of Cibicu in which Colonel Carr's troops were defeated by the Indians, seven Apaches appeared at Middleton's and asked for food. At the ranch were William Middleton and his wife, Harry Middleton, their son, and a grown daughter with four children; and Henry Moody and George L. Turner, Jr. After they had eaten, the Indians suddenly opened fire, killing Moody and Turner and wounding Harry Middleton in the shoulder. The latter promptly shot one of his assailants, and made things so hot for the others that the rest of the family managed to reach the cabin without further loss. A grim battle with death followed; and in as heroic a defense as ever took place during all the Apache wars in the Southwest, William Middleton and his wounded son fought the red warriors off for three terrible hours. This was not the same Harry Middleton who was killed six years later in an early morning attack on the Tewksbury camp.

After the Indians finally gave up the siege and retired, William Middleton secured a horse that had been left behind by the raiders and rode for help, his family following on foot with only the wounded boy to guard them. Middleton returned the next morning with only one man, all the aid he had been able to find, and they set out for the nearest settlement. At Sombrero Butte they met a rescue party from Globe, guided by Eugene Middleton, another son, and led by Captain Burbridge.[12]

CHAPTER IV

THE SHOOTING of white men in the fight at Middleton's was a different matter from the killing of a Navajo sheepherder. He was only an Indian, of no importance to either side; but white blood could only be washed out with more blood, and from that day it was a life for a life. From a general sheep and cattle war the fighting during the next few weeks developed into a sanguinary vendetta between the Grahams and Tewksburys, in which all of the hatreds of long years of pent-up bitterness blazed forth with deadly ferocity. Every man in the valley was drawn into the conflict on one side or the other. No one dared remain neutral. Both sides hunted each other like wild animals. Quarter was neither asked nor given, and death skulked behind every tree and rock.

Stirring events followed in rapid succession after the killing at Middleton's. Stung by the death of Paine and Blevins, the cattlemen sent forth a battle cry that resounded to the farthest corners of Tonto Basin, and cowboys and rustlers alike rallied against a common enemy that threatened the destruction of the range. Pitched battles, ambuscades, and duels to the death were the order of the day.

The bodies of Paine and Blevins were buried by friends a day or two after the battle. This burial party, according to Will C. Barnes, was composed of Charles E. Perkins and John Meadows. They found the buildings in ashes, and no one knows positively to this day who burned them.[1] The funeral of these two young cowboys, who, in the words of an old frontier ballad, "got shot in the body," was without service of any kind. Perkins and Meadows were not familar with such rites, but they did the best they could. Perhaps it was better so. When Sheriff Mulvenon arrived with his posse a short time later, the spot where the cabin had stood was marked by a pile of ashes, and near by were two new graves.

According to one well-authenticated version, a party of cowboys who had gathered at the Graham ranch after the news of the battle spread over the valley, hastened to the Middleton place, and followed the trail of the fleeing Tewksbury forces to a well-fortified stronghold in the mountains. Finding the enemy so strongly intrenched that it would be impossible to dislodge them without loss of life, the cowboys decided upon the more prudent course of starving them out. Accordingly they left several men on guard while the remainder went for supplies and ammunition, determined to end the war by a prolonged siege, during which they could pick the enemy off when driven out by hunger and thirst.

There was one weak spot in the defense; the only source of water supply was from a spring covered by the guns of the besiegers. The beleagured sheepmen quickly exhausted the small quantity in their canteens, for the day was boiling hot, and before night came they were sucking pebbles. Water they must have, for they well knew that it would be suicide to surrender, and there was little chance of escaping alive by attempting to force the enemy's lines. Their stronghold was a death trap as well as a safe retreat.

Jim Tewksbury, the half-breed son of a California squaw, volunteered to go to the spring. It was a daring venture with the chances ten to one that he would stop some alert cowboy's bullet. But a Tewksbury never stopped to count the cost or chances of failure, and silent as his Indian ancestors, he crept slowly down the trail in the dead of night, with his brother Ed standing guard on a rock high above. So stealthy were his movements as he disappeared in the darkness that no sound came to the vigilant sentinel.

Reaching the spring safely, he filled the canteens with the precious water and slung them over his shoulders so that his hands would be free for quick work with the deadly Winchester. Then he started cautiously back. Nothing was heard from the enemy, and he was just congratulating himself upon the success of his venture when Ed shouted a warning of danger. Jim Tewksbury had learned what few men could master—even in that frontier day—the art of shooting backwards without turning around. Suddenly throwing his rifle over his shoulder, he fired and then darted up the trail like a deer. When he reached camp his brother informed him that his pursuer had fallen at the crack of his gun. It came out long afterwards that Jim's bullet had broken the cowboy's thigh, and he bled to death before his comrades dared to move him from under the deadly menace of the Tewksbury guns. Unfortunately, the name of this man is not known today. The cattlemen withdrew after the killing and left the sheepmen masters of the field.

Joe McKinney, on the trail of a horse thief, heard of the fight at the Middleton ranch when he stopped at Al Rose's cabin in Pleasant Valley. As soon as Rose learned that his visitor was an officer, he insisted that something should be done about the killing; but it was not McKinney's fight, and he refused to make an investigation. He cannot be censured for this, for Pleasant Valley was a very unpopular locality in those days for any man from the outside who attempted to interfere unless he had a posse at his back. After McKinney left Rose's he met seven men on their way to bury the dead cowboys.[2]

When news of this killing reached Prescott, Sheriff William Mulvenon, of Yavapai County, secured ten warrants for the arrest of the Tewksburys and other members of that faction, all charged with the murder of John Paine and Hampton Blevins, and he set out immediately for Pleasant Valley with a large posse. At whose instance these warrants were issued is not known today. The Grahams had their hands full with the trouble in the feud district, and it is probable that the sheriff himself secured them on information received.

Mulvenon was joined on August 23 by Deputy Sheriff John W. Francis, of Flagstaff, who had been summoned by wire, together with Constable E. F. Odell, John W. Weatherford, and Fletcher Fairchild, also from Flagstaff, at that time in Yavapai County.[3]

From Payson, Sheriff Mulvenon proceeded to Pleasant Valley with his deputies; but they found the Tewksbury ranches deserted and there was no trace of the men they were seeking.

At Perkins' store, which figured prominently in the war as a rendezvous for the cattlemen on account of its proximity to the Graham ranch, the officers met a party of Grahamites under the leadership of Andy Cooper. As the sheriff held no warrants for these men he did not molest them at that time; but they were spoiling for a fight, and Cooper told Mulvenon plainly that if he did not arrest the Tewksburys, the cattlemen intended to take matters into their own hands and wage a war of extermination.

After promising that the parties guilty of the killing of Paine and Blevins would be apprehended, the sheriff and his posse, accompanied by Cooper and his cowboys, set out in search of the men named in the warrants. The personnel of Cooper's band that day has been forgotten, but the Grahams do not appear to have been present, as the few survivors do not recall having seen them, and the old newspaper accounts contain no mention of them.

It is strange that the name of the Grahams do not appear as participants in the early battles, and one might well doubt if they took any active part at this stage of the game. Their ranch was the headquarters for the cattlemen, and Tom Graham was looked upon as the leader; but he was opposed to violence from the beginning of the trouble. Andy Cooper apparently usurped the leadership of the Graham forces at every opportunity.

After scouting for several hours, Mulvenon's men found the trail of a party of horsemen going directly north. This led both the sheriff and Cooper's cowboys to believe that it had been made by the Tewksburys on their way to Holbrook for provisions and ammunition, and the posse camped on the spot to intercept them when they returned.[4]

Before daybreak the next morning a stranger entered the camp and requested Sheriff Mulvenon and one deputy to return with him to a certain designated point to meet a man who was waiting for them, but he refused to disclose this party's name. Members of the posse were of the opinion that this was a trap; but the sheriff could not believe that the Tewksburys would openly attack the forces of law and order.

Mulvenon left immediately, taking one deputy as directed, but, unfortunately, his name has been forgotten. They found George A. Newton waiting at the meeting place. Newton's ranch was located ten miles away on the other side of Cherry Creek, near Middleton's. Between his place and the Graham territory were the Tewksbury ranches.

Just what took place at this meeting is not known; but members of the posse reported later that when the sheriff returned he was accompanied by Newton, and they all then proceeded to the latter's ranch which they found had been burned. This mistake in the name was probably due to the fact that these men were not acquainted with the various ranches in the valley, and they naturally supposed that Newton guided them to his own place. But the error has persisted all these years, and many people will still tell you that the first fight, in which Paine and Blevins were killed, was at Newton's.[5]

Death and desolation were apparent on every side. A lone hog and some chickens were the only living things found about this dreary, God-forsaken spot. Even the very air seemed charged with some mysterious force that the men could not account for, and their hands were held ready for a quick draw while they cast uneasy glances over the surrounding country as though expecting a charge from an unseen foe. A pile of ashes showed where the cabin had stood. Two dead horses were lying in front of the ruins; and near by two newly made graves, piled high with rocks to cheat the prowling coyotes out of a meal, marked the last resting places of Paine and Blevins. Some say that Newton's ranch was also burned; but there is no record of this, and the story may have originated from the fact that the posse found the Middleton cabin in ashes and reported it as Newton's.

Tracks of a large party of horsemen, made by either the Apaches or the Tewksbury men when they fled from the ranch, led the posse to the farther side of the valley. This trail plainly showed that two men had deployed on either side of the main body to guard against a surprise and protect the others from an attack on the flank. After following it until they were almost lost in a maze of canyons and ravines, the sheriff decided that further pursuit was not only useless but might endanger the lives of his men, and so he abandoned the hunt. When it was plainly evident that the Tewksburys had fled from the valley, Mulvenon returned to Prescott, while Deputy Francis and his men went on to Flagstaff. And thus the first invasion of Pleasant Valley by the forces of law and order resulted in a dismal failure.

John W. Weatherford informs me that in the early morning of the twelfth day after the posse reached the valley the Tewksburys sent a messenger to the camp with a request for the sheriff to accompany him. Mulvenon was gone about three hours and when he returned he ordered the posse back to town. He explained that the Tewksburys refused to surrender as long as the Grahams were in the valley for the reason that they were afraid that if they left first, the Grahams would murder their families and kill their stock; but they promised that if the sheriff would procure warrants and arrest their enemies, they would follow him into Prescott and surrender. Mr. Weatherford states further that after the subsequent arrest of the Grahams the Tewksburys kept their word. This did occur after the arrest of Al Rose and Miguel Apocada, following the killing of John Graham and Charles Blevins by Mulvenon's posse during his second invasion.

That the criminal action, growing out of the killing of Paine and Blevins, was instituted against the Tewksburys by Sheriff Mulvenon is shown by the old court records in Prescott. On August 14 criminal complaint was made before Justice of the Peace John Meadows, at Payson, against John Tewksbury, Sr., John Tewksbury, Ed Tewksbury, William Jacobs, and Joseph Boyer for the murder of John Paine and Hampton Blevins on the tenth.[6] This definitely establishes the date that Mulvenon was in Payson with his posse on his way to the valley; and the warrants issued by Justice Meadows were those carried by the sheriff on his first invasion. At the preliminary hearing late in September Justice Meadows held the defendants for the grand jury. The records show that the case was continued several times, but was finally dismissed because of insufficient evidence. Further details are lacking, for all persons connected with the case are now dead.

The charge against John D. Tewksbury, Sr., was not pressed. The old man was evidently not at the Middleton ranch the day of the killing, and, in fact, it has been definitely established that he did not take an active part in the war. Hearing of the warrant for his arrest, he went to Prescott on September 6 and voluntarily surrendered to Sheriff Mulvenon. The Prescott *Journal Miner* of September 7 states that he "was not held there being no charges or evidence against him." This would indicate that the charge was dismissed at the hearing before Justice Meadows.

However, the complaint against the others named in the warrants did not end with the dismissal of the information of August 14, and a new indictment was evidently drawn, for the old court records at Prescott show that on December 3, 1887, the grand jury in session indicted Edwin and James Tewksbury, Joseph Boyer, James Roberts, George Newton, Jacob Lauffer, and George Wagner for the murder of Hampton Blevins. The reason for omitting the killing of John Paine from the indictment is not known today.[7]

The prolonged absence of Sheriff Mulvenon and his posse, with no word from them, created the utmost alarm on the outside, and many wild rumors without any foundation whatever spread like wildfire. The condition of affairs at this time is graphically described by the *Coconino Sun* in the following:

The whole community of northern Arizona has been in a condition of agitation and suspense during the last few days on account of the rumors of the murder of Sheriff Mulvenon and several of his deputies including John W. Francis, J. W. Weatherford, and E. F. Odell, of Flagstaff, in Tonto Basin. Stories are told with the minuteness of detail that compel the most skeptical to believe the many terrible circumstances related must have some truth for their origin.

Things are in a fearful condition ·in the Basin. Since the two men Paine and Blevans were killed by the parties firing from their concealed position in Newton's ranch, William Graham was shot from ambush while riding the Payson trail and died the next day. Old man Blevans is also probably killed; he has been missing for a month, and no trace can be found of his body.

An amusing story of Mulvenon's first invasion was recently unearthed in the old files of *The Arizona Silver Belt*, of Globe. This account gives us the interesting information that the sheriff, who was anxious to cover the movements of his posse with the utmost secrecy, concealed his horses in the brush after their arrival in the valley, and then reconnoitered on foot. After scouting for some time without results, the deputies returned, only to find that during their absence their mounts had been stolen, and they were compelled to walk to the nearest ranch. This was charged against the Tewksburys.

If such an incident actually occurred, the animals were either found or returned, for the posse did considerable scouting on horseback before leaving the valley. No report of anything of this kind was made by Sheriff Mulvenon or the deputies from Flagstaff; but the joke was on them, and they would naturally want to keep the story as quiet as possible.

CHAPTER V

THE PASSING
OF BILLY
GRAHAM

AFTER THE departure of
Sheriff Mulvenon and
his posse hostilities
flared up again with all
the bloodthirsty ferocity that only a cruel vendetta knows. The law had failed to apprehend
the men guilty of the killing of Paine and Blevins, and with the support of the cattlemen Andy
Cooper prepared to carry out his threat to drive
the sheepmen and their sympathizers from the
valley. On account of his prominence and leadership the cattle forces again rallied around
Tom Graham, thus drawing him further into
the deadly hand of the feud.

The Graham forces, with as many as twenty
fighting men in the field at a time, swept
through the entire Tonto Basin country; and the
Tewksburys, with from four to six and never
more than eight men, were quickly driven to the
brush like hunted animals. In spite of their inferior numbers, this gave them an advantage
that they were not slow to seize. The blood of
their Indian mother and their life in the wilderness came to their aid in this crisis; for they
were masters of this primitive mode of warfare
as old as mankind, and from the hunted they
quickly became the hunters. Working alone and

in pairs, they stalked their enemies with the stealth of a panther, sending a shot out of the night or from the sagebrush on the hillsides as a challenge to the Graham battle cry.

The next victim claimed by the cruel hand of the vendetta was William Graham, youngest of the family, who was mortally wounded on August 17 by James D. Houck, a sheep owner who supported the Tewksburys for personal reasons and a man with a reputation as a gun fighter. I have been unable to find the exact date that Billy Graham went to Arizona, but from the fact that his name appears jointly with that of George Graham in the indictment at Saint Johns in 1882 and 1883, it must have been shortly after his half-brothers, Tom and John, located in Pleasant Valley. It is generally reported in Arizona that Billy Graham was only eighteen years of age when he was killed, but this is a mistake, for he was twenty-two.[1]

Billy Graham and his nephew Louis Parker[2] went to Arizona together—two red-blooded boys of the same age in search of adventure on the wild Southwestern frontier. One found a lonely, forgotten grave; the other remained with his uncles, fighting until the end of the feud, and then settled in New Mexico.

Billy was a happy-go-lucky youth who refused to take danger seriously. He had had no part

in the feud, and he knew no reason why anyone should bother him; but death had placed its
mark upon him because he was a Graham.
While at a dance at the old Central Hotel in
Phoenix, less than two weeks before his untimely
end, friends warned him to watch for the Tewksburys on his return to Pleasant Valley; but the
devil-may-care youth laughingly replied that the
sheepman's bullet had not been made that would
get him.

Jim Houck held an appointment from Sheriff
Commodore P. Owens, of Apache County, as a
deputy, and under the guise of an officer's badge
he entered the valley alone to fight for the
Tewksburys. There is no doubt of this now, although he claimed when he returned to Saint
Johns a month after the killing that he had a
warrant for the arrest of John Graham. If this
statement was true, then his warrant must have
been a dummy secured by him in his official
capacity in order to give him an excuse to prowl
around in the feud district, a land that most men,
except participants, carefully avoided, for the
court records at Saint Johns fail to show any
charge against John Graham.[3]

At any rate Houck was scouting in the valley
alone, and to further his purpose he remained in
hiding as much as possible, watching for a
chance to catch some Graham man off his guard.

On August 17 he stopped at the Haigler ranch for dinner. Haigler had remained neutral; but fearful of Graham wrath if a sheepman should be seen at his place, he begged Houck to leave at once, and after a hasty meal the deputy departed.

Several versions of the killing have been told, but from a mass of information I believe that the following account is as correct as is possible after the passing of so many years. Part of it is taken from Houck's own story, told after his return to Saint Johns, and the remainder from the statements of residents of the valley.

After leaving Haigler's, Houck selected an advantageous point on a hillside that commanded a good view of the trail from the Graham ranch to Payson, and concealed himself in the brush where he could watch without fear of detection. According to his own statement, he expected John Graham to pass that way; but the fact that he gave no reason for this leads to the conclusion that he was simply bushwhacking. How long he waited is not certain; but when he saw a lone horseman approaching he believed this was his man, and just as the rider was opposite his hiding place Houck ordered him to surrender. When the cowboy turned with drawn six-shooter ready for action, the deputy recognized Billy Graham.

Houck afterward claimed that he told him to go on as he did not have a warrant for the boy; but young Billy Graham came from a fighting breed, and he answered the command with a shot, which was instantly returned with fatal effect. Houck was taking no chances. The wounded youth swayed limply in the saddle and almost fell from his horse, but quickly recovered and dashed away to the Graham ranch three and a half miles distant, to die the next day of a wound from a sheepman's bullet. Just before he closed his eyes forever the boy whispered to his brother Tom, who was sitting on a box at the side of the bed, that he did not know why the Tewksburys wanted to kill him.[4] And so the youngest of the Grahams passed over the long trail.

According to Charles Perkins' version,[5] Joseph Ellenwood was riding with Billy Graham that day, some distance in the rear, and when he heard the exchange of shots he put spurs to his horse and galloped out of danger. An hour or two later he ventured back, to meet Billy crawling desperately along the trail. He helped the wounded youth to Haigler's ranch, where he nursed him for nearly two weeks before he died.

This is not correct. I have the story from reliable sources that the shooting took place at the point I have already described and that Billy's horse carried him to the Graham ranch.

Very little is known of Joe Ellenwood. Perkins claims that he was a foot-loose cowboy riding the chuck line.[6] I cannot agree with this, for Ellenwood remained at the Graham ranch after Billy's death, and was wounded in the same fight in which Harry Middleton was killed on September 17. He had a wife there, or at least Sheriff Mulvenon found a woman at the ranch who claimed to be Mrs. Ellenwood.[7]

Houck's own story of the shooting of Billy Graham, which he told when he reached Saint Johns over a month later, appeared in the *Herald*, of that place, on September 29, 1887:

Hon. J. D. Houck arrived in St. Johns last Monday night fresh from the bloody acts and scenes in the Tonto Basin, and from him we gather the following interesting account of the stirring events that have transpired in that hotbed of lawlessness since the fatal affray at Newton's ranch, where the first blood was shed.

About the 9th of August some of the Graham faction, who said they were hunting for old man Blevans, rode up to the house occupied by Newton, and inquired if anything had been seen of him, receiving "no" for an answer; they then asked for dinner, and on being refused, started to leave. As they turned their horses (so they claim), fire was opened upon them from within the house, and John Paine and Hank Blevans were killed. Tucker, Gillespie, and Bob Carrington were wounded.

On the 17th of August, Mr. Houck, who had been

compelled to keep in the brush for some time by the Grahams, saw a man whom he took to be John Graham, riding along the trail. He waited until the horseman was abreast of him, when he called, and the man looked up, at the same time drawing his pistol. Mr. Houck then discovered that it was Bill Graham, and told him to go on, that he did not want him. Instead of moving, however, he took a shot at Mr. Houck, which was returned by the latter with the fatal effect. Graham succeeded in reaching his home, but died the next day.

CHAPTER VI

THE KILLING OF JOHN
TEWKSBURY AND
WILLIAM
JACOBS

THE KILLING of the youngest member of the Graham family marked the turning point in the Pleasant Valley war. From a struggle between sheep and cattle interests for the possession of the range the fighting immediately became a personal vendetta between the Grahams and the Tewksburys; and a land already stained with the blood of its pioneers soon became a shambles. Tom Graham[1] might have passed over the killing of Paine and Blevins, and the forgotten cowboy; but his own brother, the baby of the family, was an entirely different matter. Graham blood called for Tewksbury blood in atonement; and the animosity between the clan leaders became so bitter and the fighting so fierce during the days that followed the death of young Billy Graham that many of the smaller cattlemen fled from the valley rather than become further involved in a range war that had now developed into a fierce feud to the last man.

The condition of affairs at this stage was graphically described in later years by J. W. Ellison, a resident of Pleasant Valley in the early days: "At first the Grahams had the sympathy of the settlers, all of whom owned cattle and appreciated the danger to their range from the incursion of locustlike wandering sheep bands. But the fighting soon became too warm for any save those immediately interested, for the factions hunted each other as wild beasts might have hunted."

But even in his rage there is nothing to show that Tom Graham took an unfair advantage of his enemies. Bloodshed was obnoxious to his nature; but after the death of his brother he was like an enraged lion, and he was determined to drive the Tewksburys from the country. But even then he gave strict orders to his men that all fighting must be fair. This turn of events suited Andy Cooper, who made plans of his own to wipe out the entire Tewksbury family from father to son at one decisive blow.

The members of the force that attacked the Tewksbury ranch are not positively known to-day; but it is certain that Andy Cooper took a very prominent part, as shown by his own statements, and it is equally certain that Tom Graham was present. From statements of persons still living who were in central Arizona at that time, it appears that Tom was in command, and his brother John was undoubtedly present.

The blow that was to wipe out the Tewksbury family and avenge the death of young Billy Graham as well as other comrades killed in the vendetta, was struck in the early morning of September 2; but the results were not what either the Grahams or Cooper had expected. Few other events in the history of the old Arizona cow country hold as much tragic interest as the fight at the Tewksbury ranch that day. A halo of romance has been woven around the events of this battle by many campfire tales told these sixty-odd years, and by romances written around the feud. Just what actually occurred that day will probably never be known, for all of those engaged on both sides are now dead; but the bare facts available show that many events, sordid and heroic, tragic and romantic, took place at the old Tewksbury ranch that September day more than sixty years ago.

Cautiously Tom Graham advanced in the early morning with his men spread out to surround the house. So stealthily did they move, taking advantage of every cover that promised the slightest concealment, that the people at this lonely ranch detected no sign of danger in the beauty of that September morning, for September mornings are always beautiful in central Arizona; and John Tewksbury and William Jacobs were taken completely by surprise about a mile from the cabin. There was no escape. For them it was the end of the trail, and both were

shot down before they could turn in their tracks
—the first victims of Graham vengeance.[2] Who
actually did the killing cannot be ascertained,
but there is no doubt in my mind that it was
Andy Cooper or the party led by him in surrounding the cabin, for he boasted of the deed
two days later in Holbrook.

With a shout of triumph the cattlemen closed
in upon the ranch, confident of an easy victory;
but those about the place had fled to the cabin
at the first alarm, and a volley from the windows
sent the raiders scampering for safety. After
this repulse the Graham forces settled down to a
siege, and it looked for a time as if Cooper's
threat made to Sheriff Mulvenon—to wipe out
the entire family—would be successful.

Securely entrenched on the adjacent hillside
the besiegers kept the cabin under constant fire.
They had not counted on this turn of events,
but they were determined to carry out their plan
of extermination. The number of men in the
cabin that day is not known; but it is certain
that Mrs. John Tewksbury and John D. Tewksbury, Sr., were there with the two remaining
sons, Ed and Jim, and possibly Jim Roberts.

The worst atrocity of the entire vendetta, and
one of the most inhuman in all Arizona's history,
with the exception of the barbarities of the ferocious Apaches, was committed during the siege

that followed. As the beleaguered Tewksburys fought for their lives, exchanging bullet for bullet, a drove of hogs started to devour the bodies of their dead lying in full view of the cabin;³ and instead of granting a burial truce or at least driving the brutes away, the cattlemen kept up such a fusillade that it was certain death for any man to attempt to leave the shelter of those log walls. With resounding thuds rifle bullets from the hillside struck the cabin on all sides. Only puffs of smoke curling up from the rocks revealed the positions of the besiegers; the Tewksburys kept such a well-directed fire that the cowboys did not dare show themselves.

As the hogs rooted at the bodies and contentedly grunted over their ghastly feast, and bullets from the hill crashed into the log walls, the heart-rending scream of a woman came from the cabin.

"I can't stand it," shrieked the wife of John Tewksbury. "I must bury them. They'll have to kill me to stop me."

The next instant a white-faced woman appeared in the cabin door with a shovel in her hands, and with head erect, looking neither to the right nor to the left but straight ahead at the gruesome sight, she walked bravely out across the flat in defiance of the enemy's bullets. It was as brave a deed as any woman ever attempted.

John Tewksbury

An Old-Time Arizona Cow Outfit in Camp

The guns from the hillside were suddenly silenced by the chivalry of the cowboys, for it was an unwritten law of the range that no harm should come to a woman; and not a shot was fired as she drove the hogs away and laboriously scraped out two shallow graves in which she buried her husband and his comrade. Only the wailing of an infant back in the cabin, her baby and this man's who was now dead, broke the silence of that September day. It must have been a terrible, heartbreaking ordeal, but of such bravery were the women of old Arizona.[4]

As soon as she had completed her gruesome task and returned to the cabin, the enemy's guns blazed forth again with increased fury, but no further casualties occurred on either side. The Tewksburys were so well fortified in the log building that it was impossible for the cattlemen to dislodge them; and the marksmanship of Jim and Ed Tewksbury made the cattlemen keep under cover.

As the hours dragged wearily by, a gloomy foreboding settled over the besieged cabin. The Tewksburys well knew that unless reinforcements reached them before night the enemy would set fire to their fort under the cover of the darkness, and shoot them down when they were driven out. But aid could not be expected. Their own men were scattered through the mountains like hunted animals, and even if their entire fighting force was assembled, there would not be enough to cope with the situation. There was little prospect of any of them escaping alive; but they were determined to fight to the very last. The afternoon was well advanced when the firing from the enemy suddenly ceased, and a man rode from the brush and out across the flat towards the cabin.

"It's a trick," growled Jim Tewksbury as he trained his rifle through a window and lined the horseman up with his sights.

"Don't shoot; they want to parley," cried Ed.

"Well, I'll keep him covered, and see what he wants. You watch the other side of the house. It might be a trick to attract our attention while they charge us."

"That's John Meadows," suddenly shouted Ed as he recognized the advancing horseman. "He must have a posse. We're saved."

True enough it was John Meadows, the justice of the peace from Payson. In some manner that has never been revealed the news of the fighting had drifted out across the valley to this little settlement; and, hastily gathering a few men, Meadows had by hard riding reached the cabin in time to save the Tewksburys from extermination.

No braver man ever lived than John Mead-

ows, and when he ordered them away the cattlemen sullenly withdrew. It was one thing to
fight enemies who had gone beyond the law
themselves and would kill at any opportunity or
be killed as part of the game; but it was quite
another matter to defy the law in the person of
this fighting justice of the peace, backed by a
heavily armed posse of fighting men.[5]

As soon as he had raised the siege and restored order, Meadows, acting under his authority as a justice of the peace, exhumed the bodies
and held an inquest on the spot. An examination
showed that Jacobs had been shot three times in
the back, each bullet breaking the spine, and
John Tewksbury had one wound in the back of
the neck, while his head had been crushed with
a rock. The result of this inquest is not known
today, as no record of it has been found,[6] but it
is doubtful if the jury was able to name the men
who had committed this atrocious double murder. After the inquest, Meadows returned to
Payson with his posse, but not until he had
searched for the men engaged in the attack. His
man hunt was in vain for they had vanished.

The account of this affair found in the old
files of *The Arizona Silver Belt* states that
three Tewksburys were killed; but this is evidently a mistake, and I have been unable to con-
firm the report from any other source. This ver-

sion gives the names of the victims as John Tewksbury, William Jacobs, and "another person whose name we are unable to learn." According to *The Silver Belt* story, the third man had just reached John Tewksbury's ranch, and was killed with an axe while on his way to the house after he had picketed his horse. No further mention of this man has been found. John Tewksbury's cabin was some distance from his father's house.

The account in *The Silver Belt* is of interest in this connection:

We have news of another killing in Pleasant Valley, which we think is ostensibly correct. John Tewksbury, a Mr. Jacobs and another person whose name we are unable to learn, were the victims. The bodies of John Tewksbury and Jacobs were discovered by Mrs. Tewksbury some distance from her residence and near her father-in-law's house, which evidently they were trying to reach. The third man had just reached John Tewksbury's house, had picketed his horse and was on his way to the house when felled, it is supposed by an ax.

The senior Tewksbury is reported as having arrived in Prescott, and surrendered himself to the sheriff.

It is reported that U. S. soldiers have been ordered from Fort Verde to Pleasant Valley for the purpose of trying to arrest the belligerent factions.

The report that "the senior Tewksbury" had surrendered at Prescott was not correct. This refers to John D. Tewksbury, father of the brothers; but he never took an active part in the fighting except during the attack on the ranch. The statement that soldiers were sent into the valley is an error; for the military authorities never interfered with the vendetta

No further mention of this third man has been found in any subsequent account. On the day he was shot to death by Sheriff Owens, Andy Cooper openly boasted in a saloon in Holbrook that he had killed one of the Tewksburys, and a man whom he did not know, only two days before; but he made no mention of a third victim. Had there been another he would undoubtly have said so.

The Silver Belt gives the following account of the inquest:

The bodies of John Tewksbury and Bill Jacobs remained where they fell under the hand of the assassins, for eleven days. Disinterested persons who asked to be allowed to bury them were warned by the members of the Graham faction to keep away, that anyone attempting to bury the corpses would forfeit their lives. When John Meadows, justice of the peace at Payson, arrived to hold an inquest on the bodies of Tewksbury and Jacobs they were so decomposed that they had to be shoveled into coffins, and the stench was so terrible that many of the men summoned as jurors were made deathly sick.

This is another error, due to the many wild rumors that were circulated during those stormy days of 1887. John Meadows arrived on the scene the day of the murder, and two days later

Andy Cooper was in Holbrook. Thus it would
have been impossible for the bodies to have lain
unburied for eleven days.

News of the killing at the Tewksbury ranch
did not reach Prescott until a week later, and
immediately Sheriff Mulvenon prepared for his
second invasion of the valley, determined this
time to end the war. The following account,
which appeared in the *Coconino Sun* on September
ber 10, 1887, establishes the date of the killing
as September 2 and not the third as claimed by
some:

> Yesterday Deputy Sheriff Francis received a telegram from Sheriff Mulvenon from Prescott, stating that one of the Graham gang had killed John Tewksbury and William Jacobs, from an ambush on September third. These may be the men that Andy Cooper stated he had killed when he said on the morning of his own death at Holbrook, that he had killed one of the Tewksburys and a man he did not know on the Friday previous, which would be September *second*. Although Andy Cooper was known by that name, his real name was *Blevans*, and he was a brother of the other Blevans boys. It is said that he committed a murder some years ago in Texas and changed his name to avoid detection.

This was the same telegram by which Sheriff
Mulvenon summoned Francis for the second invasion, which resulted in the killing of John
Graham and Charles Blevins at Perkins' store,
the details of which are related in a subsequent
chapter.

The full extent to which Tom Graham was involved in the attack on the Tewksbury ranch is
not certainly known today. That he was present
as leader of the cattlemen there seems to be no
doubt, if the statements of some of the old-
timers are correct; but it is very doubtful if he
sanctioned the cold-blooded murder of John
Tewksbury and William Jacobs. This looks more
like the work of Andy Cooper, especially in view
of the latter's own boasting statement on the
morning of the fourth. This is borne out by the
fact that there are no records of charges or indictments against him for the double murder,
for Cooper was dead. Both Tom and John Graham sought revenge for the killing of their
younger brother. The expedition against the
Tewksbury ranch was undoubtedly organized
for retaliation and as a measure of self-defense,
for all the casualities to that date, with the exception of the Indian herder, had occurred on
the Graham side. The attacking force was scattered, and in the heat of battle a man will commit acts that in his cooler moments he would
never countenance. This probably explains the
refusal of the cattlemen to grant a burial truce
until Mrs. Tewksbury bravely forced the issue.
Those who knew Tom Graham best state that he
would fight when necessary; but no man ever
accused him of cold-blooded murder. On the

other hand, Cooper was a killer of the old frontier type, and would take advantage of any break.

Mary Ann Tewksbury, the widow of the slain John Tewksbury, married John Rhodes in 1887, and on December 24, 1950, died at the home of a daughter, Mrs. Ann Mognett, at Florence, Arizona, at the age of eighty-nine years. After her marriage to Rhodes, they lived in Pleasant Valley until about 1900, when they moved to Mesa; but a short time later they located at Mammoth, a mining town in the San Pedro River Valley. She was the mother of two sons and four daughters by her second husband.

This little, gray-haired lady was a child when her parents emigrated from California to Arizona, where she spent more than eighty years of her long life. She saw the territory grow from one of the wildest frontiers America has ever known to a peaceful and highly productive state; and when she died she was believed to be the last survivor of any of those directly connected with the sanguinary Pleasant Valley War of the 1880's. She was a pioneer in every sense of the word.

The Tewksbury Ranch

Jim Roberts

CHAPTER VII

COMMODORE OWENS'
BATTLE WITH THE
BLEVINS GANG

ON SEPTEMBER 4, 1887, just two days after the battle at Tewksbury's ranch, one of the bloodiest and most thrilling gun fights of old Arizona occurred at Holbrook between Sheriff Commodore Owens and four members of the Graham faction.[1] For individual bravery it stands above all other encounters, even eclipsing the famous Earp-Clanton feud at Tombstone, in which Billy Clanton and Tom and Frank McLowery were killed in a sanguinary battle with Wyatt, Morgan, and Virgil Earp and Doc Holliday on October 26, 1881. Wyatt Earp and his three comrades were pitted man to man against four; but Owens alone faced four, three of whom were known as dangerous fighters.

For several years Andy Cooper had kept a few head of cattle in Pleasant Valley as a blind to cover rustling. He was regarded as one of the most daring cattle thieves in the territory, and his operations became so bold that a warrant for his arrest was issued in the summer of 1887; but there were few men, even in gunfighting Arizona of the 1880's, who cared to serve the warrant on account of Cooper's reputation as a dangerous man. However, he did not tempt fate too far, and he remained in Pleasant Valley most of the summer, where he felt safe from officers of the law.

On the morning of September 4, 1887, he ventured into Holbrook, and while relating the latest news of the feud to a crowd of saloon loafers he boasted of killing one of the Tewksburys and another man just two days before. After strutting about the street for some time, he went to his mother's cottage on the north side of the railroad. Holbrook was a typical Arizona cow town of the 1880's, and it boasted of several men rather proud of their ability to handle a gun; but none of them had "lost" any bad men that morning.

During the afternoon, however, a man with the courage of a lion, in the person of Commodore P. Owens, sheriff of Apache County, rode into town while making his round of official duties, summoning the grand and trial jurors for the next term of court. Owens had received his early range education in the rough school of Texas trail driving, and by the time he reached Arizona he was ready to meet trouble more than halfway. This was just the caliber of man the law-abiding citizens had been looking for; and Sam Brown,[2] a sheepman who was also chairman of the Democratic county committee, and Frank Wattron, a druggist, succeeded in having him elected sheriff for the purpose of cleaning the rustlers out of Apache County. This had taken place only a short time before, and Owens was performing one of his first official duties when he rode into Holbrook that September morning of 1887.

At that time Holbrook was noted as one of the wildest towns in all the wild Southwest. It was fairly itching to try out its new sheriff, for it had its doubts of this good-looking young officer with his long hair hanging well below his shoulders, and with a face without a hard line. In addition to the long hair and pleasant face he dressed in cowboy chaps and wide sombrero, carried a Winchester, and wore his long-barreled Colt on the left side with the butt turned forward in perfect disregard for all local ideas of how a gun fighter should carry such an implement of his trade. A man who wore his gun on the left side was immediately branded as a tenderfoot; but there was an occasional exception among those old-time fighters. Holbrook did not believe that the new sheriff would stand the test. He was too picturesque. That kind of stuff might be all right back East where he came from, but not in Arizona. There was one thing, however, that Holbrook did not know; this new sheriff was a dead shot with both rifle and six-shooter, and he could get into action with surprising speed, even if he did wear his gun on the left side with the butt turned forward.

The versions of this famous gun fight all agree as to the main details; but there is a difference of opinion as to just what took place before Sheriff Owens went to the Blevins house to arrest Andy Cooper. In the old courthouse at Saint Johns the record of the testimony of the witnesses at the inquest, which was taken down verbatim, was buried for more than forty years. Finally this valuable document was unearthed for me by Mr. Dodd L. Greer, county attorney of Apache County, and as I write I have before me a transcript that he kindly furnished. The testimony of eyewitnesses, including the sheriff's own story, is given here for the first time since this fight of long ago.

One popular version still told informs us that as soon as Owens arrived in town he was informed of Cooper's presence, and told of the killer's boast of murdering two men in Pleasant Valley. According to this old tale the sheriff paid no attention and made no attempt to serve his warrant for horse stealing until several saloon bums declared that he was afraid of the rustler. Then he seized his Winchester and hurried to the Blevins cottage. There is nothing in the testimony of either Owens or of the prin-

FROM PHOTOGRAPH TAKEN AT ALBUQUERQUE, NEW MEXICO.
BY COURTESY OF ELIZABETH BARRETT OWENS, HIS WIDOW

Commodore P. Owens, Sheriff of Apache County

PHOTOGRAPH BY COURTESY OF W. H. CLARK

The Blevins Cottage in Holbrook

cipal witnesses to show that anything of the kind occurred.

The testimony shows that after his arrival in Holbrook that morning Cooper did not remain long at the Blevins house; in a short time he was back on the south side of the railroad. That the rustler knew a warrant had been issued for his arrest is shown by the testimony of his brother John, Frank Wattron, and Owens. About two hours before the sheriff arrived, Cooper told Frank Wattron, in front of the latter's drugstore, that he would never surrender to any officer, but that if he lived through his present trouble, he would go to Saint Johns and stand trial at the spring term of court. While Cooper did not so state, his "present trouble" probably referred to the part he was then playing in the Pleasant Valley war.

In order to properly understand the events of that bloody day in old Holbrook it will be necesary to give a description of the location of the Blevins cottage. This house stood on the north side of the railroad facing the street now known as North Central Avenue, which runs parallel to and along the north side of the Santa Fe Railroad tracks. On the south side was the main business street of that time on which Frank Wattron's store was located. The Blevins house stands about fifteen feet from the street line.

On the next lot to the east is the old Armbruster blacksmith shop, which played an important part in the fight, and directly on the west side is a stone house with walls sixteen inches thick. Both of these buildings stand on the street line. To the west of the stone house is a row of shacks, and across the alley beyond is the building that was Brown and Kinder's livery stable in 1887. All are still standing, although time has changed their appearance.[3]

John Blevins was sitting in a room at Brown and Kinder's livery stable repairing his violin when Sheriff Owens rode up and dismounted. Young Blevins did not know Owens, but he suspected that this long-haired stranger who wore his six-shooter on the left side and carried a Winchester in his saddle scabbard was the new sheriff, and he immediately went to warn his brother.

When he found Cooper talking to several men in front of the post office, he said: "Andy, Owens is in town, ain't he?"

"Yes," replied the rustler, which shows that he had seen the sheriff ride in. He then told his brother that he was going to the ranch, meaning Canyon Creek, and he directed him to take his horse to the house. John hastened back to the livery stable to carry out these instructions, while Andy went direct to the Blevins cottage.

Commodore Owens put his horse up at the stable, and had just started to clean his six-shooter when Sam Brown and D. G. Harvey entered. That the sheriff was not holding the warrant for Cooper as a bluff is shown by the fact that he asked both if they had seen the rustler, and when they informed him that Andy was in town he stated positively that he intended to arrest him. While they were talking John Blevins came for his brother's horse, and as he led the animal away Sam Brown informed the sheriff that his man was getting ready to leave town.

Hastily putting his pistol together, Owens left instructions to have his own mount ready. Then he seized his Winchester, and when he came out of the stable he saw Cooper in the act of saddling his horse in front of the Blevins cottage. The rustler immediately went inside when he saw the officer.

Besides Andy Cooper, John Blevins, Sam Houston Blevins, and Mose Roberts, there were four women in the Blevins house that day— Mrs. Mary Blevins, widow of Mart Blevins and mother of the two brothers[4] killed in the fight; Eva Blevins, the wife of one of the Blevins boys; and Mrs. Amanda Gladden[5] and her nine-year-old daughter, Beatrice.

Like all other affairs of this kind, the details of this famous gun fight vary according to the source of information. The three adult women declared that Cooper was unarmed; but John Blevins admitted that his brother carried a gun while in town, and it is hardly likely that he would have taken the weapon off when he expected to leave for the ranch so soon.

According to Commodore Owens' testimony he went straight to the Blevins house. As he approached he saw a man watching him from the open door, and when the officer drew nearer it was slammed shut. Walking boldly up on the porch, the sheriff saw Cooper and three other men through a window; and when he ordered the rustler to come out, Andy hastened into an adjoining room. Cautiously opening the door with his left hand, he stood facing Owens with a six-shooter held in his right. At the same instant John Blevins, his own gun ready for action, opened the door at the side just far enough to look out, and thus the officer found himself between two brothers.

Never in all his adventurous life, either before or afterwards, was Commodore Owens nearer death than at that moment when he faced Andy Cooper, one of the most treacherous and deadly man-killers of old Arizona. Quick as lightning and a dead shot, no one has ever been able to explain just why he hesitated that fraction of a second to ask the sheriff what he wanted when he already knew. And as he stared death in the face in the person of Andy Cooper, Commodore Owens never flinched; he was not that kind. Had his gaze wavered for a second from the outlaw's eyes he would have been killed in a flash.

Coolly facing this cold-blooded killer who would stop at nothing to gain the advantage of an adversary, the sheriff calmly and with scarcely an inflection in his voice, said: "Cooper, I want you." He might have been discussing the weather with a friend for all the difference it seemed to make.

"What do you want with me?" the bad man demanded gruffly.

"I have a warrant for you," was the curt reply.

"What warrant?" Cooper was plainly sparring for time.

"The same warrant for horse stealing I told you about some time ago." This was for stealing Navajo ponies.

"Wait, an' I'll see about it," replied Cooper.

"No, I'll not wait; you must come at once," replied the sheriff in the same cool, even tone. Something ominous and deadly about that voice held the outlaw's trigger finger in check; for it carried a warning that this was a man not to be underestimated.

"I won't go," was the rustler's final ultimatum.

Just who fired the first shot is a matter of dispute to this day. Both Mrs. Blevins and her daughter-in-law declared at the inquest that Cooper was unarmed. The account in the Saint Johns *Herald* of September 8, 1887, states that when Cooper refused to submit to arrest both he and Owens fired, the two shots being almost simultaneous, the outlaw receiving his death wound and the officer escaping uninjured.

In his testimony at the inquest Owens made no mention of Cooper's firing. The sheriff simply said, "I shot him," when the rustler refused to surrender; but this officer was not the type who would shoot an unarmed man.

Almost instantly with the discharge of Owen's gun John Blevins fired from the side door. Missing the sheriff by a narrow margin, he hit Cooper's horse that was still standing in front of the house, waiting for its master to start back to the ranch.

Quick as a flash Owens whirled half around. That deadly Winchester, still at his hip, roared again, and John Blevins staggered back with a bullet in his shoulder.

Mrs. Blevins was standing beside Cooper at the door, and when he staggered back, fatally wounded, she led him to a trunk in the room.

Immediately after shooting John Blevins,

Owens ran to the street where he could watch both sides of the house. Through the window he saw Cooper, but at that instant he disappeared, and the sheriff fired through the thin walls in an effort to hit him between the shoulders. This is probably the origin of the story that instead of wounding the rustler, as related here, Owens shot him by firing through the house when he saw him crouching at the window.

The action in this fight was very rapid and the whole affair probably did not cover more than sixty seconds. As a bullet from the sheriff's rifle crashed through the boards beneath the window Mose Roberts leaped through a door or window at the northeast corner with a six-shooter in his right hand. The fact that Commodore Owen's brain and trigger finger worked in perfect unity again saved his life. Instantly leaping to one side of a wagon that stood between them, he fired before his adversary could get into action; and Mose Roberts ran back of the building with a mortal wound that quickly sapped his life away.

Inside of the house young Sam Houston Blevins, a sixteen-year-old boy (some say fourteen), asked his wounded brother John for his gun; but the latter refused to let him have it. The excited youth, determined to end the fight and avenge his brothers, seized the dying Cooper's weapon and the next instant leaped through the front door, his frantic mother trying to hold him back. While in the act of cocking and throwing the pistol down to fire, the deadly Winchester cracked again. The boy halted abruptly, staggered back a step or two, and fell across the threshold in his mother's arms with a bullet wound through his heart.

According to the account published in the *Coconino Sun* of Flagstaff, a few days after the fight, young Blevins was shot through the hips and died half an hour later; but this is an error.

With his smoking Winchester in his hands Commodore Owens stood there like an avenging specter of death, waiting and watching for any others who might take up the fight; but none were left. The body of the boy lying in the doorway was the only thing in sight. Enough blood had been spilled that day to more than satisfy the sanguinary lust of old Holbrook. Its bad men had discovered that the new sheriff was more than a match for the worst of them, and they were satisfied; and when that officer found that no one else wished to dispute his victory, he returned to the livery stable, his back turned to his enemies—a gesture of contempt for their courage, for he well knew that their fighting spirit had vanished. This ended the most desperate battle Commodore Owens ever fought in his long career as a man hunter, and the bloodiest day in Holbrook's history.

One version states that Owens had retreated to the corner of the Armbruster blacksmith shop when John Blevins opened fire and that he did his fighting from that point; but the testimony of Frank Wattron, who witnessed the shooting, and the sheriff's own story, told at the inquest, show that Owens stood in front of the house until the fight was over.

After the battle the inside of the cottage was like a shambles; blood was everywhere, over the floor, the walls, and furniture. Stretched out on the bed was the body of Mose Roberts. Cooper was down on the floor in the agony of death, with a bullet through his abdomen, imploring someone to shoot him. Covered with blood from his wound, John Blevins lay in a chair, all of the fight taken out of him. He subsequently recovered, but Cooper died the next day. Lying across the threshold of the front door was the body of Sam Houston Blevins, the youngest of the clan. And thus three fighting members of the Graham faction were wiped out by Commodore Owens' deadly Winchester within the passing of not more than sixty seconds. Those bad men had discovered, too late, that this good-looking sheriff with long hair, the soft voice, and the pleasant face was not to be trifled with. That Owens escaped with his life or without even injury is little short of miraculous.

After the publication of the first edition, Mrs. Evelyn Blevins, the wife of John Blevins, who was living in Phoenix in 1939, gave a somewhat different version. She was a bride of seventeen at the time of the fight, and was in the living room of the Blevins cottage when she heard a knock at the door. She opened it to find Commodore Owens standing there with a Winchester in his hand. She did not know him at the time, but from his gun she believed him an officer.

"Is Andy Cooper here?" Owens asked.

"Yes, he is here," Mrs. Blevins replied.

"I want to speak to him," Owens said.

"All right," she replied, and going to the dining-room door she called to Andy, who was with his mother and brothers. "Andy, you are wanted at the door."

When Cooper entered the living room, Owens said, "I want you," and at the same time he raised his Winchester and fired without giving him a chance to say a word. Mrs. Blevins declared further that Cooper was unarmed.

After shooting Cooper, according to Mrs. Blevins' version, Owens backed off the porch into the street and went to the corner of the house where he could see both sides. Just at this instant John Blevins ran to the porch and fired at Owens, missing him and killing Cooper's horse. Owens returned the fire and wounded young Blevins.

Mose Roberts was in the sitting room writing a letter to his mother when Owens first appeared, and when John Blevins was shot, Roberts started to crawl out of the window at the northeast corner. Mrs. Blevins declared that he was unarmed, and that when Owens saw him, he fired. Roberts fell to the ground, but scrambled to his feet and ran to the kitchen door and fell on the floor. He lived for about a week.

After John was wounded, his brother, Sam Houston Blevins, a boy of twelve, seized John's gun and ran out on the porch to kill Owens, in spite of his mother's efforts to hold him back. Owens fired and the boy fell into his mother's arms, dead. Mrs. Blevins said that Owens regretted the shooting of young Sam, and, because of this, he resigned his office of sheriff. This, however, is an error. According to the best information I can secure he completed his term, but refused re-election. Mrs. Blevins also stated that before the fight Cooper and Owens had been friends, but fell out over a woman.

However, this version is not corroborated by the evidence given by Mrs. Eva Blevins (evidently the same woman as Mrs. Evelyn Blevins) at the coroner's inquest. My original account of the fight was taken from the testimony of witnesses at the time and I am of the opinion that it is the correct version.

CHAPTER VIII

AFTER THE
BATTLE

IMMEDIATELY AFTER the fight Frank Reed, a friend of the dead outlaws, attempted to raise a mob to lynch Owens by creating sentiment against him; but the leading men of Holbrook promptly told him to" cheese his racket," a command that he obeyed without quibbling, for he soon discovered that a large majority of the citizens thoroughly approved of the new sheriff's action, and that they were in no mood to be trifled with. With the exception of a few friends of the dead men, who remained discreetly silent after they heard the warning given to Reed, Commodore Perry Owens received the unanimous support of every resident in town.

The inquest into the death of Andy Cooper was held in Holbrook on September 6 by D. G. Harvey, a justice of the peace. Sheriff Owens told his story of the killing in a simple straightforward manner that carried conviction with the jury. In my account I have accepted his version as correct, for it was corroborated by Frank Wattron, who witnessed the fight from the other side of the railroad; but I have made several additions to his story, taken from the testimony of others. Among the important witnesses at this inquest were John Blevins and Mrs. Mary Blevins, the mother. After hearing all of the testimony, the jury returned the following verdict:

We, the undersigned, coroner's jurors, in the case of the inquest of the killing of Andy Cooper, alias Andy Blevans,

Find that the deceased came to his death from the effects of a gun shot wound, the gun being in the hands of Sheriff C. P. Owens, while in the discharge of his duty.

From testimony adduced we fully exhonerate [sic] Sheriff Owens.

(Signed) W. P. Yaney, Foreman,
Sam'l. Brown,
J. Q. Adamson,
Henry Killsby,
Jas. M. Higgins,
J. H. Wilson.
Holbrook, A. T., Sept. 6th, 1887.

Charged with assault with intent to murder, John Blevins was placed under arrest for his part in the fight and lodged in the county jail at Saint Johns; but the old court records of Apache County show that a year passed before he was brought to trial, for the grand jury did not return an indictment until September 15, 1888. The reason for this delay is not known, unless it was to give the prisoner an opportunity to recover from his wound. No time was lost, however, after the action of the grand jury, and five days later young Blevins was called for trial before Judge James H. Wright. A verdict of guilty was returned the next day (the twenty-first), and on September 24 he was sentenced to serve five years in the territorial prison at Yuma. There were no railroads at that time between Saint Johns and Yuma, and it is interesting to note that Judge Wright stipulated that the sentence should not start until November 1, 1888. The reason for this is not given, but the court probably thought that the sheriff would not be able to deliver the prisoner to the warden of the penitentiary before that date.

In the first edition I stated that John Blevins served a sentence of five years in Yuma, but I have since been informed by a descendant that this was a mistake, for he was never in the penitentiary. I made an investigation, and, under date of February 22, 1939, Alva L. Weaver, secretary of the Arizona State Prison, wrote that after a careful search of the records he was unable to find that John Blevins was ever committed to that institution.

The explanation for John Blevins' failure to reach the penitentiary, as given to me by his descendant, is undoubtedly correct. This explanation may seem rather strange today, but those who lived in Arizona in territorial times will understand, as conditions were different then. The sheriff started for Yuma with his prisoner, taking him from Saint Johns to Holbrook, the nearest railroad point. After they were on the train the conductor handed Owens a telegram ordering him to release Blevins. The sheriff paid no attention, for he was determined that John should be taken to Yuma.

Later, another telegram was sent to Owens instructing him to release his prisoner, and at the same time the train conductor received a wire asking him to read the communication to Owens in front of Blevins. After the conductor read the telegram, he told Owens that he had better release his prisoner. (It is probable that only one wire was sent and it was this later one.)

According to this old story, Owens got off the train at a town en route and turned Blevins over to the sheriff at that place. The latter said that he did not want the prisoner, and told John that he was free. The name of this town is uncertain, but it was probably Flagstaff as that was the only place with a sheriff at that time. Commodore Owens and John Blevins met on the street several times after that, but they never spoke.

Just what brought about the release of John Blevins is not known today. The Board of Pardons and Paroles at Phoenix has no record of a pardon; but the capital was then at Prescott, and the records may have been lost in the change to Phoenix. Governor Zulick evidently issued the pardon by telegraph, and probably kept no record. But the fact remains that John Blevins did not serve a term in prison. This is established by the old penitentiary records.

That the Arizona press of that time thoroughly approved of Sheriff Owens' part in this bloody affair is shown by extracts from the Saint Johns *Herald* and the *Coconino Sun*, the only newspapers published in the northern part of the territory. These accounts are quoted in full.

The following, taken from the *Herald* of September 9, 1887, was the first published story of the fight:

From private parties and from parties up from Holbrook, we are enabled to gather the following particulars of the good work done by Sheriff Owens in that town on last Sunday, in ridding the territory of two, perhaps three, of the worst characters that ever infested any country. It appears that in the afternoon of last Sunday, Sheriff Owens rode into Holbrook on his rounds summoning the grand and trial jurors for the present term of court. He had scarcely dismounted from his horse, when he was informed that Andy Cooper was in town, and that he made the assertion that he would not be taken by any officer in Apache county. Owens thereupon inquired as to the whereabouts of Cooper, and the hostler pointed to a house only a short distance from the stable, and told the sheriff they were in there. He searched among his papers and found the warrant for Cooper, and then started for the house in question. Cooper was standing on a porch in front of the house, and saw the sheriff approaching—before he reached the house Cooper went inside and shut the door. Mr. Owens went to the door and called for him to come out. Instead of doing so, Cooper passed from the room which he first entered into one on the east, opened the door slightly and stuck his head out, holding the knob of the door in his left hand and a six-shooter in his right. Owens then told him that he had a warrant for his arrest, and wanted him. Cooper asked him what it was for, and was told that it was for stealing some ponies from the Navajoes. He then said, "Wait a while and I will see about it;" but the sheriff was not disposed to wait, and told him that he must come now. Cooper then replied that he would not go, when Owens opened fire on him, and was fired on in turn from the door through which Cooper entered the house—the two shots being almost simultaneous. There was a general firing from the inside on Owens then and he retreated to the corner of Brown and Kinder's stable, and had scarcely reached his place of partial shelter before a man known as Mose Roberts turned the corner of the house in which the Blevans were, with a gun in his hand. Owens turned loose on him, the ball striking Roberts in the side passing entirely through his body. Samuel Blevans, a boy about 14 years old, then ran out of the house and took a shot at Owens, which was returned with fatal effect.

The names of the two killed are Andy Cooper and Samuel Blevans, half-brothers. John Blevans and Mose Roberts wounded, the former slightly and the latter mortally. The men killed and wounded have been members of a desperate gang of cattle thieves, who have been a terror to the law abiding citizens of Yavapai and Apache counties, and openly boasted that the officers of the law were afraid to undertake to arrest them.

We take the following extract from a private letter received yesterday morning from a prominent citizen of Holbrook, which tells the story in a nut-shell, and also gives the feeling of the people of that town in regard to the affray:

"Owens went to Blevans' house and there found

Cooper and the other parties. Cooper resisted and was killed. John Blevans then fired upon Owens, and he in turn was shot. Roberts appeared from the corner of the house and was in turn laid out. Young Blevans then sprang out and fired his little pop, and was killed on the spot; thus ended the bloody day in Holbrook. Owens was not hurt, and did it all without assistance. Frank Reed raised a cry against Owens, when he was informed by the citizens of Holbrook to 'cheese' his racket. Outside of a few men, and a very few at that, Owens was supported by every man, woman, and child in town."

Too much credit cannot be given to Sheriff Owens in this lamentable affair. It required more than ordinary courage for a man to go single-handed and alone to a house where it is known that there were four or five desperate men inside, and demand the surrender of one of them. And when one takes into consideration that the combatants were separated by only a few feet at the commencement of the difficulty, it seems miraculous that Mr. Owens should come out of it uninjured.

While this story was written just a few days after the fight it contains several errors. I have already pointed out that Brown and Kinder's livery stable, behind the corner of which the *Herald* stated that Owens took refuge, is some distance from the Blevins house, and at the time of the fight there was and still is a stone house between the two buildings, which would make it impossible for him to have fired upon his assailants from this point.

The following account is taken from the *Coconino Sun* of September 10, 1887:

A shooting affray occurred at Holbrook Sunday last, in which Sheriff Owens killed two men, one of them a noted desperado named Andy Cooper, and probably mortally wounded another. Cooper is a half brother of the Blevans family of boys, and has been one of the most notorious of the rustlers and dangerous characters which infest Tonto Basin. There has been a warrant out for the arrest of Cooper for a long time, but he has kept out of the way or has been in such a position as to defy arrest when he has been seen.

On Sunday morning last Andy Cooper was on the street at Holbrook and stated openly that he had killed one of the Tewksburys and another man whose name he did not know, on Friday and that those with him had wounded several others. It is understood that Cooper had come in that morning, and was stopping at a cottage on the north side of the railroad back a little way from town, occupied by Mrs. Blevans, mother of the Blevans boys. A short time after, Sheriff Owens was met by some parties and told of what Cooper had said. He immediately procured a Winchester rifle and started out to arrest his man. On approaching Mrs. Blevans' house Cooper was found standing in the doorway. On being informed by the sheriff that he had a warrant for his arrest issued at a place named Taylor, for a crime committed some time since, Cooper replied that he would not be arrested, and knowing the desperate character of the man, before he could make any break, the sheriff fired and shot him through the center of the body. At this time the fight became general, there being four men in the house. John Blevans came to the door and shot at Sheriff Owens, but the ball missed him and killed a horse standing near by. Before he could fire another shot the sheriff's rifle put a ball under his right arm and disabled him. Hewston Blevans then came to the door with a pistol in his hand. His mother caught him and endeavored to drag him inside the house, but before she could do so a ball from Owens' rifle went through his body at the hips and he died half an hour afterwards. He was only a boy about fourteen or fifteen years of age but said to be a desperate character.

The fourth man, Mose Roberts, got through a window of the house and was shot through or under the shoulder blade. He is not expected to live. Andy Cooper lingered until Sunday evening when he died. The coroner's jury which held an inquest on the body of the boy Hewston Blevans, exonerated Sheriff Owens from blame. The men were all desperate characters who made a practice of killing anyone who stood in the pathway of their crimes, and openly boasted of their murderous deeds afterwards. Sheriff Owens seems to have shown an amount of bravery in the discharge of his duties which he deserved credit for. That he should have gone single handed, and succeeded in getting the best of four such desperate men, without being killed or injured himself, is almost miraculous.[1]

These are the most authentic newspaper accounts that I have been able to find of this noted gun battle of the days when the law was slowly fighting its way across the northern Arizona frontier. It will be seen that they differ somewhat as to the details, but in the main both stories are substanially correct. From that day Holbrook was a peaceable town. Bad men had little use for a sheriff who could handle his guns with such deadly accuracy, and in spite of his long hair and pleasant face, they gave him a wide berth.

Commodore Owens was one of the few fighting sheriffs of old Arizona who survived those stormy days. After a long life of thrilling adventures among bad men, outlaws, and Apache and Navajo Indians, he died with his "boots off" from natural causes at Seligman, Arizona, on

May 10, 1919, and was buried at Flagstaff. This gun-fighting peace officer was a typical product of the days when Arizona, as the last frontier, was the refuge for the old-time type of bad men and outlaws wanted by sheriffs in other sections of the vanishing West; but with blazing six-shooter and Winchester, Commodore Owens carried the law into the desert with a thoroughness that has always marked the Arizona sheriff.

I am indebted to his widow, Elizabeth Barrett Owens, who still lives at Seligman, for much valuable information on his adventurous life. Commodore Perry Owens, as he was christened, was born July 29, 1852, on a farm in eastern Tennessee; and at the time of his famous battle with the Cooper-Blevins gang he was thirty-five years of age. Following the trail of many other young Southerners of the reconstruction period after the Civil War, he went to Texas in the early 1870's, and spent eleven years as a cowboy during the wildest of the trail-driving period. It was in this hard-riding, quick-shooting school that he received his training for the dangerous life of a man hunter in the old Southwest, where he later played such a prominent part as a peace officer.

I have before me a story written by A. L. Spellmeyer, published in an adventure magazine, giving a very fantastic version of how

Owens was christened "Commodore." According to this tale, Owens was with the Hash Knife wagon in 1879 when it forded the Picketwire, a shallow stream, to scatter cattle in the cedar brakes to the south; but when the outfit returned on its way to Holbrook, the cowboys found this shallow, trickling stream had become a raging torrent that they believed could not be crossed.

Throwing his rope over several logs floating down the muddy water, Owens succeeded in bringing them to the bank. After he had secured enough for his purpose he lashed them together into a raft upon which he embarked on the swirling current, and finally succeeded in landing on the opposite shore five miles below his starting point and almost opposite Holbrook. Thereafter he was known as the "Commodore of the Picketwire."

In the first place, the Hash Knife outfit was not in existence in 1879, and the Picketwire[2] is a river on the plains east of the Rocky Mountains, several hundred miles from Arizona. The stream near Holbrook is the Little Colorado River.

Mrs. Owens informs me that her husband was christened Commodore Perry Owens by his parents, and baptized under that name, in honor of Commodore Perry of Lake Erie fame.

Drifting westward into New Mexico about

1882, Commodore Perry Owens became foreman
of a cow outfit at Navajo Springs. The stock-
men of that section were having trouble with Indian rustlers, and singlehanded he killed three
Navajos whom he caught stealing cattle. By
this act he incurred the enmity and respect of
the renegades of that tribe; but many another
bloody battle was fought before they decided
that he was a good man to let alone.

His reputation attracted the attention of Sam
Brown and several other prominent citizens of
northern Arizona who were looking for a gun
fighter with "guts" enough to clean up the outlaws of the section, and after looking up his
record they decided that this long-haired cow-
puncher from New Mexico was the man for the
job. Pooling their interests, the reform element
elected him sheriff of Apache County in 1887;
and for three years he held the job—three years
which were as wild and stormy as any Western
sheriff ever survived.

During this period indictments were returned
against sixteen outlaws and cattle rustlers by a
special grand jury impaneled for that purpose
by Judge Robert E. Morrison. Owens and his
posse killed three of the most desperate at their
camp on Blue River, one of whom was the
notorious Ike Clanton, of Tombstone fame. The
officers waited at the outlaws' rendezvous and

when Finn Clanton, leader of the gang, returned, he was neatly trapped. This was enough for the rustlers, and the remaining twelve against whom indictments had been returned, fled to safer parts. Finn Clanton was convicted of cattle stealing, and sentenced to ten years in the Yuma penitentiary.

When his term as sheriff expired, Owens refused re-election to accept a position as special officer tendered him by the Atlantic and Pacific Railroad, now the Atchison, Topeka, and Santa Fe; later he entered the service of Wells, Fargo and Company as an express messenger. His next position was that of deputy United States marshal, in which capacity he served for several years.

He gave up the man-hunting game about 1900 to engage in the mercantile business at Seligman; and when he died nineteen years later, he left an estate of ten thousand dollars.

Love never came into his busy life until shortly after locating at Seligman, where he met Miss Elizabeth Barrett, and on April 30, 1902, they were united in marriage.

In personal appearance Commodore Owens was the Eastern ideal of the frontier gun fighter. In those days the Southwest had come to believe, and not without reason, that a man with long hair would not measure up when put to the test; but many a bad man discovered, too late, that this good-looking young fellow with the pleasant face, and hair that almost reached his waist, could draw and shoot with swift, deadly accuracy. He always carried his long-barreled six-shooter on his left side with the handle turned forward, something rarely done by old-time fighters, for a fraction of a second longer is required to reach across and draw than to drop the hand to the hip. It was a swift hand, indeed, that ever attempted such a feat. Standing five feet ten inches in his stockings, he was built like an athlete, with muscles that worked like steel springs. He never hunted trouble, but when it came his way he was always ready to meet it; and it was often said of him that he would not only "fight at the drop of a hat," but would "fight before the hat dropped." There was something in the steel-blue eyes that warned the observing man to let him alone; he had a personality that won friends wherever he went.

The Blevins cottage where this famous battle was fought nearly fifty years ago is still standing. A grim relic of the bloody days when Holbrook's reputation as a tough town was not surpassed by any other in all Arizona, it has been a peaceful home these many years, with flowers blooming around the yard and vines climbing over the little porch. While the building remains unchanged by time, it is in good repair, and the little yard in front, shut off from the street by a wire fence, is always attractive. Its sanguinary story is told to the casual visitor with many embellishments; and if you are fortunate enough to find some old-timer who knows the spot in the old boot hill cemetery, he will show you the graves of these three men who died with their boots on when the law of the six-shooter ruled the land. But you will be fortunate indeed, to find such a man, for today there are hardly half a dozen left in that part of Arizona who actually know the details.

From a roaring cow town of the old frontier, in which killings were of frequent occurrence and attracted little more than passing notice, Holbrook has grown to a prosperous community of two thousand inhabitants, where the jingling spurs of the old-time cowboy clinking along the plank sidewalks are heard no more; and sleepy cow ponies that once lined the hitching rails in front of the saloons of yesteryear have given place to an army of Fords, varying from an ancient vintage down to the latest models. Since the days of the feud Navajo County has been created with Holbrook as the county seat. Surrounded on all sides by the Arizona desert land, it is an interesting little town, with as thrilling a past as you will find in all the Southwest.

CHAPTER IX

THE RAID ON THE
TEWKSBURY
CAMP

IT WAS NOW a war of extermination to the last man, with quarter neither asked nor given —a personal feud in which the fires of bitterness and hatred blazed out so fiercely that many of the fighting men of both sides were soon wiped out, and the survivors were glad enough before the end of September to declare a truce by mutual consent. Like all vendettas embittered by the vindictiveness of men who had once called each other friend, whether in civilized communities or in the wilderness, the authorities were powerless to cope with the situation and stop bloodshed. The expeditions led by Sheriff Mulvenon and Justice of the Peace Meadows in August had failed to accomplish any real good, and these officers might as well have saved themselves the trouble and danger of invading the feud district. The men wanted on warrants could not be found, and hostilities ceased only when the posses appeared on the scene; but it was a war to the death, and as soon as the officers had departed, the fighting flared out again with renewed fury.

Early in September a report reached Globe

that Mart Blevins had been seen at his ranch on Canyon Creek; but this was a mistake.

The next casualty occurred on September 17 when Harry Middleton and a cowboy named Joseph Underwood[1] were wounded in a skirmish with the Tewksburys. Several versions of this affair have been told, and it is impossible today to state which is correct, as the last man who really knew the truth was Jim Roberts. Will C. Barnes[2] says that Middleton and Underwood were ambushed by the Tewksburys. The former fell from his horse mortally wounded; Underwood escaped uninjured and quickly scampered to the shelter of a near-by tree. The fight then developed into a sniping contest, which lasted for several hours until a rifle bullet drilled a hole through the calf of Underwood's leg; but still the plucky cowboy fought on, holding the Tewksbury forces at bay until night fell and he escaped in the darkness.

Joe T. McKinney,[3] who was in the valley with Sheriff Mulvenon during the second invasion, relates that Jim Roberts pointed out to him the scene of the fight in which these two men were wounded, one mortally. Roberts told few of the details, but he showed McKinney the position of each man. It must have been a fight of some duration, for Roberts stated that the Tewksbury men lay flat on the ground behind small rocks.

After it was over they retired to a small knoll just north of the battleground and allowed the cattlemen to carry off their wounded.

A version that I heard on the Arizona range years ago gives more of the details, and is probably nearer correct. It seems that a Graham scout on September 16 reported that several Tewksbury men were camped on Cherry Creek, below the Tewksbury ranch; and plans were carefully made by the cattlemen for an early-morning raid. It would be an easy matter to dash through the camp just at dawn and wipe out the entire band while they were still rolled in their blankets.

The name of the leader of the attacking party was never disclosed, and the number on each side is not known. During the night, the Graham men took their position and patiently waited for dawn. Then in the early morning when there was just enough light for shooting, and while the Tewksbury forces still slept, the cowboys charged, fully expecting to catch their enemies off guard and wipe them out at one blow. But they had failed to take into consideration that cool, desperate Tewksbury fighting spirit that arose to meet all emergencies; and they paid dearly for this oversight.

Only the most expert marksman can hit a man from a galloping horse, and no casualties oc-

curred among the sheepmen. Both Jim Tewksbury and Jim Roberts fired from their blankets
as the cowboys charged through the camp, and
Middleton and Underwood received severe
wounds. As the raiders swept past, the Tewksbury men seized their arms, and scattered in the
brush from which they could repel another attack; but after this hot reception the cattlemen
retreated to the Graham ranch, all of the fight
taken out of them. Two days later Harry Middleton died of his wound, making the ninth
man who had given his life since the beginning
of the vendetta. This corroborates in a large
measure the story told by Jim Roberts to Joe Mc-
Kinney. After the Tewksbury forces took the
positions as related by Roberts they undoubtedly
made it so hot for the enemy that they were glad
enough to call it a day and retreat.

Whether Underwood was wounded in the
charge through the camp or during the fighting
that followed is not fully known; he took no
further part in the war, and by the time he had
recovered, hostilities had ceased. He was taken
to the Graham ranch house, where he was found
by Mulvenon on the twenty-first, but was not
disturbed. The wound did not improve, and he
was later removed to the Apache Indian agency
at San Carlos, where he remained for several
weeks under the care of Dr. Davis, the govern-

ment physician. Just why he went to San Carlos for medical attention is not known, unless he was afraid of being arrested if taken to either Prescott or Globe. He eventually recovered, and on January 13, 1888,[4] he was in Globe, after which he dropped out of sight, and nothing more is known of him.

The Silver Belt, in the issue of January 14, 1888, notes Underwood's return from San Carlos and states that he was under arrest on a bench warrant. This must be a mistake, for I can find no record of a warrant issued for this man.

Harry Middleton was buried in the little graveyard that was started on the Graham ranch when Billy Graham was killed. Charles Perkins told Will C. Barnes that he helped make a coffin out of boards from old packing boxes found at his store; and in that case Harry Middleton received a more pretentious funeral than most other victims of the vendetta who were generally rolled into some shallow grave without covering of any kind. Men killed in the feud received only the most primitive obsequies; but this was the best their comrades had to offer.

CHAPTER X

THE KILLING AT
PERKINS'
STORE

IN 1887 the greater part of the Pleasant Valley country and all of what is now Coconino County were included in old Yavapai County, and when news of the continued fighting reached Prescott, the county seat, Sheriff Mulvenon and the authorities decided that it was time for drastic measures. The law was not only openly defied by the feudists, but they had laughed in the sheriff's face on his first invasion. Anxious to secure the support and sanction of higher authority for any radical action that might be taken, Sheriff Mulvenon and District Attorney John C. Herdon on September 7 sought the advice of Governor C. Meyer Zulick.[1] During this conference the chief executive decided that there was just one thing to do: the sheriff must raise a posse large enough to sweep the valley and arrest every man of either side he could lay his hands on; and the force must be adequate to fight both Grahams and Tewksburys if necessary.

Billy Mulvenon's fighting blood was up. He had been elected to keep the peace in Yavapai County, and he made up his mind to end the war this time, even if it were necessary to kill a few men. On the ninth he wired Deputy Sheriff John W. Francis at Flagstaff to meet him at Payson with what men he could gather for another invasion of the feud district; and the next day he left Prescott with Deputies George Bristow, E. M. Tackett, and S. J. Sullivan. Others were undoubtedly with him at that time, but their names are not known today.

Old-timers recall that Mulvenon left Payson with about twenty men. Among those who accompanied Deputy Sheriff Francis from Flagstaff were Constable E. F. Odell, a member of the first posse in August, and two men by the name of Jacobs, possibly brothers or other relatives of William Jacobs, who was so brutally murdered at the Tewksbury ranch on the second. The sheriff was undoubtedly joined by others at Payson.

Because of delays in raising and outfitting a large expedition, Mulvenon's posse did not reach the valley until after the fight of the seventeenth, in which Harry Middleton was killed. If he could have proceeded without delay, the raid on the Tewksbury camp on Cherry Creek would not have taken place.

About this time Deputy Sheriff Joe McKinney[2] with John Scarlett, Lon Hawes, Joe Herschey, and Osmer D. Flake started in the direction of Pleasant Valley in pursuit of bandits who had robbed a Santa Fe train at Navajo Springs;

they lost the trail, and when they met Sheriff Mulvenon's posse camped above Haigler's ranch they decided to join him for the big adventure. This was certainly a formidable force of fighting men.

Pleasant Valley at that time was so far removed from any seat of justice that law and order had never been known there, and Sheriff Mulvenon decided that the quickest way of restoring peace was to arrest the leaders; but for some unknown reason practically all of his activities during this second expedition were directed against the Grahams and their henchmen. This may be explained by the fact that Jim Houck and George Newton, both Tewksbury partisans, joined the posse at Payson and probably exerted every means to that end. The fact that Houck held a deputy sheriff's commission in Apache County and claimed to have warrants for the arrest of everyone in the valley undoubtedly had considerable influence with Mulvenon.

Deciding that the quickest way of accomplishing his purpose was to capture the entire Graham outfit, the sheriff made his plans with that end in view. The utmost secrecy was necessary for the success of the scheme; and as a precaution every person encountered after the expedition left Payson was placed under arrest so that news of the invasion could not be carried to the Graham headquarters.

Before daylight on the morning of the twenty-first, twelve days after the first move from Prescott, Mulvenon and his men arrived at Perkins' store, a stone building erected during the Apache wars of the early 1880's as a fort for the settlers of Pleasant Valley. It stood within sight of the Graham ranch and Al Rose's cabin, the latter an active Graham fighter. The influence of Houck and Newton is seen in the sheriff's subsequent actions. The natural course would have been to surround both Graham's and Rose's and demand the men wanted; but another plan was executed.

Taking possession of Perkins' store that night, Mulvenon secreted his men in the building, and concealed his horses some distance away where they could not possibly be seen from the valley. Before daylight he sent five men with McKinney on a circuitous route over the foothills to the south, with instructions to return to the store just after sunrise by riding past the Graham and Rose houses, hoping that the appearance of strangers would decoy the Graham forces out. The remainder of the posse was placed in ambush behind the walls of an unfinished stone building about five or six feet high, which stood opposite the store. Perkins was erecting this for a residence.

Shortly after dawn the six men rode leisurely past the two houses as planned, and then tied their horses in front of the store; but when no one appeared after the passing of several minutes, Mulvenon sent five of these men and one of his own posse on McKinney's horse with instructions to ride away in the opposite direction. The trick was partially successful; and a few minutes later a signal of two shots fired from Rose's cabin was answered by three from Graham's. Considerable activity at the Graham ranch followed. Men were seen hastening to the corral, and a few minutes later Charles Blevins and John Graham rode to the store and cautiously circled the building, evidently looking for more men

Everything was quiet, ominously quiet; but behind the gray stone walls of the half-completed building death stalked the two luckless horsemen. Finally they rode up to investigate this one place that they had not examined, and just as they raised in their stirrups to look over the walls Billy Mulvenon stepped out with a double-barreled shotgun ready for action, and ordered them to throw up their hands. But John Graham and Charley Blevins had been schooled in old Arizona where life was always a courageous fight with death. Instead of complying with the demand they wheeled their horses and reached for their guns at the same time.

Mulvenon's shotgun roared twice in quick succession. The rifles of the posse belched death from the stone walls. The two unfortunate men were swept from their saddles by the rain of lead, and the next instant they lay sprawling in the dust, one dead before he struck the ground. A charge of buckshot had left a gaping hole in Blevins' back[3] from which his lifeblood gushed in a sickening stream.

John Graham was still living, desperately wounded with a rifle bullet through his body. The pallor of death was upon his face, and in answer to a feeble request McKinney gave him a drink of water. Billy Mulvenon told afterwards that he did not want to kill Graham and shot his horse through the neck, hoping that John would surrender; but the sheriff had forgotten that his man was afflicted with a nervous trigger finger.[4]

Other business demanded their immediate attention, for Tom Graham and his fighting henchmen must not escape; and so leaving the partisan leader's brother John to die alone as best he could, the posse hastened to Graham's and Al Rose's ranches. As they approached the Graham cabin, two horsemen, who were recognized as Louis Parker and a man named Bonner, galloped away. They were not pursued, for Mulvenon wanted Tom more than any of the others, and he was afraid that if he reduced his force, the Graham leader might escape. But he could have saved himself the trouble. As the posse closed in, a woman with a baby in her arms and a little child clinging to her dress came down from the cabin door, and slowly advanced towards them.

When the sheriff hastened to her, she informed him that the only men left in the house were Miguel Apocada and her husband, Joe Underwood, who was wounded and not able to move about. The poor woman, evidently under the impression that the approaching horsemen were Tewksbury men on a raid, was terrified beyond measure; but Mulvenon reassured her by stating that he did not want her husband. However, he did arrest Apocada, the Mexican, after which he proceeded to the cabin of Al Rose, one of the best of the Graham fighters. Rose was inclined to fight it out when Mulvenon demanded his surrender, but when he saw the size of the posse he wisely decided that the odds were too great and gave up. In view of the subsequent events it is plainly evident that bloodshed could have been averted had the sheriff proceeded to Graham's and Rose's cabins in the first place instead of resorting to a subterfuge.

On their way to the Tewksbury ranch, their next objective, Mulvenon told McKinney that the members of that faction would be there ready to surrender. That there must have been some secret understanding between the sheriff and the Tewksburys is shown by this statement and by the fact that seven of that faction were waiting for the posse. When the officers arrived they found Ed and Jim Tewksbury, George Newton, Jim Roberts, George Wagner, Joe Boyer, and Jake Lauffer waiting, and they surrendered without a word. George Newton had met the sheriff at Payson, but he had evidently left the posse by prearrangement on the night of the twentieth, before the ambush at Perkins' store, and had hastened to gather the Tewksbury forces.

The sheriff's well-planned scheme to capture Tom Graham had failed. In some manner the clan leader had slipped through his fingers; and so Billy Mulvenon came to the conclusion that his best course of action would be to return to Prescott with his nine prisoners before some escaped. However, before he left the valley, Sheriff Owens arrived with a posse of thirty men from Apache County, and took up the search for the Grahamites who had escaped, for it was believed that Tom was with them. Their trail was plain; but after following it for many miles through the hills and mountains, even these veteran trailers were forced to give up and return empty-handed. It is an interesting fact that during the war Tom Graham proved too wily for his enemies, and was never captured by any sheriff,[5] or caught off his guard, until his murder five years later.

Mulvenon's prisoners were given a preliminary hearing before Justice of the Peace Meadows at Payson, and Al Rose and Miguel Apocada were discharged, for there was no evidence of any kind against them; but the Tewksbury brothers and their five henchmen were held for the grand jury for the killing at the Middleton ranch on August 10. They were taken to Prescott where they were subsequently released under bond for their appearance before the next grand jury, and within a few days they were all back in the feud district.

The return of Sheriff Mulvenon's second posse was noted by the *Coconino Sun* of September 24, 1887, in the following item:

Deputy Sheriff John Francis, E. F. Odell, the two Jacobs boys and several others composing the posse that went from Flagstaff to join with Sheriff Mulvenon in his last attempt to restore law and order in Tonto Basin, returned Thursday afternoon, after being held in the saddle twenty days.

It seems probable that this last effort to make a peaceful abiding place of Pleasant valley will be successful. All of the Tewksburys who have not been killed in warfare are now under arrest, and only one of the opposite faction, Tom Graham, is at liberty. There are of course, some hangers-on, on both sides that have not been captured, but they will cause but little trouble now that their leaders are dead, or in the clutches of the law.

The sheriff's party, when they had joined forces at Payson, numbered nearly 20; still much caution was required in their operations. An attempt to lead the Graham party into a trap for their capture, was successful in bringing John Graham and C. Blevans within range. When Sheriff Mulvenon stepped out and ordered them to hold up their hands, instead of doing so they went for their guns, and the next instant there were two dead men on the ground. The Tewksburys surrendered peaceably when the officers approached them, and Ed and Jim Tewksbury, Joe Boyer and a man named Roberts were placed under arrest with Al Rose and McGill,[6] of the Graham party, were taken to the Prescott jail.

The officers of the law are to be congratulated upon having apparently put an end to a bloody and disgraceful feud in which eleven men have been killed during the past two months and as many seriously wounded. Of the Blevans family numbering six who took sides with the Grahams, only one remains alive, John, and he is in jail at St. Johns, having been wounded while resisting arrest by Sheriff Owens, at Holbrook.

The *Sun* was a little in error when it stated that the posse had been in the saddle for twenty days. Deputy Sheriff Francis did not leave Flagstaff with his men until the tenth, and he was back again on the afternoon of the twenty-second. As this was the day after the killing of

John Graham and Charles Blevins, it shows that Mulvenon must have left the valley immediately after the capture of the eight prisoners already noted in order to cover this distance by hard riding.[7]

In its account of the killing of John Graham and Charles Blevins *The Arizona Silver Belt* gives the following opinion on the propects of peace:

It is believed that peace has been restored to that ensanguined neighborhood until the courts have probed the matter and determined who are the instigators in the affray, accountable for so many lives which have been sacrificed. We do not share the belief, however, that the feud can be settled for all time in the courts. As long as men remain in both factions, bearing wounds inflicted by their enemies, thirsting for revenge, the lives of those who have in any way been connected with the quarrel will be in imminent jeopardy.

CHAPTER XI

TOM GRAHAM
FALLS IN
LOVE

THE PREDICTION made
by *The Arizona Silver
Belt* that the vendetta
could not be settled by
the courts proved well-founded, as subsequent
events showed; but for a time after Sheriff Mulvenon's second invasion, Pleasant Valley was
quiet. This was due, however, to the constant
vigilance of both sides, and not through any fear
of the law. The fighting had been so desperate
that they were all a little weary; and as a matter
of fact, hostilities never broke out again with
the ferocity that marked those bloody days of
August and September, of 1887. It is true that a
few men were killed from ambush; but there
were no raids and no pitched battles.

It was at this period that a seventeen-year-old
girl unexpectedly entered upon the bloody stage
of Pleasant Valley, and her restraining hand did
more to bring about peace than all the sheriffs
and courts in Arizona had been able to accomplish. This fair apostle of peace was Anne Melton by name, the daughter of Elder W. J. Melton, a Baptist preacher who resided near Tempe.
Old-timers who remember her will tell you today that Anne was unusually good-looking;
hers was a face that attracted more than pass-

ing attention, and her vivacious, affable disposition won her friends wherever she went.
Therefore it was not strange that Elder Melton's
home was a popular gathering place for young
men of the Salt River Valley, from far and near.
And those same old-timers will tell you that
Elder Melton was of that type of frontier min-
ister who could preach a regular "hell-fire and
brimstone sermon that made you shake and
shiver in your boots and repent your sins in
short order." Whether the conversions lasted is
another matter. But in spite of her friendly disposition, his daughter had inherited a good
share of his fiery temper, as subsequent events
will show.

One day several years after he settled in
Pleasant Valley Tom Graham made a trip to
Phoenix. There was nothing unusual in this,
for settlers of central Arizona went there as
often as business would permit. This was their
one touch with the outside world; but the events
of this trip were destined to change the whole
course of Tom Graham's life, for it was then
that he met Anne Melton. Just when and where
this meeting that had such far-reaching effects
occurred, we cannot say, but it was sometime in
1886 or early in 1887. The circumstances of
their first meeting are not known today; but in
spite of the fact that he was sixteen years her

senior, the fair Anne was attracted to the handsome young cattleman from Pleasant Valley,
who was endowed with that greatest quality
of human nature—the ability to make friends.
Their brief courtship was interrupted by the
fighting days of that summer of 1887; but in
spite of the sanguinary events of August and
September, Tom Graham did not forget the girl
down in the Salt River Valley; and even though
sudden death from a Tewksbury bullet constantly stalked his trail, his thoughts never
strayed far from her fair face. Even when the
fighting was at its worst he dreamed of the return of peaceful times when a man would no
longer have to ride the trail with his hand on
his six-shooter and his eyes on every rock and
bush—when he would no longer have to watch
every man with suspicion—and in all those
dreams the face of this girl was constantly at
his side. Tom Graham was very much in love;
and for love of a woman a man will do a great
deal, as later events proved.

Mulvenon's second invasion was followed by
a short period of peace. The Tewksburys and
their principal fighting men were held safely in
jail at Prescott.[1] Now was the time to act.
Nothing could happen during his absence; his
men would watch the valley carefully, and so
the last of the Grahams decided to put his sweet-

heart to the test. A decision meant immediate action, and one day in early October Tom Graham rode the trail to the Salt River Valley. Never was a girl put to a greater test than Anne Melton, when the fighting partisan leader in a bloody vendetta that had already cost many lives asked her to be his wife. At any moment a bullet from an ambushed foe might make her a widow; but without a moment's hesitation she accepted, for she was very deeply in love with Tom Graham, and during the trying days that followed, this seventeen-year-old girl with the attractive face and personality proved her sterling character many times.

And so Tom Graham and Anne Melton were united in marriage at her home near Tempe by her father on October 8, 1887.[2] The bride was just seventeen and the groom was thirty-three. The names of the guests at that wedding we do not know, for none of them are now living. However, we do know that two of those present were Samuel Graham and his brother-in-law, Mr. Parker, who arrived from their homes at Boone, Iowa, on October 6. Mr. Parker was the father of Louis Parker who had accompanied his young uncle Billy Graham to Arizona several years before, and fought on the side of his relatives during the feud. The two fathers made the long journey to Phoenix with the hope that they could induce their sons to leave the valley; and the wedding took place after their arrival. Louis Parker accompanied Tom Graham to Phoenix for the purpose of meeting his father, and he was probably present at the wedding.

But this meeting between fathers and sons was useless. In vain old Sam pleaded with his boy to leave Arizona; but Tom Graham's was a fighting spirit that makes leaders of men in both war and peace, and he refused to abandon the ranch and his dream of becoming a cattle king. He was a proud man, this Tom Graham, and he told his father point-blank that he would not have it said that the Tewksburys had chased him out of the valley. Sam Graham had something of his son's fighting spirit, and he wanted to return with him to Pleasant Valley; but Tom refused to permit him to enter the danger zone, and friends advised the old man that he would probably be killed. He returned to Iowa a few days later.

During this conversation Tom Graham told his father that northern sheepmen who wanted to drive through the Tonto Basin country to a winter range had started the trouble. His ranch, with plenty of grass and water, was the most desirable in all Pleasant Valley; and he stated that the Tewksburys in the beginning had boasted that they were going to get it for their sheep, even if they had to kill the Graham brothers.[3]

Tom Graham's young wife now had something to say in his affairs, and on October 12, four days after the wedding, the partisan leader went to the office of Sheriff Halbert in Phoenix and inquired if that officer had a warrant for his arrest. When informed that none had been issued in Maricopa County, he requested Halbert to notify Sheriff Mulvenon that he would go to Prescott for trial whenever wanted, if assured of protection.

Mulvenon acted upon this information by going to Phoenix immediately, and on October 16 he placed Tom Graham under arrest. The prisoner retained Attorney A. C. Baker to defend him, and the next day he went to Prescott with the sheriff. He was released immediately under three thousand dollars bail to appear before the grand jury in December at the same time as the Tewksburys and their followers. There was practically no evidence upon which to hold Tom Graham, and as far as I have been able to learn the grand jury failed to indict him.[4]

After his release on bail Graham returned to Tempe, and a few days later he rode away with his young bride to spend their honeymoon on his ranch in Pleasant Valley. What a honeymoon that must have been for a seventeen-year-old girl, right in the very heart of a bloody vendetta that had already cost many lives! But the love of a maid for a man is a wonderful thing, something unexplainable. She will leave her home, her parents, her friends, and a life of ease for that love, and endure all manner of suffering, privations, and hardships just to be with her man; to share his life, his hardships, his disappointments, and his dangers; and even though she knows all this before hand she will gladly go with him. Such was the love of Anne Melton for Tom Graham.

Pleasant Valley was one of the most remote outposts of this far-flung Arizona frontier of the 1880's. It was lonely with that terrible, dreary loneliness of the wilderness that men love and that often drives women mad. But Anne Melton was a daughter of old Arizona. Her father was a pioneer, and she had been born and reared on the edge of a civilization that had no room for the weaklings of either sex. The old Arizona frontier was no place for a woman; and those who defied its hardships and heartaches were endowed with a far greater courage than any man ever possessed. The Arizona of those days was a big adventure for the men. They loved its wild loneliness and its hard, cruel life with death stalking them on every trail; but to the women it was a terrible nightmare.

Possessed of a warm, friendly disposition, nature had also endowed Anne Melton with a capacity for great love—a love that has remained constant during the fifty-odd years that have passed since her husband's murder. This handsome, dashing factional leader in a bloody vendetta that had already made widows of several wives, was a romantic figure that would have appealed to the heart of any seventeen-year-old girl. Well knowing that at any instant the crack of a Winchester might end her dream of love, Anne Melton had gladly cast her lot with this man. Henceforth for all time his life was her life; his battles were hers, and his enemies were her enemies. Without a word of protest she went with him to this lonely cattle ranch in Pleasant Valley to live in the one-story log cabin that is still standing in a state of sad dilapidation. But from that day they rode up to their home in a land surrounded by their enemies, she never knew another happy hour, and the short bliss that she had enjoyed during the few days that had followed their marriage was soon broken by the terrible hand of the vendetta that clutched this valley in its death grip. Grim tragedy stalked her trail down through the years and cast its black shadow over her life. Other widows of the vendetta married again, but not Anne Graham; and down through all the rest of her life she has carried the memory of that cowboy sweetheart who rode out of war-torn Pleasant Valley and won her heart. He was her first and only love, this sweetheart of her girl-hood years, and no other man ever came into her life.

CHAPTER XII

THE BATTLE IN THE COURTS

THE FALL of the year is the most beautiful of all the seasons in central Arizona. The intense heat of the summer is gone, but there is enough warmth left in the sun's rays to keep back the frost that threatens. The air exerts a vigorous influence upon the body not felt at any other time of the year; and as you breath it deep into your lungs it sets your blood on fire and goes to your head like rare old wine. You fairly drink it in by the lungful, and no matter what your troubles are, you feel that it is good to be alive. But you must get out in the open to feel its exhilaration to the highest degree before you are capable of understanding; you must ride over a land where fences and plows and farms and crops are unknown—a land where your neighbors are miles apart and spend their lives on the hurricane deck of a cow pony—to enjoy to the fullest extent the glorious intoxication of a beautiful fall day in central Arizona. Those clear, crisp days of October and November, with just the proper proportion of the tang of frost in the air, certainly made life worth living on the old-time cattle range.

The fall of 1887 brought a welcome respite

to the people of war-torn Pleasant Valley. The feud was still as bitter as ever but the leaders, by mutual consent, were apparently glad enough to adopt a policy of watchful waiting; and the seventeen-year-old girl whom Tom Graham had taken to blood-soaked Pleasant Valley as his bride did more to hold the factional leader in check than all the sheriffs and courts of Arizona ever accomplished. Her influence was the greatest factor towards a permanent peace that could have entered the vendetta; for war, whether a clan feud or a battle between nations, is always a horrible nightmare for the women. By the time Tom Graham returned to his ranch, the Tewksburys and their henchmen had all been released on bail, and tensed nerves were so near the breaking point that the slightest provocation would have precipitated another bloody battle. It was the restraining hand of Anne Graham that held both sides in check. As long as they were not attacked, the Tewksburys were willing enough to remain quiet, for they did not wish to commit any overt act that would place them in a bad light in court unless forced to do so in self-defense; and Tom Graham was held in check by his wife.

The Saint Johns *Herald* contains the interesting information that Ed and Jim Tewksbury took advantage of this tranquil period to slip quietly into Holbrook about the middle of October to replenish their almost exhausted stock of ammunition.

An interesting story, of an alleged attempt by Ed Tewksbury to kill a woman of the opposite faction one day in Holbrook, came to me in a rather roundabout way; and I am unable to verify it from any other source. It was first told by Mrs. Amanda Gladden, who was living with the Blevins family at the time. All of the old-timers who would have known the truth were either dead when I heard the story or had left Holbrook long before. However, I am giving it for what it is worth; the reader should remember that it might be only a product of feud hatreds. On the other hand, there is always the chance that it is true.

According to this old tale, Ed Tewksbury and some friends were in a saloon in Holbrook one day when the clan leader saw a Graham girl pass the door. Like a flash he drew his gun, but was seized by friends before he could fire.

He is quoted as saying: "There isn't any use in letting any of them live."

The date of this supposed incident is not known, but if it did occur, it was probably during the visit of Ed and Jim Tewksbury in Holbrook in October, 1887. One flaw in this story is that Anne Graham was the only girl of that clan in Arizona. The brothers had a half sister, but she was never in the Southwest; and Tom Graham would hardly have permitted his young wife to venture into Holbrook when he well knew that the Tewksburys and their men often went there for supplies. If such an incident did occur the woman was either Eva Blevins, the wife of one of the Blevins brothers, or Mesa Blevins, their sister, who was about twelve years of age at the time. And it was probably Jim Tewksbury instead of Ed, for the former had a quick, nasty temper that was almost uncontrollable at times.

With the Graham fighters held in check by seventeen-year-old Anne and the Tewksburys on constant guard against surprise, Tom Graham changed the plan of attack for the time being, and during the last days of November, 1887, the vendetta battleground was shifted out across the mountains from Pleasant Valley to Prescott, where the members of both factions went in force to attend the grand jury that would meet the first part of December. That a conflict did not occur on the way was due to the fact that both leaders were careful to keep their men together and see that the opposing forces did not meet on the trail.

The details of this stage of the feud were related to me by the late C. P. Hicks,[1] of Prescott, who was a member of the grand jury that later indicted the Tewksburys. While court was in session both factions camped side by side at the old O K Corral and Store, where Mr. Hicks was employed as a clerk. Living in such close proximity where every movement was watched, it was the general opinion that a clash was inevitable; and never in all its thrilling frontier history was this county seat under such tense excitement. While every man connected with the feud was very careful, it was felt that at any instant some insignificant, unforseen incident might precipitate a general fight. An indiscreet word uttered by some half-drunken man would have been enough. Sheriff Mulvenon had a number of extra deputies ready for a crisis, and most of the citizens as well as the members of both clans went heavily armed at all times. No man dared lay his guns aside. Prescott was over a mine of clan hatreds that might explode without the least warning.

Both leaders realized that a conflict under such circumstances would bring disaster to both sides and cost the lives of innocent persons who were in no way connected with their differences, and nothing occurred. It can be said to the credit of both chieftains that when they met in towns where the lives of others would be in danger they held their men in with an iron hand, and in spite of their bitterness towards each other, they only engaged in fighting when in their own territory.

Mr. Hicks informed me that while camped side by side at the O K Corral the members of both factions conducted themselves as gentlemen, coming in close contact, brushing elbows, but never speaking to each other. Because of his connection with the grand jury, Mr. Hicks became well acquainted with those fighting men of old Arizona, and they were all on friendly terms with him.

The old court records at Prescott show that on December 3, 1887, the Grahams succeeded in having Edwin and James Tewksbury, Joseph Boyer, James F. Roberts, George A. Newton, Jacob Lauffer, and George Wagner indicted for the murder of Hampton Blevins, who was killed in the fight at the Middleton ranch on August 10. As I have already stated, the reason for the omission of John Paine's name from this indictment is not known.

This shows beyond all doubt that George A. Newton had openly and actively lined himself up with the Tewksburys. The fact that a cattleman espoused the cause of sheepmen is one of the unexplained mysteries of the war. No one has ever been able to give the reason for this action on Newton's part.[2]

As previously stated, the grand jury failed to indict Tom Graham, while Al Rose and Miguel Apocada were released at the preliminary hearing before Justice Meadows at Payson.

Nothing occurred to mar the peace of Prescott; and after the grand jury's indictment, the Tewksburys and their friends were released under bond to appear for trial. The cases were called in the district court at Prescott in June, 1888,³ but the members of both sides, as well as neutrals, were afraid to testify for fear of assassination, and the county attorney's motion for dismissal on the grounds of insufficient evidence to convict, was granted by the court. Thus the dreaded hand of the feud held the courts powerless to end the vendetta.

Will C. Barnes informs me that the Tewksburys retaliated by having Tom Graham charged with the murder of the Navajo sheepherder, and the battleground was shifted again, this time to the little Mormon settlement of Saint Johns, county seat of Apache County. Once more the difference in the names appears, for the old court records at Saint Johns show that George and William Graham were charged with felony in 1888; and thus George Graham appears upon the stage again for the first time since 1883. Unfortunately, the nature of the crime and disposition of the case are not given. The court records have disappeared from Saint Johns courthouse, probably borrowed by someone who failed to return them; and thus what might have been a very important source of information has been lost. Personally, I am of the opinion that some old friend of the Grahams took this means of wiping that family name from the legal slate. But for the clerk's old minute book which still lies among the musty court records at Saint Johns, together with the memories of Alfred Ruiz, this would have been successful, and the name of George Graham would never have been known in connection with the vendetta.

Mr. Barnes must be mistaken in saying that Tom Graham was arrested when both the old court minute book and Mr. Ruiz gave the name as George. That these two men are not speaking of different occasions is shown by the fact that Mr. Ruiz's discription of George Graham is exactly the same as that of Tom Graham given to me by Mr. Barnes.

I am inclined to believe that George Graham voluntarily appeared for trial, as there is nothing to show that a warrant was ever served. In the absence of the old court records, the reason that the name William Graham appears when he had been dead for nearly a year will probably never be explained. That there was also a mistake in the name of William is hardly probable because it was well known in Saint Johns and throughout Arizona that William and John had been killed the previous summer, and that Tom was the last of the brothers. The only logical explanation is that the old charge of cattle stealing in 1882 and 1883 had been resurrected.

The old minute book at Saint Johns also gives the interesting information that James Tewksbury was under indictment in Apache County; but the nature of the crime or the disposition of the case are not noted.[4]

Mr. Barnes gave me a vivid description of that gathering of fighting men of both clans at the little Mormon settlement for the trial of a Graham, when a word from either side would have started a bloody battle that would have wiped out many lives. As at Prescott, both leaders realized the tense situation and watched their men carefully; for Saint Johns was a typical frontier town where the citizens went armed and were expert shots, and a fight would have resulted disastrously to both factions.

The Graham leader was described by Mr. Barnes as a large man, attired in a black sombrero and a long black coat of the style popular with Southern planters, preachers, and Kentucky colonels of that period. Huge bulges under his coat at each hip indicated that he was well armed. This description tallies exactly with that given me by Alfred Ruiz.

Alfred Ruiz, who is still living at Gallup, New Mexico, was clerk of the district court at Saint Johns at that time, and I am indebted to him for definite information that there was really a George Graham. Mr. Ruiz was personally acquainted with the Graham on trial at that time, and he gave me the name of the defendant as George, thus establishing the identity of this man beyond all doubt. His story of the events that occurred in Saint Johns on this occasion follows:

"As I recall the details now I was on my way to open my office in the court house about eight o'clock one morning. The district court was in session, and the Graham and Tewksbury men were in town for the trial of George Graham. Just as I was opposite Walter Darling's saloon I heard loud talking, and I went in to investigate.

"The first person I saw was George Graham who was introduced to me. He was a man about twenty-five or twenty-six years of age,[5] and weighed about two hundred pounds, well built, good-looking and a good talker. He was neatly dressed in a long black coat and a large black hat, and he reminded me of a Methodist preacher.

"He had been indicted in the district court, and was in Saint Johns for the trial. After talking with him for a few minutes some of the men told him that I was the clerk of the court. He was immediately interested, and said that he would like to go to the courthouse, but was afraid that he might have trouble with the Tewksbury gang. I informed him that as I was an officer of the court I would protect him, and that while he was with me there would be no trouble.

"Graham was very much excited, and as we walked to the courthouse together he told me that his brothers[6] had had some trouble with the Tewksburys in Tonto Basin. He was armed with two pistols, and seemed constantly on guard against surprise; but no one molested us in any way. My recollection is that George Graham was discharged at that term of court. I afterwards heard that Tom Graham, a brother of George, was killed by Ed Tewksbury near Phoenix. The trouble was brought about by cattle rustling in the Tonto basin country."

After the charge against George Graham was dismissed at Saint Johns, the scene of the war shifted back to Pleasant Valley.

CHAPTER XIII

WAR TO THE
LAST MAN

WHEN the courts failed to punish those implicated in the war and stop further bloodshed, the vendetta broke out again, but not with the same fury that had marked the early engagements. After the first few sanguinary weeks all participants except those closely associated with the Grahams and Tewksburys had withdrawn, and most of them left the country. The pitched battles and raids that had marked those bloody days of August and September, 1887, were no more. Now it was a war of ambush and assassinations. A life was the price of an unguarded moment. Both sides skulked through the brush and timber of the rugged mountains like hunted wild animals, shunning the open places by day. Men were shot down as they rode along lonely trails or when they opened their cabin doors in the early morning. At night, armed bands swept down upon some cabin or lonely camp, and the bloody hand of the feud gripped another victim. The number killed during this stage will never be known.

The statement has been made, frequently without contradiction, that hired gunmen were imported from Texas and other sections, but this is very doubtful. Central Arizona was a danger ous land for even a peaceable stranger during those stirring days—a land shunned by every man except those actually engaged in the feud. Professional fighters are a very expensive luxury, for they are engaged in the most dangerous occupation in the world, and they always demand high wages. The war had been so costly that neither the Tewksburys nor Tom Graham had the money to buy fighting men. Some claims have been made that the cattle companies brought men in from Texas, but the only big outfit involved was the Hash Knife (Aztec Land and Cattle Company), and before the close of 1887 it had practically withdrawn from the conflict. If any men were brought in from the outside at any time, they disappeared and were never seen again. It is possible that Daggs Brothers, who financed the Tewksburys from the beginning to the end, may have imported hired gunmen, but there is no evidence of this kind.

Dates from this time on are hard to obtain; but the fighting was all over by the end of 1888, for it was early in 1889 that Tom Graham, weary of the strife, left the valley at the solicitation of his young wife to make a new start in a land that did not hold so many tragic memories. The vendetta dragged itself through the weary months of 1888, neither side daring to relax its vigilance for an instant. With death as the price of a careless moment, the men left in both factions were constantly alert; but casualties continued in spite of all this caution. Held in by the restraining hand of his wife, Tom Graham remained on the defensive; and the Tewksburys continued to skulk through the brush.

It was during this period that Al Rose, one of the most noted of the remaining Graham fighters, was killed near the Houdon ranch on Spring Creek. During those bloody days of September, 1887, someone had fired at him from ambush and missed; but the newspapers reported that he had been killed. The exact date of his death is not known, but it was evidently early in November.[1] With two companions, one of whom was Louis Naeglin, he had camped at the Houdon ranch; and while his comrades were busy getting breakfast the next morning he went out to look for their saddle horses that had been hobbled the previous night and turned loose to graze. Scarcely had he disappeared when several shots startled the men in the cabin and when they rushed out to investigate they found Al Rose stretched out in the grass, dead with a bullet wound in his back.[2] The tracks on the ground told a plain story. A shot from ambush had ended the career of another Graham fighting man, and his assassins had walked up to the body to make certain of his death. His comrades packed the corpse back to Graham's, slung across his saddle horse and lashed on with his lariat, and sadly buried all that was left of Al Rose in the little boot hill graveyard near by. Now it held five victims of Tewksbury vengeance.[3]

According to Joe McKinney,[4] it was Glenn Reynolds who killed Al Rose. His authority for this statement is no less a person than Ed Tewksbury, who told McKinney that they (evidently meaning a party of Tewksbury men) were concealed behind a brush fence at the Houdon ranch "looking for some parties." When they saw Rose come out of the cabin in the early morning, Reynolds beckoned to him, but Al seemed undecided as to just what he should do. Several times he started forward and then stopped, but when he finally turned towards the house Reynolds killed him with a shotgun. This would account for the story that he was hit so many times.[5]

That bushwhacking was not carried on by the Tewksburys alone is shown by the attempt to kill Jacob Lauffer, a Tewksbury man; and in view of subsequent events it is probable that some Graham partisans had been "gunning" for him for some time. On August 4, 1888, a shot crashed from the brush as he came from his cabin door, and a forty-five Winchester bullet smashed his arm. Jake's life was saved by the speed with which he got back into the house.

Two other men named Cody and Coleman were fired upon that same day while on their way to Lauffer's ranch, and the former's horse was wounded.

The names of the parties who tried to murder these men were never known, but Jim Houck used both incidents as an excuse to explain his own questionable actions in connection with the lynching of Stott, Scott, and Wilson,[6] the details of which are related in a subsequent chapter.

Charles Perkins states that after the killing of Al Rose, he and two others buried a man named Elliot,[7] who had drifted into the feud district from the "land of nowhere" and married a widow named Mrs. Bishop. This was undoubtedly the widow of W. H. Bishop, one of the early settlers in the valley who was indicted at Prescott in 1884 with other members of the Tewksbury faction for cattle stealing. Elliot's part in this vendetta is not known; but he must have become mixed up in it in some way, and paid the price with his life—and found a lonely, unmarked grave, now long forgotten, in the Arizona wilderness.

Mr. Perkins believes that at least six men[8] were shot from ambush as they rode lonely trails in the feud country during those bushwhacking days in the latter part of 1887 and in 1888. It is a fact that unknown men, thirsting for reputations as bad *hombres*, were lured into the valley by glamorous tales of the war and killed before they even had a chance to show their skill with a gun. Strangers were in more danger than those known to be either Graham or Tewksbury partisans. The fighting men of both sides would kill them on sight, for they did not know what to expect from a stranger, and they were taking no chances.

Many tales of other battles are still told in Arizona; but old residents of the valley declare that most of them are pure fiction born of the feud, for open warfare ceased after Sheriff Mulvenon's second invasion in September, 1887.

The story of a big fight at the Graham ranch, in which several men are said to have been killed, is an example of these groundless tales. According to one version, Tewksbury men concealed on a hill near by shot away a corner of the house; but Miss Ola Young, who has lived there since 1889, informed me that this is not correct. The never-relaxing Graham vigilance made an attack, even by night, impossible. The Tewksburys, on account of their inferior numbers, were compelled to fight on the defensive; but as their force was never more than eight men at any one time and as they were generally scattered in pairs, they simply did not dare risk an open attack or raid against the superior numbers mustered around Tom Graham by the cattlemen. From information gathered from many sources I am very strongly of the opinion that most of the Tewksbury fighting was done by the brothers Ed and Jim, and Jim Roberts and John Rhodes. Jim Houck figured in it to some extent when he could do so with safety under cover of his deputy sheriff's badge; but from what I have been able to learn he was never willing to take the chances necessary in an open attack.

The many conflicting stories of the vendetta have thrown a sort of mystery around the fate of Jim Tewksbury. This is especially true during the last few years, for most of the men who knew him are dead; and in the land where he died, the majority of people do not know his fate. These tales that have come to me from many sources state that he was killed during the fighting in Pleasant Valley, murdered in the Salt River Valley, still living as a hermit in the mountains, and emigrating to California. Strange how people forget with the passing of the years.

As a matter of fact, Jim Tewksbury, the most deadly fighter among all the vendetta's clansmen and the man who is credited with starting the first clash at the Middleton ranch, passed

over his last trail in a very unromantic manner,
for I have learned positively that he died of
quick consumption at Prescott in 1888, following an attack of measles that settled on his
lungs. I have been unable to learn the date, but
Will C. Barnes quotes the Phoenix *Herald* of
December 6, 1888, which states: "Jim Tewksbury died of consumption at 5:30 p. m., December 4, at his sister's home in Globe."[9]

These tales that have come to my attention are
worth repeating, not that they have any historical value, but to show how easy it is to build
up fables that may be accepted by another
generation as the truth.

Sam Brown, of Gallup, New Mexico, once told
me that many years after the feud was over he
heard that Jim Tewksbury had settled in the
Salt River Valley where he and Tom Graham
became warm friends. Then Jim was murdered.
Just think of it: a Tewksbury friends with a
Graham. Mr. Edw. E. Johnson, of Phoenix, former deputy county attorney, tried to trace the
origin of this story for me among some of the
old-timers still living in the capital. Even they
had forgotten, for all agreed that the vendetta
leader was killed in Pleasant Valley; but they
were unable to give any details.

Another story comes from William MacLeod
Raine, of Denver, the noted author who wrote

the first account of the Pleasant Valley war as a magazine article many years ago. He informs me that once while in a barber shop in Phoenix about 1918 he was told that Jim Tewksbury was living the life of a hermit in the mountains.

During the summer of 1930 a young man named Smith appeared in Tucson and claimed to be a son of Jim Tewksbury. According to his tale, the clansman went to California after the war, changed his name to Smith, and was married. However, this man told some other stories that were known to be untrue, and his claim was branded as fictitious.

TOM HORN   MUCH HAS been said, especially in later years, of the part played in the Pleasant Valley war by Tom Horn, the Wyoming cattle detective who was hanged at Cheyenne on November 20, 1903, for the murder of Willie Nickells, a fourteen-year-old boy. That Horn was associated with the Tewksburys there is no doubt, for I have found considerable evidence among people who knew him at that time to show that he was in their company frequently during the latter days of the fighting at least. The full extent of his activities will never be known, for only one man who lived in recent years could have told the entire story, and he carried it to the grave. Some say that Tom Horn went into the valley as a spy; but who employed him and for what purpose is uncertain. Whether he gained the confidence of either side is not known.

That Tom Horn was a brave man, an excellent shot, and a first-class cowhand as well as one of the best trailers in the Southwest is a matter of history. He could throw the longest rope of any cowboy in old Arizona, a land famous for good ropers; and today a special brand of lariat is called the "Tom Horn." In a field against many contestants he won the roping contest at Globe

Tom Horn

A Cowboy of Old Arizona

on July 4, 1888, and at the Phoenix state fair
that fall he again carried off first honors. But
Tom Horn threw a wide loop in more ways than
one, for he was often inclined to allow his imagination to soar when relating his exploits, as a
careful reading of his autobiography will show.
During the Apache wars of the early 1880's he
served as a packer under Al Sieber, Arizona's
most famous scout and Indian fighter; and, according to his own statement, Horn was the man
who ended the Apache wars.

Will C. Barnes, who was personally acquainted with men on both sides of the Pleasant
Valley war, informs me that he never heard
them mention Horn's name. In his opinion
many of Horn's tales of adventure in the Apache
wars are pure fiction. This opinion is worthy of
consideration, for Mr. Barnes himself is a man
who speaks with the authority of a veteran of
those same Apache wars and he is one of the best-
informed men on the history of that period. He
remembers Tom Horn as a "scrub" packer
about San Carlos and other army posts in the
early 1880's.

Regardless of any opinion we may have
formed of Horn's reputation for truth, it is a
historical fact that he did see some hazardous
service with United States troops operating
against hostile Apaches in Old Mexico. The au-

thority for this is no less a person than Lieutenant Charles B. Gatewood, the one man above all
others who induced Geronimo to return to the
United States and surrender to General Miles.
Lieutenant Gatewood trusted the Apaches to the
extent that he boldy entered their camp with
only a few men as an escort, one of whom was
Tom Horn; and it would have been very easy
for those human tigers of the desert to have
wiped out this little band of men.

In his own narrative of the surrender of the
Apaches, Lieutenant Gatewood states that in
August, 1886, with an escort of six or eight
men, and Tom Horn and Jose Maria as additional interpreters, he left Fronteras, Mexico, in
search of the hostiles reported by scouts to be
somewhere in the Sierra Madre Mountains. The
camp was located after a long search, and on the
twenty-fourth this young lieutenant rode boldy
into the Apache stronghold with his little escort
of less than a dozen men and delivered General
Miles's message to Geronimo and Natchez. Only
a man of heroic courage dared to trust his life in
Geronimo's hands in those days; and only men
of uncommon bravery would have dared accompany him. And Tom Horn was one of that in-
trepid little band.

In spite of his courage Horn loved to boast
of his exploits; and a spirit of bravado fre-

quently led him far from the truth. That this tendency to romance got him into trouble in Wyoming and resulted in his execution for murder, there is now little doubt; for the passing of almost fifty years has practically established the fact that he was "framed." However, that is another story and has nothing to do with his part in the Pleasant Valley vendetta.

Horn claimed to have been sent into the feud district by Sheriff "Buckey" O'Neill as a mediator; but a thorough investigation of his life in Arizona fails to reveal anything upon which to base this claim except his own statement in the autobiography[1] he wrote while in jail at Cheyenne before his execution fifteen years later. This statement of the part he claims to have played in the Pleasant Valley war follows:

"Early in April, 1887, some of the boys came down from Pleasant valley, where there was a big rustler war going on and the rustlers were getting the best of the game. I was tired of the mine and willing to go, and so away we went. Things were in a pretty bad condition. It was a war to the knife every time the two outfits ran together. A great many men were killed in the war. Old man Blevans and his three sons, three of the Grahams, a Bill Jacobs, Jim Payne, Al Rose, John Tewksbury, Stott, Scott, and a man named "Big Jeff" were hung on the Apache and Gila county line. Others were killed, but I do not remember their names now. I was the mediator, and was deputy sheriff under Buckey O'Neil, of Yavapai county, under Commodore Owens, of Apache County, and Glenn Reynolds, of Gila county. I was still a deputy for Reynolds a year later when he was killed by the Apache Kid, in 1888.

The mine referred to was in Arivaipa Canyon, where Horn worked a claim for some time after the close of the Apache wars. A careful reading of his autobiography and a comparison with historical facts show that he allowed his imagination to soar when relating his own exploits.

In his statement he gives the impression that the war had been in progress for some time before he received that visit "early in April, 1887," from some of the boys from Pleasant Valley. However, the records show that hostilities did not break out for several weeks after that date; and no man ever went into the feud district in the role of a peacemaker between the warring factions. Those officers who tried to stop the fighting did so with six-shooters and Winchesters as their mediators, and even they failed to bring peace to that blood-soaked land.

As a matter of fact, the old records at Prescott show that William O. (Buckey) O'Neill was not sheriff until 1889, and he served until the close of 1890. The fighting was over before he took office, and he never entered the valley or made an attempt to restore order. Therefore it would have been impossible for O'Neill to have sent Tom Horn there as a deputy. Sheriff Owens led one expedition into the valley in September, 1887, but there is nothing to show that Tom Horn was a member. Sheriff Reynolds did take some part in the vendetta, but not in the capacity of a peace officer as far as I have been able to learn. His activities were all on the Tewksbury side.[2] Horn is in error in regard to the year of Reynold's death, for he was killed by the Apache Kid on November 2, 1889.[3]

In an effort to secure some exact information of this man's activities, a resident of Pleasant Valley (since 1889) recently made inquiry for me among the few old-timers still living there, and they all declare that Tom Horn was not engaged on either side, at least not in the early stages[4] of the war. However, this party learned that he did go into the valley with Ed Tewksbury and John Rhodes after most of the fighting was over. That Horn was on very friendly terms with the Tewksbury faction is shown by the fact that when he left Arizona about 1890 or 1891, Ed accompanied him to Wyoming, but he returned a short time later with the explanation that that country was too tough for him. It must have been a wild land, indeed, that was too tough for Ed Tewksbury; but he was probably tired of trouble.

Mr. Robert Scott, of Mesa, an old Arizona pioneer who was acquainted with Tom Horn in the 1880's, has also given me some interesting information on this subject. While on his way to Pleasant Valley, Horn stopped one night with

Mr. Scott, but he did not disclose the nature of his mission into the feud district. It was the general opinion at that time that he was sent in as a spy by someone; but for what purpose and by whom has never been revealed. However, there is not the least shred of evidence to show that he was a deputy sheriff at any time during the war. Mr. Scott stated that in reality Horn took sides with the Tewksbury faction, and while riding through the Pleasant Valley country some time later he camped one night with six Tewksbury men, one of whom was Tom Horn. This is borne out by the other information that Horn was associated with Edwin Tewksbury and John Rhodes.

Tom Horn never returned to Arizona. Remaining in Wyoming and Colorado until the outbreak of the Spanish-American War in 1898, he entered the service as a packer for General Shafter's army in Cuba; but he contracted fever before hostilities ended, and went to John C. Coble's ranch in the Iron Mountain country of Wyoming to recuperate. This section was infested with rustlers, and the leading cattlemen employed Horn as a stock detective as soon as he was able to work. In order to inspire fear among the cattle thieves he built up a reputation as a killer by boasting of the number of men he had slain. To quote his own words, this reputation was his "stock in trade"; but there is nothing on record to show that he ever actually killed anyone. When he met a man suspected of tampering with brands he immediately gave detailed accounts of his many victims. This accomplished the desired result, and the rustlers soon grew to fear and hate him. The war between the big outfits and the cattle thieves became very bitter. There were numerous killings that the rustlers blamed on Horn, and in order to add to his reputation, he encouraged these stories.

A personal feud developed between the Miller and Nickells families, both nesters; and in the summer of 1901, Kels Nickells brought a band of sheep into the district. This was an unpardonable sin on the Wyoming cattle range in those days, just as it had been years before in Arizona, and the feeling against Nickells was very intense.

On July 19, 1901, Willie Nickells, fourteen-year-old son of Kels Nickells, was found dead. The evidence pointed to one Victor Miller, but there was not enough to warrant an arrest. The Millers, with the help of the rustlers in the district, threw suspicion on Tom Horn. They wanted him out of the way, for his reputation as a killer had inspired a deep fear in their ranks, and it is now a well-established fact that they considered this the easiest way of getting rid of him. The evidence against Horn was very flimsy; but he was convicted, and on November 20, 1903, he was hanged at Cheyenne. Boasting, especially when intoxicated, was Tom Horn's greatest fault, and it is doubtful if he ever killed unless in self-defense. At any rate, time has practically proved him innocent of the murder of Willie Nickells.

James W. Stott

James W. Stott

CHAPTER XV

LYNCHING OF STOTT, SCOTT, AND WILSON

THE TRIPLE lynching of Jim Stott, Jim Scott, and Billy Wilson one day in August, 1888, is generally regarded as one of the last incidents of the war in the Pleasant Valley country; and in view of the well-established fact that these three men were entirely innocent of any crime and were not affiliated with either side, this was the most dastardly act of this bitter vendetta. Tewksbury sympathizers were charged with this outrage; but neither Jim nor Ed, nor their close associates, had any part in the affair. The evidence points conclusively to Jim Houck as the instigator.

Will C. Barnes declares that this lynching had nothing to do with the feud; but there is no doubt that it was carried out by some of the men affiliated with the Tewksburys, aided by others, who used the wounding of Jake Lauffer as an excuse. Later events have proved that this was only used as a pretext to carry out a private grudge. It shows how completely lawless was the spirit that ruled that bloody land in the latter 1880's; and as this condition was a direct result of the disorder in Pleasant Valley, this act must be charged to the vendetta.

Young Jim Stott[1] was a native of New England. His parents were weavers in a manufacturing town in Massachusetts; and with frugality and industry they had accumulated some property. At regular intervals they sent money to their son in Arizona; and in Western parlance this placed him in the class known as remittance men. I have been unable to learn the reason that led him to the Southwest; perhaps he was in search of adventure; perhaps the old home town was a little tame.

During a trip to Arizona his parents made the acquaintance of Sam Brown, who conducted a livery stable in Holbrook at that time and was interested, with Daggs Brothers, in the sheep business.[2] A typical Westerner of the 1880's, bluff and outspoken and honest to the core, Sam Brown quickly gained the confidence of these New England folks. Strangers in a strange land where life was so utterly different from their own quiet, easygoing Massachusetts town where every day was a repetition of the one just passed, the Stotts turned to the Arizonian in their hour of need and asked him to watch over the son they were leaving in this wild western land, and see that the money they intended to send him was wisely invested. And Sam Brown, in his turn, attracted to these quiet, trusting New England folks, promised to watch over their boy. Consequently, young Stott placed a great deal of confidence in Mr. Brown, who knew every business transaction he ever made.

Jim Stott located at Bear Spring, near the old Stinson ranch in Phoenix Park in the Mogollon Mountains, sixty miles south of Holbrook. Phoenix Park is forty miles from Pleasant Valley as the crow flies; and like other ranchers and settlers in the country bordering the feud district, Stott had remained neutral, for he had other troubles.

Stott made one grave mistake when he purchased horses with blotched brands.[3] While it is impossible to say definitely whether or not this had anything to do with his subsequent murder, for the names of the parties associated with him in these questionable transactions are not known today, the general opinion among some of the old-timers is that this was the real cause of the lynching. Mr. Brown was very much opposed to this business of dealing in stolen horses, and he advised Stott to buy sheep as the safest investment. But the youth had enough of the wild, adventurous spirit to take a chance for some easy money, for the profits were larger. Had he followed Sam Brown's advice, the lives of three men might not have paid the penalty. While Stott had taken no part in stealing horses, he had purchased them from the rustlers and he was

196 ARIZONA'S DARK AND BLOODY GROUND

one of the very few who knew their identity. At that time Sheriff Owens had given the thieves something to worry about, for he was hot on their trail, determined to drive them out of the country. The supposition is that they were afraid that Stott would talk, and so they followed the old safety-first maxim that "dead men tell no tales."

One day in the early summer of 1888, a young man suffering from consumption got off the train at Holbrook. All his worldly possessions consisted of ten dollars. He was without friends; but warm-hearted Sam Brown's sympathy was aroused by the young "lunger's" apparent hopelessness, and he told him to stick around until he could get a place for him. Accordingly, when Stott rode into Holbrook a few days later, Brown introduced these two, both strangers in a strange land, but there for entirely different reasons; the one to seek health in the pure, life-giving air, and the other his fortune and adventure. The one found health; but all the other ever got out of it was the adventure—and a lonely grave in the wilderness. Stott was a sympathetic young man, and when Brown suggested that the invalid could make himself useful about the ranch in exchange for his board, he was immediately taken with the idea. As a result of this meeting the consumptive went to

Phoenix Park to "keep the beans warm" and guard the chickens from hawks. In other words, he was to be "chief cook and bottle washer."

The spring days passed into summer, the busiest time of all the year for the men of old-time rangeland; and after the regular spring branding was over, they spent their time hunting strays and horses. Consequently, it was August before Stott was again in Holbrook. As usual he went to Sam Brown's livery stable where he met Billy Wilson,[4] a wandering prospector on his way with saddle and pack horse from the mining camp of Durango, Colorado, to try his fortunes at Globe. He alternated prospecting with work in mines. The night before Stott rode into Holbrook, Wilson had stopped at Brown's stable; and as the trail to Globe passed through Phoenix Park, Stott invited the prospector to accompany him back to his ranch the next morning. Unfortunately for Billy Wilson, he accepted. He was an utter stranger who was just passing through the country, and it is doubtful if he even knew of the feud in Pleasant Valley; but the very fact that he was a stranger probably led to his death, for the rustlers and feudists were suspicious of him for this very reason.

Of the four men who spent the night of August 10[5] at the Stott ranch, only the consumptive

lived to tell the story of the tragic events that occurred there the following morning. Two days
later he staggered into Holbrook on foot and
reported the lynching to Sam Brown. In addition to Stott, Wilson, and the lunger, there was a
young Hash Knife cowboy named Jim Scott,
who was riding bog on Silver Creek between the
Little Colorado River and Snowflake. Brown
knew this young puncher intimately, a pleasant
lad from Weatherford, Texas, who came of
good, God-fearing parents, and who bore an
excellent reputation in Arizona.

Joe T. McKinney had known Scott in New
Mexico, where they had both worked on the ALC
Ranch. He described him as a small man, about
twenty-six years old, with one brown eye and
one blue one. He was always very agreeable,
and was a man of courage. According to McKinney's story, Jim Houck held a grudge against
Scott because, one night in Holbrook, the young
cowboy called Houck's hand when he was "shooting off his head recklessly." Houck backed down,
but he never forgot the incident. Scott had
loaned his pet saddle horse to Louis Naeglin and
was bringing the animal back from Pleasant
Valley when he stopped that night at Stott's
ranch. McKinney says that when Houck found
him there, he paid off this old grudge by taking

him out with Stott and Wilson. Joe McKinney keenly felt the shock of Scott's death.

According to the story the lunger breathlessly related to Sam Brown, a band of ten or twelve men rode up to the cabin and dismounted just before breakfast the morning after Stott returned from Holbrook with Wilson. That Stott was acquainted with some of the party is shown by the fact that he called them by name and invited them to eat. The custom of "taking the victim for a ride" did not originate with the modern gangster, for bad men and outlaws of the old frontier often invited men they had marked for death to take a "ride" with them.

But in this case it was a "walk" instead of a "ride"; and after the meal was over the strangers quietly invited their host and his two companions to take a "walk." That the doomed men knew that death awaited them at the end of that "walk' there is no doubt, and Wilson refused to submit quietly; but by their superior numbers the strangers forced their victims to accompany them. Why they failed to include the consumptive will never be known. The only theory that can be advanced is that his ailment aroused their pity; and as he had only been there a few weeks, he was not acquainted with any of them. Therefore they felt safe in allowing him to escape.

From the doorway the lunger watched the strange horsemen until they disappeared among the trees and brush. He was filled with apprehension for the safety of his friends, for he well knew by the actions of the visitors that something was wrong. The minutes dragged into hours without bringing any sign of the missing men; but he waited, hoping for their return. When noon came and went he was convinced that something terrible had happened. In spite of their apparent cheerfulness that morning, before they were taken away, he had sensed a feeling among his three friends of impending calamity. Finally when he could stand the suspense no longer, he crept cautiously out to investigate. Some distance from the cabin he beheld three objects swinging from the limb of a tree. Could such a thing be possible? Fear almost drove him away. His eyes fairly bulged, and his heart beat so rapidly that it almost choked him. He wanted to run from the accursed spot as fast as his legs could carry him, but he conquered the impulse and cautiously advanced until he could obtain a better view.

Yes, it was true. Those three ghastly objects swaying in the wind and casting long shadows under the big pine tree were the bodies of Stott, his benefactor; young Scott, the cowboy; and Billy Wilson, the prospector. Their purple faces

were terribly drawn and distorted, as though
they had died in great agony, and their necks
were stretched to an unusual length.

In terror he fled. Not even stopping to catch
a horse, he ran and walked all the way to Holbrook, where he told his terrible story to Sam
Brown. Scarcely able to believe the lunger's
tragic tale, the liveryman hurriedly rode to
Phoenix Park only to find that it was true.

Sam Brown told me that he himself cut the
victims down, and then scooped out three graves
under the pine tree that had been their gibbet.
Stott and Scott were only boys whom he had
known intimately, and Wilson was a stranger
far from home and friends; and he felt that he
could not bury them in that lonely wilderness
without some sort of Christian service. Like
most frontiersmen Sam Brown had long forgotten most of the religion he had ever known,
but he remembered enough of his Christian
mother's teachings to say a benediction over
their graves. Then he marked each grave with a
wooden stake.

The only theory that can be advanced for this
lynching is that it was committed by rustlers
who had been selling stolen horses to Stott, and
they were afraid that he would disclose their
names to Sheriff Owens, who was very actively
engaged at that time in cleaning up both cattle

and horse thieves. Unfortunately for Scott, he probably knew the lynchers and paid the penalty with his life; and they were afraid of what Billy Wilson might tell. In fact, they may have suspected that he was a detective sent in by Sheriff Owens to gather evidence. Although Scott was a Hash Knife cowboy, there is nothing to show that he had ever taken any part in the feud, which at that time was practically over; but in attempting to justify this cowardly murder the story was later circulated that the three victims were the men who had attempted the life of Jacob Lauffer. However, there is no foundation for this charge.

That this story originated with Jim Houck when he was in Flagstaff about the middle of August is shown by the following item from the Flagstaff *Champion* of August 18, 1888:

Jim Houck, who is from the Tonto Basin, says Jake Lauffer was shot at and his arm broken by ambushed assassins at his ranch about two weeks ago, August 5. Two other men, Cody and Coleman, on their way to Lauffer's ranch were shot at. Only Cody's horse was wounded. This, says Mr. Houck, was done by Jeff Wilson, Jim Scott and Jim Stott who were arrested by Houck and his posse, on warrants sworn out for their capture. The persons, however, were taken from them by an armed mob of some 40 masked men who hung them after taking them some distance down the road.

Houck certainly did not live up to the traditions of Arizona sheriffs by protecting his prisoners; but the idea of an armed mob of forty men taking them from him is ridiculous.

It is very doubtful if forty men could have been gathered on such short notice in all the Pleasant Valley country, or the entire Tonto Basin for that matter.[6] The Tewksburys never had forty men associated with them during the entire war, and in August of 1888 they were satisfied to let matters rest quietly. Suspicion fell upon Jim Houck,[7] who at that time was running a band of sheep at a water hole called Houck's Tank. Sam Brown describes him as a bad man with long hair to give him as much Western atmosphere as possible; but at that date long hair had gone out of style in Arizona, and the man who wore it had to prove his mettle before he was taken seriously.

Excitement reached a high pitch by the time Jim Houck rode into Holbrook a few days after the murder. Feeling a deep responsibility on account of the promise made to Stott's parents Sam Brown was anxious to find out who was responsible. He was very suspicious of Houck, and so he decided to force the issue if possible. With Frank Wattron's help he cornered the sheepman in the livery stable and demanded to know where he had been on the day of the lynching.

"What the hell is that to you?" snarled the

bad man as he started to draw, but before he could get his gun out, both men had him covered. However, their attempts to make him talk resulted in failure beyond the fact that he was unable to give a very clear account of his actions on the day of the murder, for Jim Houck did not bluff easily.

It was whispered that John Rhodes, a Tewksbury man, and Nook Larson were members of the self-appointed vigilance committee. The affair was soon forgotten, for no evidence was ever found that pointed towards the guilty men; but in relating these stirring events of forty odd years before, old Sam Brown told me that he believed Jim Houck and his gang were responsible. This is the story of the lynching of Stott, Scott, and Wilson as related for me by Sam Brown, a very old man whose days of life were numbered by illness when I last heard from him in 1931.

But another version of this affair as given to me several years ago by no less a person than Will C. Barnes, who, in the days of the Pleasant Valley vendetta, operated the Esperanza Cattle Company with headquarters at the Long Tom ranch, located not far from Stott's cabin. He did not know any of the events that led up to the hanging, which he claimed took place during the night and was discovered the next morning by a cowboy from his ranch. According to this story,

Mr. Barnes and his men cut the bodies down and buried them in old frontier fashion, without ceremony of any kind.

I am not prepared to say which account is correct, as both of these old-timers speak with the authority of men who lived during those times.

Mr. Barnes informed me that Stott's broken-hearted parents came out from Massachusetts and removed the remains of their boy to his old New England home, while Scott was later sent to his mother in Texas; but Billy Wilson, the wandering prospector, still sleeps under the pines of the Mogollons. For many years their graves (even though two were empty), marked by pine stakes, were pointed out to the wilderness traveler who passed that way as relics of the lawless days of old Arizona. On the other hand Sam Brown claims that all three still sleep in that lonely spot in the Arizona wilderness.

Since the account of the lynching of Stott, Scott, and Wilson was written, Mr. Arthur H. Burt,[8] of Hyde Park, Massachusetts, a cousin of James W. Stott, has furnished me with much valuable information on the murder of the young New Englander not heretofore made public. In the material furnished was a letter written by F. A. Ames[9] to Stott's parents and an account of the story told by the heartbroken father and mother after their return from Arizona.

This information differs somewhat from the narratives of Sam Brown and Will C. Barnes but it has the ring of truth, and, coming from such a trustworthy source, the evidence submitted by Mr. Burt shows conclusively that this is the correct version.

This information gives the most plausible theory for the lynching that I have yet heard; in short, it was to get possession of young Stott's ranch, which was considered a valuable location. It is significant that through all the different accounts of the lynching—Sam Brown's, old newspaper stories, F. A. Ames's letter, and the statement of Stott's parents when they returned from Arizona—the name of Jim Houck appears very consistently.

James Warren Stott was born September 13, 1863, in North Billerica, Massachusetts, where his father, James Stott,[10] was superintendent of the Talbot Woolen Mills for forty years. Reared in a Christian home by God-fearing parents young Stott's character was above reproach. And looking at the pleasant, handsome face of the young fellow in the photograph before me as I write I can well believe the truth of this.

After attending the schools of his native town James Stott graduated from the Wilmot, New Hampshire, Academy. He was evidently of an adventurous turn of mind, for after completing his schooling in 1882 he decided that the life of a cowboy held just the attractions he was looking for, and, like many another young Easterner, he turned his face to the Wild West.

Early in February, 1883, he set out for Texas. The next we hear of him was on March 28, when he wrote to his sister, Hattie from Castroville, Texas, where he was working on a horse ranch, that he could rope horses as well as the average. By the latter part of November he was on a ranch near Bartlett, owned by a Mr. Talbot, brother of Governor Talbot mentioned below; but early in January, 1884, he was on the Day Ranch in Coleman County.

In May he was back at Castroville, on the famous Circle Dot ranch owned by William Noonan, a brother of Judge Noonan. He remained there until February, 1885, when he wrote from the Day ranch again; but in March he was back at the Noonan ranch.

Thomas Talbot, twice governor of Massachusetts, who lived across the street from the Stott home in North Billerica, was financially interested in the Aztec Land and Cattle Company (the Hash Knife). In the spring of 1885 he told the elder Stott that if James would go to Arizona he could secure work with the Hash Knife outfit.

At that time Arizona was attracting attention as the future cattle country of the Southwest, and when young Stott received this word from home he decided to go. Accepting horses in payment for his work in Texas, he set out with another cowboy for this new land of adventure. They stopped for a week at the Day ranch to rest Stott's horses, and on June 14 he wrote from the Running Water ranch, fifty miles out on the plains, and on the Blanco Canyon trail to Fort Sumner, New Mexico, where he had killed a buffalo, probably one of the last in that section. After a journey of eight weeks across the plains they reached Fort Sumner on August 16. They remained in that vicinity for several weeks, working on a ranch; but by October 13 they were in Holbrook, Arizona, the Hash Knife headquarters.

It was there that Stott met F. A. Ames, another Massachusetts boy employed by the Aztec Land and Cattle Company. But Stott was disappointed in receiving the promised employment, for he found that so many stockholders had sent sons and relatives from the East to work for the outfit that there was no room for him.

F. A. Ames[11] gives the most authentic account of Stott's life in Arizona prior to his death. During the winter of 1885-86 Stott purchased the homestead right of a man located at Aztec Spring south of Holbrook.[12] This was one of the best claims in that section, and the new owner erected good buildings, fenced pastures, and conformed to all legal requirements for final title from the government.

Located on the rim of the Mogollons, Stott was on the border of the feud district when the Pleasant Valley war broke out in the spring of 1887. Literally between two fires, with the Tewksburys on one side and the Grahams on the other, his position was unfortunate, for he must either remain at the risk of his life to protect his property or abandon all he had gathered through years of saving and hard work. In addition to his ranch he owned two hundred head of horses that ranged through the surrounding mountains. His sympathies were with the Grahams, but he remained neutral. Although well aware that threats were made against his life by Tewksbury sympathizers, he courageously decided to stay in the danger zone.

Ames says that the persecution and murder of young Stott was "a deliberate and skillfully planned scheme to get possession of his ranch," and that Jim Houck boasted repeatedly that he "intended to run his sheep on Stott's ranch." When threats and intimidations failed to force the youth to abandon his property, whispered charges were made against him. In this connection Ames states that no man in that section had a better character or credit than Stott, and he was respected by all his neighbors.

When he warned his friend of the danger of remaining on his claim, the young New Englander said: "Some people have judged me guilty without taking the trouble to investigate the charges or giving me a chance to defend myself. These men are not friendly to me so I shall not take the trouble to change their opinion. If they desire to know the facts they would see me before forming an opinion. If I should abandon my ranch and stock these people and many others would think it an acknowledgment of guilt. I would lose all my property and also be doing just what the Tewksbury gang desire me to do. I have done nothing wrong and do not intend to be bulldozed or intimidated. No man will believe me guilty until he has received some reliable evidence of the fact; such as prefer to are welcome to their opinion."[13]

Stott's father sent money regularly to invest in the ranch and business; and Mr. Burt informs me that Sam Brown was not asked to watch over the young man and advise him in his investments. As Mr. Burt points out, James Stott was not a tenderfoot, for he had had two years' experience in Texas, and if the father had not had confidence in him he would not have sent him money.

Mr. Burt has also informed me that Stott's parents never met Sam Brown until they visited Arizona after their son's death. The young man wrote regularly and had evidently intended to pay his old home a visit in 1887, but conditions brought about by the vendetta prevented him from going, and so his mother and sister[14] spent a week that summer at his ranch. That was the last they ever saw of him.

It seems that Floyd Clymer, the "lunger" mentioned by Sam Brown, was at Stott's ranch during the visit of Mrs. Stott and her daughter in 1887. I am unable to say how long he remained, and there is nothing to show that he was not there when the lynching took place a year later.

In the letter already referred to, Ames places the blame on Jim Houck. According to this information, Houck wanted the ranch for his sheep, and when every other means failed he decided that something had to be done quickly, for Stott expected to prove up on his claim in September and would then acquire legal title. A great amount of rustling was going on in that section, and Ames says that some men thought that Stott was mixed up in it from the fact that he lived near the known thieves and was friendly with them.[15]

He not only denies that Stott took any part in

this nefarious work but he says that these stories were circulated by the young man's enemies—the parties who wanted to get possession of his ranch. The Graham-Tewksbury vendetta had driven many other settlers from that section. The Mormon settlements of Heber and Wilford, seven miles apart, each of which had twenty-five families in 1886, were entirely abandoned in 1888.

Ames declares that there were about twenty-five men in the party that lynched Stott, Scott, and Wilson, and that they were acting as a posse under fraudulent warrants. It is significant in this connection that Jim Houck held a commission as a deputy sheriff at that time.

That fictitious warrants were used is shown by two accounts of the lynching that appeared in the Phoenix *Weekly Herald*. The first was in the issue of August 16, 1888:

Holbrook, August 15.—Information has reached here of the lynching of James Stott, James Scott and Jeff Wilson by outlaws in the southwestern part of this county. The affair grew out of the recent war in Tonto Basin between the sheep and cattle raisers. Warrants were issued to unauthorized persons, and the prisoners were taken across the mountain in Yavapai county, where they were met by a pre-arranged mob of outlaws and hanged.

The following account appeared in the next issue on August 23, 1888:

In response to a telegram sent to Holbrook for further information concerning the lynching in Pleasant Valley, the *Journal-Miner* (of Prescott) has received the following:

Holbrook, August 16.—Reports from Pleasant Valley of the lynching by outlaws of James Stott, James Scott and Jeff Wilson near Stott's ranch on the afternoon of the 11th, received here up to date are as follows: The parties were arrested on fictitious charges and were in charge of James D. Houck and five others. They were enroute to Pleasant Valley, and when near the Canyon Creek trail were met by masked men who ordered Houck and his men to move on. Houck arrived in Holbrook on Monday, August 13 and the latest intelligence received from the scene was on Tuesday morning, when the bodies were reported as still hanging. From the best information today the county authorities are taking no action in the matter.

Ames says that he knew one of the men murdered with Stott, but he was not acquainted with the other. The first was undoubtedly Jim Scott, the Hash Knife cowboy. The fact that the other victim was unknown to him bears out Sam Brown's statement that this man was a stranger in the country; for if he had been the Jeff Wilson referred to, Ames would have known him.

In speaking of the charges against Stott, Ames says:

"Never was there a particle of evidence produced which would have had the slightest weight with an unprejudiced man. There is not a man in Arizona knowing Jim who believed him guilty and all people there look upon his death as a cowardly, brutal murder as was ever committed."

From the newspaper accounts just quoted it seems that the bodies were not cut down the next morning as reported by Barnes, but they hung there under the pine tree for at least four days. If that is true, then Sam Brown's story that he buried them may be correct.

As soon as they received word[16] of their son's death James Stott and his wife went to Arizona and were driven from Holbrook out to the ranch. It may have been at this time that Brown first met them. Jim Houck was at the ranch when they arrived, and Mrs. Stott afterwards related that he boasted of "his part in it."

"Somebody will have to suffer for this," the heartbroken mother declared. But he only laughed at her and told her that nothing would ever be done about it; and nothing ever was.

Forty-six years later Mr. Burt's niece, Mrs. Miriam McIlvene and her husband, while driving through from Massachusetts to California, stopped at Holbrook to secure what information they could of the murder. Few people living there today remember the facts, but after making some inquiry Mrs. McIlvene met a doctor who hailed an old-time cattleman passing along the street. This man refused to give his name, but he declared that he knew all about the lynching of nearly half a century before. He was very reticent, however, and refused to divulge any details.

He did tell Mrs. McIlvene that George Bailey, of Snowflake, homesteaded the claim some time after Stott's death and has owned the ranch since 1903. In view of the statement that this man did not own the place until 1903, fifteen years after the lynching, it is evident that he had nothing to do with the affair. From this it appears that Houck never proved upon the claim, but he may have used it for his sheep without the formality of residing on the property. No one is living there at present. The McIlvenes started for Snowflake and the ranch, but were forced to turn back on account of bad roads.

Will C. Barnes' statement that Stott's parents removed the body of their son to the old home in Massachusetts is not correct. Mr. Burt informs me that as far as the family knows all three are still buried in Arizona; but the name of James Warren Stott, with the dates of his birth and death, appears on the family monument at Lowell, Massachusetts.

From this it is safe to say that the body of James Scott was not removed to Texas as related by Barnes, and that Sam Brown was correct when he informed me that all three victims

still sleep in that lonely spot under the pines of
the Mogollons, awaiting the end of time.

After the publication of the first edition,
Arthur H. Burt already mentioned, furnished me with copies of letters written by James
Stott to his sister, Hattie, after his mother and
sister, Hannah Louise, had returned East from
a visit at his Arizona ranch in the summer of
1887. These add some interest to Stott's life.

In a letter dated October 2, 1887, he says that
between fifteen and twenty men were killed in
the war in Pleasant Valley and several more
were wounded. The last one known to have been
killed (before he wrote the letter) was a young
man his mother and sister had met when they
left his ranch on July 4, 1887. He was placed in
charge while Stott went to Holbrook with his
relatives. He says that this young man "was
killed more than a week ago," which would place
the time as the latter part of September. Unfortunately, he did not give the cowboy's name,
but he may have been Harry Middleton, who was
mortally wounded September 17, 1887 (see
pages 140-43), and who died at the Graham
ranch two days later. Stott expressed the opinion
that the war would cause many to leave the country, but he was determined to remain. This
shows that James Stott possessed plenty of cour-

age, for only men with "gravel in their gizzards" stayed on in the feud country.

The fact that Sam Brown took Stott's parents to the ranch after their son's murder is proved by a letter written by Mrs. Stott from Holbrook, August 23, 1888, to her daughter, Hattie. In this she says that Mr. Brown, "the stabler," intended to go with them to their son's ranch. Proof that it was Sam Brown who buried the victims is also contained in this letter. Mrs. Stott referring to the lynching, says, "Mr. Brown helped bury him," meaning her son.

According to a second letter written that same day, it was J. P. Burdett, a young Texan with the Hash Knife, who sent a telegram to Stott's parents in Massachusetts, telling them of the murder. He had known Stott from the time he arrived in Arizona, and they were warm friends. Quoting from this same letter, Mrs. Stott says:

Dear, Dear Child, his hopes and expectations, so suddenly destroyed, and be cut down by cruel, wicked outlaws. A man pretending to be an officer with a false warrant, and did not even have the warrant with him, arresting him falsely, a band of 28 men got there about daylight. He [meaning Stott] gave them all breakfast, they pretending to take him to Prescott. Took the three to a place between 20 and 30 miles, there killed them.

In a letter written from Holbrook, August 28, 1888, Mrs. Stott states that they reached their son's ranch on the twenty-fifth. They found that Motte Clymer (evidently the Floyd Clymer referred to by Sam Brown) was taking care of the stock. Two days later they were back in Holbrook, and after settling their son's affairs they returned to their home.

These letters give some interesting information in regard to young Stott's character, and refute the opinion expressed by some old-timers to this day that he dealt in stolen stock. A Mrs. Day at Snowflake told Mrs. Stott that her son "was so honest in all his dealings and so kind and good to everyone." And she knew him well.

D. G. Harvey, the justice of the peace at Holbrook, under date of October 10, 1888, wrote to Stott's father:

> I am fully convinced, after a thorough inspection of James' books and papers, that he purchased and paid a good round price for every head of stock on his ranch. But I do think that he was imposed upon by designing parties and through his kindness he had to suffer; and I believe this opinion is concurred in by every law-abiding person in the country.

Mrs. Stott died in 1916 at the age of ninety-six years, bright and vigorous to the last.

In July, 1942, fifty-four years after the lynching of Stott, Scott, and Wilson, the graves were opened. Stott was easily indentified by the fact that he was the taller of the trio. Only a few bones that had once been Jim Stott were found —the large leg bones, the large arm bones, and the back of the skull. There was nothing else—no ribs, no vertebra, no fingers or toes could be distinguished, all dust of mother earth. The back of the skull crumbled when exposed to the air. The body had been wrapped in a brown, woolen blanket, scraps of which were left, and some rotten pieces of rope had been tied around the the blanket. A piece of red and white plaid shirt, about six inches square, and portions of an undershirt were found. Copper rivets from the overalls (Levi's) were found, and the soles and heels of the boots were still in good condition. A small gold band ring, worn smooth, a rusty pocket knife, about fifteen coins— nickels, dimes and quarters—and two or three white pearl buttons were found. A knot about three inches in diameter from a sawed pine board that had been placed over the face, completed the contents of the grave.

The leg bones were those of a man who had been about six feet tall, and the men living at that time remembered that Stott was tall and that Scott and Wilson were short. Whether the bones were reburied I cannot say, but this ends the story of Jim Stott.[17]

CHAPTER XVI

THE MYSTERY OF
GEORGE NEWTON'S
DISAPPEARANCE

WITH THE exception of Tom Graham's murder ten months later, no other incident in all the history of the Pleasant Valley war, that kept Arizona in a turmoil for years with its gun battles and court trials, created as much excitement as the disappearance of George A. Newton, while on his way from Globe to his ranch in Pleasant Valley in September, 1891. It will be remembered that he took a very active part in the chain of events that followed the killing at the old Middleton ranch on August 10, 1887, and although a cattleman, he was drawn into the vendetta on the side of the Tewksburys for some reason that has never been revealed.[1]

George Newton, a jeweler at Globe in the early days, was one of the camp's most popular men, and his influence made that place a Tewksbury town even to this day. In the early 1880's he engaged in the cattle business with J. J. Vosberg, and together they established the Flying V outfit, with headquarters near the old Middleton ranch, which they later purchased.[2] Newton was a man well liked by all who knew him, and before the Tewksburys drove that band of sheep over the rim of the Mogollons he did not have an enemy in the world; but the law of the vendetta recognized no friendships in opposing factions.

While he continued to operate his business in Globe he made frequent trips to his ranch in Pleasant Valley, even during the days when the feud was at its worst; and there were men in the Graham faction who wanted nothing better than to plant a Winchester bullet in George Newton's anatomy; but this had always been too dangerous an experiment, for, like Tom Graham, he was never caught off his guard during those stirring days of 1887 and 1888. But with the passing of years Tom Graham had removed from the valley and the Tewksbury faction was left in possession, victors of the bloody vendetta. While peace reigned over the feud district there were still a few Graham sympathizers living in the valley who thoroughly enjoyed the sensation of firing a shot from ambush now and then if they could do so without danger to themselves. With the passing of time the general opinion that the war was over seemed well founded.

During all those dangerous days of 1887 and 1888, when men of opposing factions shot it out when they met, George Newton had never hesitated to ride the lonely trail to Pleasant Valley. Three years had passed since the last hostile shot had been fired, and what was there now to fear?

As he threw the saddle on his mount and loaded his pack horse with supplies one bright day in September, 1891, and rode out of Globe, he was fully justified in a feeling of security. What danger could there be on a trail he had traveled a hundred times and more?

The fate of George Newton remains a mystery to this day. As he left Globe that morning for his ranch in Pleasant Valley, sixty-five miles away over rugged mountain trails, he disappeared as completely as if the earth had swallowed him up, for none of his friends ever saw him again. His fate is another mystery of the vendetta that the passing of many years has failed to solve. Even his body was never found.

As the days passed and nothing was heard from George Newton, a rumor was circulated that he had been murdered on the trail. Excitement reached a high pitch, especially when the story was told that he had been shot from his horse while crossing the deep water of the Pinal Creek ford. A man named Crampton, on his way to Globe that morning, met Newton and advised him to return home and wait until the water should fall. This was good advice, for Salt River at flood tide is hazardous for even the most experienced frontier travelers; but George Newton had ridden that trail many times, and he knew the hidden danger of every eddy and quicksand at the crossing. With the remark that he would change his saddle to his pack horse, a long-legged, rangy animal, the cattleman rode on—to his death. That was the last ever seen of him either dead or alive.

Searching parties immediately set out; and spurred by his wife's offer of a large reward for the recovery of his body, they carefully combed both sides of Salt River for miles. With its load still in place, the pack horse[3] was found half buried on a sand bar; but no trace of either George Newton or his saddle horse were ever discovered. That he died in the ford, there can be no doubt; but whether by an enemy's bullet or the dangerous, swirling waters that clutched him in their death grip will never be known; for Salt River holds its dead with a jealous hand, and his body was forever buried in its quicksands.

A heavy life insurance made it necessary to establish the fact of his death before payment would be made by the company, and the reward offered by Mrs. Newton for the recovery of the body or positive evidence of his death was finally increased to ten thousand dollars. Stimulated by this sum, the hills and mountains between Globe and Pleasant Valley were combed by the best hunters and trailers in the Southwest; but Salt River still guards the secret. Seven years later the company paid the insurance in full; and the case was placed in the pigeonhole of unsolved deaths.

CHAPTER XVII

TOM GRAHAM LEAVES   JIM TEWKSBURY'S death
PLEASANT VALLEY   left only one Graham
                     and one Tewksbury to
carry on. The courts had failed to punish those
guilty of bloodshed; and there is little doubt
that both leaders would gladly have ended hostilities if they could have done so with credit to
themselves, but neither would make the first
overtures of peace.

After his marriage, Tom Graham, the last of
his family, returned with his bride to his lonely
ranch in Pleasant Valley. He had few followers
now. Tom Tucker, Tom Pickett, Roxy, and
Peck, and other hard-fighting Hash Knife cowboys had drifted to other ranges, for old-time
punchers were ever wanderers; and raiding
bands of cattlemen no longer rode the night
trails of Pleasant Valley. After those first few
weeks in the summer of 1887, the quarrel had
ceased to be a sheep and cattle war, and the new
men working for the Hash Knife did not care a
rap. They had lost no blood; it was none of their
affair, and the feudists could settle their differences among themselves as far as they were con-
cerned. While this outfit never openly supported
the Graham cause, there is no doubt that its
leaders had secretly approved of the action of

its men as a protective measure to the range. But the sheep had been driven out; the range was safe from invasion, and the Hash Knife was no longer interested in the result.

Thus Tom Graham, deserted by all except his close friends, was left almost alone to carry on the fight. Opposed to bloodshed in the beginning, he now adopted a policy of armed neutrality, thus placing responsibility for further hostile acts directly upon the shoulders of the Tewksburys. If they had followed this same policy, the trouble would probably have died out; but their Indian blood would not let them forget. It was still an eye for an eye.

The last of the fighting Grahams had other things to think of after his marriage. His courage was beyond question, for he had stood the test many times; and a braver woman never lived than that seventeen-year-old girl wife who volunteered to share his life in the heart of the feud district. Determined to carry on, he settled down on his ranch, resolved to act only on the defensive, and for nearly two years they lived there, always under the menace of a Tewksbury bullet; but Ed Tewksbury was apparently satisfied to let matters rest. However, neither leader could control his followers, and during the remaining months of 1887 and 1888 several ambuscades occurred as already noted.

But this state of affairs could not continue forever. Some day a bullet would crash out of the brush, and Tom Graham would go over the long trail to join his brothers. His young wife wanted a life of peace and happiness and she was determined that the grim hand of the vendetta should not snatch her husband from her arms if she could prevent it. She pleaded with him to leave, to seek a new home amid peaceful surroundings far away from this bloody land. At first Tom Graham turned a deaf ear to all his wife's entreaties. It is true that he was tired of fighting, but if he went away Ed Tewksbury would boast forever that he had driven him out; and a Tewksbury would be left in possession of the range—the range that he had fought for, that had cost the lives of his two brothers and some of his best friends. This was just what Ed Tewksbury wanted. But he was Tom Graham; he would remain and fight it out to the end. Still the young wife refused to give up. She wanted a peaceful home somewhere, far away from the Tewksbury menace; and when a woman with the determination and courage of Anne Graham sets her mind to these things, she generally gets what she wants. She was very much in love with her husband. She would ride with him, fight for him if necessary. That was a factor that counted in such a crisis, for this girl had been born on the frontier and she could ride and shoot like a cowboy. But what could be gained by remaining? she argued. Even if Ed Tewksbury finally left them in possession of the range, would their victory be worth the cost of that dread of sudden death at the hands of the vendetta? With this fear hovering over them constantly they would not be able to look after their cattle properly, and it would be hard to employ men willing to work in the feud district.

During all these months, the one friend who remained true to Tom Graham was Charley Duchet, the Frenchman, and as strange a character as the feud produced. The circumstances of their first acquaintance and the reason for their devotion will probably never be known, for theirs was a friendship that stood all tests and was only ended by death. Strange as it may seem the name of Charles Duchet does not appear in connection with any of the battles during those sanguinary days of 1887; but he was constantly with Tom Graham all through those trying times. This attachment was so strong that Duchet acted as a self-appointed bodyguard for the Graham leader, and he never allowed him far out of his sight. And Charley Duchet, gun-fighting frontiersman, was a force to be reckoned with; but with his constant boasting he kept matters in a turmoil long after the two

leaders had ceased activities. He was the last
person in the world who would have brought
harm to Tom Graham, yet he could not keep his
mouth shut.

Anne Graham never gave up hope of per-
suading her husband to leave Pleasant Valley,
no matter what sacrifices it might mean; and
finally Tom began to listen. Then another very
important reason developed; the Grahams were
expecting an addition to their family. This put
an entirely different complexion on his former
decision to remain, for the partisan leader did
not want his children reared in this sanguinary
land, overcast with clouds of personal hatreds
that might carry down to the second generation.
He was weary with the constant vigilance. He
had had enough bloodshed to last him for the
remainder of his life; and so in the summer of
1889 he turned his cattle[1] over to S. W. Young[2]
to manage on shares, and sought peace with
his young wife on a farm near Tempe. His
dream of becoming a cattle king was over. The
price already paid in blood had been too great,
and he decided to spend the remainder of his life
in the more peaceful occupation of farming.

Miss Ola Young, daughter of S. W. Young,
still lives on the old Graham ranch in Pleasant
Valley. Her memories of Tom Graham are entirely different from the pen pictures of the

heartless killer drawn by fiction tales of the war. She remembers him as a good-looking man, with a short mustache[3] and wavy, brown hair, a pleasant man who made friends wherever he went; and to the end of his life he deplored the terrible vendetta into which he had been unwillingly drawn as one of the clan leaders.

Ed Tewksbury and his few followers were left as masters of the situation in Pleasant Valley; but they had learned a hard lesson, and no further attempts were made to take sheep over the rim of the Mogollons. This was a cattle country, and the Tewksbury forces were apparently glad enough to let the matter rest at that, without bringing down the fresh wrath of the cattlemen upon them again. They had had enough of sheep.

With the passing years Tom Graham prospered on his farm just as he had prospered in the cattle business before the vendetta. Charley Duchet, close friend of the Pleasant Valley days, accompanied him to his new home, still acting in the role of self-appointed bodyguard, and he remained with him to the end. Pleasant Valley was a terrible memory of wasted years that Tom Graham wanted to forget; but he was still a young man, and the future was bright with promise. Surely the feud was over. That he made many friends in the Salt River Valley

is shown by the bitter feeling against the two
men accused of his murder, and only the prompt
work of officers saved them from a lynching at
Tempe. A daughter[4] born a few months after he
settled on the farm brought great happiness to
this man whose soul had been seared with the
vendetta's bitterness.

As the years passed, Tom Graham's cattle
in Pleasant Valley increased under the management of S. W. Young, and finally in June of
1892 he decided to return to the old ranch for
a division of the herd.[5] After thinking the matter over, he decided that if he went back with a
large force of men, Ed Tewksbury would naturally believe that he came to revive the feud.
He decided that he would go alone if necessary;
but his faithful old friend, Charley Duchet,
readily agreed to accompany him. In fact, it
was difficult for Tom Graham to even leave his
house without this shadow at his heels; and so
with this one comrade he rode back unarmed
into the land of his enemies—a land that held
the graves of two brothers and many bitter
memories.

Stories of a revival of the feud were quickly
spread on the outside, and it was reported in
Phoenix a short time later that both men had
been killed but nothing occurred while they
were in the valley. Ed Tewksbury seemed will-

ing to let his enemy come and go in peace, and the clan leaders did not meet. When reports of the killing of Graham and Duchet were at their height, the two men walked into the office of the Phoenix *Herald*, and gave an account of their only meeting with their former enemies of the vendetta.[6]

When they entered the valley a party of Tewksbury men met them, but neither Ed Tewksbury nor John Rhodes was present. Both parties stopped as soon as they recognized each other as former enemies; and then Bill Colcord[7] rode out from the Tewksbury force with a gesture of peace.

"Well, boys, is it peace or war?" he asked as he approached.

"It's peace; we don't care for war. We only want our rights," replied Tom Graham. "I have too much involved here to be bluffed. We prefer peace if it's possible."

This met with Colcord's approval, and he shook hands with Graham and Duchet as a token that the bitterness of the past was buried.

With the aid of S. W. Young and a few hired cowboys it was an easy matter to round up the cattle. Bill Colcord's promise of peace was kept to the letter, for no opposition was offered by the Tewksbury forces. The hills and draws were combed, and they staged such a round up as the valley had not known since the day the three Tewksburys and Bill Jacobs had driven that band of sheep over the rim of the Mogollons. As Tom Graham once more rode the range he loved so well, he drifted back over memory's pages to those old days when he was at peace with all his neighbors and had dreamed of the day when he might become one of Arizona's prominent cattlemen, with his herds grazing on a thousand hills. But the hand of a terrible vendetta had wrecked all of his plans and dreams. He had hitched his cow pony to a plow; he had traded his saddle and six-shooter for a reaper and binder, and instead of living the free, roving life of a cowboy that appealed to him with all the love of a red-blooded man, he was just another farmer. He had not given up without many a pang; but this new occupation had its compensations, for he had the best wife and the sweetest baby in the world. The old life held too many bitter memories. He was satisfied now if he could just live in peace.

The cattle were bunched at his old ranch and divided according to the agreement made three years before. Then, with the help of several of Young's cowboys, he and Charley Duchet drove his share to Tempe; and during all this time no attempt was made by Ed Tewksbury or any of his men to interfere. The vendetta was apparently at an end.[8]

CHAPTER XVIII

THE LAST OF THE GRAHAMS

WITH THE MURDER of Tom Graham and the exciting chain of events that followed, the curtain fell on the final and most tragic act of this bloody range drama of the old Southwest. No other incident in all the thrilling history of the old Arizona cattle country ever created as much excitement; and to this day old residents of the Salt River Valley love to reminisce over the details of this bold assassination right in the heart of a settled farming community, and on the subsequent attempt made by Anne Graham to shoot John Rhodes during his preliminary hearing before Justice of the Peace W. O. Huson in Phoenix, for the murder of her husband. All this occurred four years after hostilities had ceased in Pleasant Valley, and after the vendetta had apparently been forgotten.

Ed Cummings, now a guide at the Grand Canyon, was a boy during the years Tom Graham lived in Salt River Valley, and he remembered him with all the vividness of childhood. In telling me the story of the clan leader's murder, he stated that Graham never carried a gun again after settling near Tempe, although both his wife and Charley Duchet still feared Ed Tewksbury, even more than during the fighting days in Pleasant Valley. Like a sword the terrible thought hung over this plucky frontier woman that some day the last Tewksbury would exact the vendetta's price in the blood of the last Graham. It was her terrible dream at night, her constant fear by day; and then it happened. Time and again she implored her husband to go armed; and in spite of all entreaties and the advice of Charley Duchet, Tom Graham always gave the same answer: that he had left Pleasant Valley to get away from the gunplay and fighting of the vendetta, and he declared that he would never carry a weapon again, not even to save his own life. This decision was in keeping with his fearless character; and he paid the price.

Like a bolt from a clear sky the last of the Grahams was shot from ambush near the Double Butte schoolhouse on August 2, 1892, while he was hauling grain from his ranch to Tempe, and the entire Salt River Valley was plunged into the wildest excitement it had known since the days of Indian raids. The feud had been revived, but the reason for his murder will never be known. For three years he had lived in peace, unmolested by his enemies; and even when he returned to Pleasant Valley a short time before his assassination, Ed Tewksbury had permitted him to

gather and drive his cattle away without raising
a hand. Now he had paid the price of the blood
feud. Why no attempt was made on his life
when he returned to the feud district is a mystery that even time has failed to reveal, for he
could have been killed there with little chance of
detection. One story is told that after his return
home he foolishly boasted that Ed Tewksbury
was afraid to molest him; but such a statement
was not like Tom Graham. It sounds more like
the bragging of Charley Duchet.

On the day before the killing, a Mexican
ranch hand left Graham's employ without giving any reason, and went to work for Daggs
Brothers, whose sheep, driven over the rim of
the Mogollons six years before, had furnished
fuel for the smouldering flames of hatred between the Grahams and Tewksburys. Although
part of this man's work was hauling the grain
then being threshed, to town, nothing conclusive
was ever brought out to connect his action with
the murder the next day.

The slump in wool during Cleveland's first
administration brought financial disaster upon
Daggs Brothers. Following so closely on this
reverse, the loss of their sheep during those
early raids in Pleasant Valley had dealt another
hard financial blow that practically forced them
out of business. P. P. and A. A. Daggs then

went to Tempe, where they secured control of the Bank of Tempe, and were still there when Tom Graham was killed. Naturally they were still very bitter; but nothing was ever brought out to show that they were in any way implicated in the assassination, and no one ever accused them of any connection with the plot.

That the Graham ranch was closely watched by someone is shown by an incident that occurred the night before the murder. During the evening Mrs. Graham heard a noise outside a window, and quickly blew out the light, a caution born of the vendetta days she had spent in Pleasant Valley. The next morning the tracks of two men around the house showed that some enemy had been watching, possibly in hopes of an opportunity for a chance shot under cover of the night.

The tragedy of August 2 was witnessed by three children—Ed Cummings, then a lad of twelve; his sister, Molly, whose father lived two miles from the Graham farm; and a girl named Betty Gregg. The story of this shooting, as told to me years later by Cummings, who was one of the chief witnesses at Ed Tewksbury's trial, is given here in detail for the first time.

According to Cummings, the action of the Mexican left the ranch force shorthanded, and Tom Graham decided to take the grain to town

himself. Alarmed by the strange footprints discovered that morning, Mrs. Graham begged her
husband to carry his six-shooter, and in this she
was joined by Charley Duchet; but even his
wife's entreaties failed to shake Tom Graham's
determination never to go armed again. Even
had he carried a weapon that morning, he would
have had no chance to defend himself, for he
was shot from ambush.

In my description of the murder I have followed Ed Cummings' story as the most authentic
account, for the details are still as clear to him
as they were that August day of 1892. The
three children were on their way to a neighbor's
when they witnessed the last tragic act of this
sanguinary vendetta. They had taken a short
cut and were out of sight of the road. As they
walked around a cottonwood tree that had been
blown down in the rear of a mesquite thicket at
the side of the road near Double Butte schoolhouse, they suddenly came upon two horsemen
hiding behind the brush.

Tom Graham was just driving past with a
four-horse team and a load of grain, and both
men had their guns raised when the children
first came upon them; but one, attracted by
some slight noise, turned his head just at that
instant, and young Cummings saw the man
whom he afterwards identified in court as Ed

Tewksbury; and to this day he declares that this man was the clan leader. When Tewksbury saw the youngsters, he lowered his weapon, but his companion pressed the trigger, and Tom Graham toppled over on the grain with a bullet in his back. The man who fired the shot was John Rhodes,[1] Cummings told me. Rhodes fought with the Tewksbury forces throughout the war, and afterwards married John Tewksbury's widow.

"I'll never forget those horses," Ed Cummings said as he continued his story. "They were the finest I ever saw. Ed Tewksbury rode a dark brown that was almost black, and Rhodes was on a fine buckskin. Immediately after the shot was fired they galloped away in different directions."

Tom Graham was mortally wounded, and when he fell back on the wagon the team ran a quarter of a mile to the ranch house of W. T. Cummings, father of Ed Cummings, where the last of the Grahams died that afternoon.

The children spread the alarm, and in a short time neighbors had gathered from far and near. Expert trackers followed the trails of the two fugitives, which plainly showed that they had separated after the shooting and had met on the opposite side of the section, where they parted again. Rhodes was captured after a chase of ten

Thomas H. Graham

Mrs. Thomas H. Graham

miles, but his companion was mounted on a fast horse and made his escape.

Anne Graham was soon at her husband's side. It was a pathetic scene, that last parting between this brave twenty-two-year-old wife and mother, and her lover, the dying chieftain in as bitter a vendetta as ever ravaged any land. That his lifeblood was ebbing away Tom Graham well knew, and he told his wife that he had only a short time to live. With the courage that had dominated her entire life Anne Graham faced her loss bravely. The blow that she had been expecting every day for five years and had hoped was a groundless fear, had fallen at last. Henceforth she must face life alone; and with only her memories of this sweetheart of her girlhood days to keep her company she has come down through all the long years alone.

Bravely Tom Graham faced the unknown, just as he had met every danger in an adventurous life. When his wife asked who had shot him the dying man replied in the presence of several witnesses: "Ed Tewksbury and John Rhodes." He told them that one of his slayers wore a red band around the crown of his hat; and when Edwin Tewksbury was arrested, a red ribbon was on his sombrero. About four o'clock that afternoon the last of the Grahams started on his journey over the long trail. He was buried the next day in the old graveyard at Phoenix under the auspices of the A. O. U. W., of which he was a member.

John Rhodes refused to talk after his arrest; and even when faced with the damaging evidence that the tracks of one of the horses found at the scene of the murder were identified with the shoe marks of his own horse,[2] he still refused to betray his comrade. But Tom Graham's dying statement and the testimony of the three children pointed to Edwin Tewksbury as the second man, and a warrant was issued for his arrest.

Some of the old-timers will tell you that Ed Tewksbury tried to elude the officers, but this is not correct. Instead of giving an impression of guilt by attempting to leave the country or remaining in hiding, he played a trump card by surrendering three days later. Criticisms were heaped upon the head of Sheriff John Montgomery, of Maricopa County, for not capturing him immediately, and that officer wrote to the fugitive, who was then working in Tonto Basin for a ranchman named Wilson, and advised him to give himself up.

Sheriff Findlay, of Pima County, who was well acquainted with Ed Tewksbury, went direct to Wilson's ranch, arriving there on August 5. When told that the former clan leader was wanted for the killing of Tom Graham, Wilson went out and brought in Ed. When informed that he was wanted in connection with the murder, the last of the Tewksburys voluntarily returned to the ranch and surrendered. From the beginning to the end Ed Tewksbury maintained his innocence. This and his subsequent actions, when he had several opportunities to escape, were certainly not those of a guilty man. There was either some mistake in his identification by Tom Graham and the three children or he was willing to take a long chance. I might add here that the man with the red hatband has never been positively identified beyond the damaging statements already quoted, and his reason for wearing this distinguishing badge is a mystery to this day.

The accused man was turned over to Deputy Sheriff Tom Elder, of Maricopa County, and on August 11 he arrived in Tucson with his prisoner after a horseback journey of over three hundred miles. During the five days of this lonely ride Ed Tewksbury undoubtedly could have escaped had he so desired. The reason for taking him on the long route to Tucson instead of direct to Phoenix is not known; but in view of the attempt to lynch John Rhodes, Elder probably took this precaution to avoid the danger of mob violence.

The following from the Tucson *Star* of August 13, 1892, is of interest in connection with the arrival there of the prisoner:

Tewksbury looks as if he had Indian blood in his veins, but he declares he has none. He is very bitter against what he called the persecution of himself and John Rhodes, and hinted that those at the head of it were not all they might be themselves. When the proper time comes he was sure he could get plenty of witnesses to prove an alibi.

"All I came here for," he continued, "was to get protection. Rhodes surely would have got it down there if the deputies had not saved him from the crowd." Tewksbury went on to say that he was at Desert Wells on the twenty-sixth and twenty-seventh, and started back to his ranch that day. He was looking for some lost.horses. On the fifth of August, Wilson, his employer, told him Sheriff Findlay was looking for him. Wilson told him Graham had been killed on the second and that he, Tewksbury, was wanted for the crime. "When I heard Sheriff Findlay was at the ranch," he said, "I went and gave myself up."

"Charley Duchet," he said, "is the prime mover against me. His real name is English. Anyone knows he would do or say anything to injure me. That is all I care to say now. These witnesses," he added, "will all swear they saw me when I was miles away on the third."

That the Maricopa County officials had some intimation of a plot to lynch Ed Tewksbury is shown by the precautions taken to transport the prisoner safely to Phoenix. The utmost secrecy was observed, and as Elder was probably being closely watched, Deputy Sheriff Henry DeNure quietly arrived in Tucson on August 13. In order that there might be no possible chance of a leak in the carefully laid plans, DeNure did not make himself known to the Pima County officials until shortly before he was ready to depart. Arrangements had already been made that he should leave with his prisoner at four o'clock in the morning of August 14 on the westbound train. The reason for this secrecy was to forstall the chance that some spy might send a wire from Tucson; for public feeling over the murder was so intense in the Salt River Valley—and especially at Tempe—that the Phoenix officials were afraid the train would be stopped en route. The greatest danger from a mob would be on the branch line from Maricopa Junction on the Southern Pacific to Phoenix. The engineer had received instructions to slow down when he saw a prearranged signal six miles south of Kyrene station; and Ed Tewksbury, followed by DeNure, quietly dropped off at this point.

Deputy Sheriff Henry Garfias, with two saddle horses, was waiting for them, and the trio rode leisurely away as though they were ranchmen. They attracted no particular attention; and on the outskirts of Phoenix, Tewksbury and Garfias dismounted and walked quietly through the streets to the sheriff's office. No one noticed them, and in a short time Ed Tewksbury was safely lodged in the Maricopa County jail to pass away the long weeks until his trial for the murder of the last of the Grahams should be called.[3]

Tom Graham was buried in the old cemetery at Phoenix, which has not been used for many years. In 1944, at my request, A. Lloyd Ozanne of that city located the grave, marked by a stone monument which gives the date of Graham's birth as July, 26, 1853. At the top is an anchor with a shield upon which are the letters "A. O. U. W.," showing that he was a member of the Ancient Order of United Woodsmen.

CHAPTER XIX

ANNE GRAHAM'S
ATTEMPTED
VENGEANCE

THE KILLING OF Tom Graham plunged the Salt River Valley into the wildest excitement it had ever known in all its turbulent history. The murdered man had made many friends during his three years' residence near Tempe; and an attempt to lynch John Rhodes after he was lodged in jail at Tempe was only prevented by the courage of the officers. That there was a plan of some kind to lynch Ed Tewksbury is shown by the precautions taken in transferring him from Tucson to Phoenix, the details of which have been given in the previous chapter.

The events that took place after the prisoners were arrested have been so garbled that very few people today know exactly what did occur; but the old court records of Maricopa County are the best evidence of the legal action against Tewksbury and Rhodes. Although it is a matter of public record, buried deep in the archives of Phoenix courthouse, the legal disposition of these cases has been forgotten with the passing of nearly sixty years; and the story is still told without contradiction that Tewksbury was tried at Phoenix and convicted of murder in the first degree, but was granted a new trial when his lawyers found that the indictment had not been properly entered. This is not correct. Edwin Tewksbury was never tried at Phoenix, for he secured a change of venue to Tucson after his preliminary hearing before a justice of the peace.

I am indebted to Mr. Edw. E. Johnson, former deputy county attorney of Maricopa County, for copies of the old court records of the murder of Thomas H. Graham, which give some interesting and forgotten history of the last act in the bloody drama of Pleasant Valley. There is nothing to show that the prisoners were charged jointly. In fact, it appears that there were separate charges, for each was given a separate preliminary hearing.

According to an old story I once heard, John Rhodes narrowly escaped death at the hands of Charley Duchet on the day of his arrest; but I have been unable to learn many of the details.

However, Duchet fired point-blank at the prisoner, and the quick action of Deputy Tom Elder in knocking up the Graham fighter's arm saved Rhodes's life. Curtis Miller, now editor of the Tempe *News*, still points to a bullet hole in the door frame of his office as a relic of the affair.

Rhodes was the first to be given a hearing. This was before Justice of the Peace W. O. Huson; and strange to say, all of the magistrate's records of the case have disappeared from the courthouse, but attached to Edwin Tewksbury's affidavit alleging bias and prejudice in the whole county as a reason for a change of venue were old clippings from *The Arizona Daily Gazette*. These, together with the testimony of the few old-timers who were present, tell the story of the most exciting day in Arizona's legal history—a day in which another tragedy of the vendetta was only averted by a hair's breadth. From these clippings and from the stories of eyewitnesses I am able to give a fairly accurate account of the events that transpired in Justice Huson's court during the preliminary hearing of John Rhodes.

This hearing was more in the nature of a court trial, for ten days[1] were required to take the testimony, and lengthy arguments were made by the counsel of both sides. District Attorney Frank Cox represented the Territory of Arizona, while Attorney Joseph Campbell defended Rhodes.

The most dramatic episode of the whole war occurred at this hearing. It is a tale that is still told among the traditions of old Arizona—a story handed down from generation to generation. Day after day the case dragged on. The lawyers fought back and forth over the admission of bits of testimony until even the spectators became weary with it all.

Then the climax occurred on the day that the three children testified that John Rhodes was one of the two men they saw waiting in the roadside thicket. Without the slightest warning the courtroom was plunged into the wildest excitement by an act that is without parallel in all the thrilling history of a land noted for desperate deeds. Shortly before this episode, Anne Graham had testified that just before he died her husband had told her that he had been shot by Ed Tewksbury and John Rhodes. This was followed by the story of the three children who identified Rhodes as one of the men they had seen skulking in the brush just before the murder.

A hush had fallen over the courtroom. No one spoke; not a sound could be heard. Suddenly the widow of Tom Graham drew her murdered husband's heavy six-shooter from an umbrella,[2] pressed the muzzle against the defendant's back and pulled the trigger before a hand could be raised to stop her. Rhodes never moved a muscle, and the hammer fell with a loud click as the gun missed fire. Only men of iron nerve can go through such an experience with unshaken nerves; and John Rhodes stood the test.

For the smallest fraction of a second everyone in the room seemed paralyzed; then the wildest excitement broke out. Women and children screamed, and the men crowded around the defendant in a seething mob. Before she could make another move Mrs. Graham was seized by friends and hurried out.

Two men still living in Phoenix, who were present when the distracted widow attempted to avenge the murder of her husband, claim that a handkerchief prevented the hammer from exploding the cartridge. The confusion following this failure to take Rhodes's life was so great that these men were unable to see the subsequent events clearly. This was the generally accepted version; but this story told all these years that the hammer caught in a handkerchief or shawl may well be doubted, for the old frontier type of six-shooter was equipped with a large hammer heavy enough to drive a nail, and a long, sharp firing pin that would cut through any handkerchief.

The real reason why Tom Graham's six-shooter failed that day, when his widow pressed it against John Rhodes's back and pulled the trigger, came out with the story of Ed Cummings told to me years later. While on her way to Phoenix with her mother to attend the hearing, Mrs. Graham stopped at the Cummings ranch. Molly Cummings afterwards told that she saw Anne Graham lay her husband's gun on the table in the front room, concealed under her hat and veil; and while her daughter was in the next room Mrs. Melton quickly removed the cartridges. This is the most logical explanation.

Will C. Barnes[3] quotes the story of the reporters for two Phoenix newspapers to show that Mrs. Graham did not press the weapon against Rhodes. The account follows:

Mrs. Graham was sitting beside her father near the reporter's table. Suddenly she put her hand into her dress, pulled out a .44 caliber revolver. She sprang towards the prisoner with the avowed intention of "Putting out his light." She would have succeeded had not her father held her.

"Let me shoot him, for God's sake, let me shoot him;" she screamed. Porter Moffat threw a chair between Mrs. Graham and Rhodes which undoubtedly saved Rhodes' life, as in another minute the pistol would have been discharged. Mrs. Graham was led from the room by her father, still crying out in a loud voice: "Let me kill him, let me kill him; they will turn him loose."

However, after my talk with Ed Cummings and after hearing the stories of the two men still living in Phoenix, I believe that the version I have given is correct. The reporters, like everyone else in the room, were not prepared for such a dramatic episode, and their testimony as to just what occurred would be no better than that of other spectators, especially under the stress of the intense excitement that followed. Edwin Tewksbury in his petition for a change of venue also corroborates my version, in his statement that "the widow of said Graham attempted to kill said Rhodes by shooting him in the back, and only failed in so doing because of the entanglement of the hammer of the pistol in the cloth with which it was wrapped."

The result of John Rhodes's hearing seems to have been forgotten in the maze of excitement that followed the attempt on his life; and after this dramatic episode public interest centered in the legal battle to save Edwin Tewksbury from the gallows. You may question every man in the Salt River Valley today, and with the possible exception of some few old-timers no one can tell you the real reason John Rhodes escaped a court trial before a jury. As already stated, Justice Huson's records have disappeared; but I find from old newspaper clippings unearthed among the Maricopa County courthouse records by Mr. Johnson that Rhodes was discharged at the preliminary hearing.[5] From the fact that accounts of the result of this hearing appeared in both the Phoenix *Gazette* and the Tucson *Star* on August 20, Justice Huson's decision must have been rendered on the nineteenth.

The old items disclose the interesting information that Mr. Joseph Campbell, attorney for the defendant, "made a forceful and eloquent argument, closing only at the noonday hour."

That District Attorney Cox conducted the prosecution with vigor is shown by this extract: "The argument of Mr. Cox was one of which our district attorney has a good cause to be proud. He spoke for two and one-half hours in his most effective, yet rapid style, and showed that into the case he had thrown his best energies and talents."

Justice Huson had evidently decided upon his course of action long before the arguments were concluded, for a clipping from the Phoenix *Gazette* of August 20, already mentioned, gives an interesting account of the close of the hearing:

Upon the conclusion of the District Attorney's argument there was hardly a pause before Justice Huson rendered his decision. He said in a rather indistinct voice, "I have listened carefully to all the testimony in this case and, although I was at first inclined to believe the defendant guilty of the murder, the defense has so conclusively proved their alibi that I must release the prisoner."

A look of disgust and amazement spread over the uplifted faces of his hearers. There is no doubt but that the decision pleased very few. Knots of men gathered all over the streets and discussed, somewhat angrily, the situation.

A number of wild propositions were made, the most popular being to hang the judge in effigy. But a milder reaction followed and none of the foolish schemes were carried out. Rhodes had a few friends well armed and ready with a saddle horse, but he preferred to stay in jail today and return in broad daylight tomorrow.

It is unfortunate that we do not know the nature of this alibi today; but it, like many other important events of the vendetta, seems to have been forgotten with the passing of so many years. The excitement that followed Rhodes's release and the quick interest that centered in the hearing and later trials of Edwin Tewksbury are partly responsible. That this alibi was probably not very strong is shown by the outburst of indignation that blazed forth. Public opinion throughout southern Arizona over this action is expressed in the following editorial that appeared in the Tucson *Star* of August 20:

It appears that Rhodes did not have a hand in the killing of Graham. So Justice Huson of Tempe thinks, if he is honest in his decision which turns Rhodes loose on the community.

If the Phoenix Press reported the evidence correctly, and we have no good reason to believe otherwise, we cannot conceive upon what grounds the defendant was discharged. Why go to the useless expense of an examination which is but a travesty upon law and justice?

Public feeling became so bitter over Rhodes's release that on August 24 a mass meeting was called at Tempe to consider Justice Huson's action. The justice of the peace was condemned in no uncertain terms, and it was declared on all sides that he had exceeded his authority. The call for this meeting, signed by forty-five leading citizens, follows:

We, the undersigned, respectfully request the citizens of the South Side to meet in mass meeting, Saturday, August 27th, 1892, at 3 P. M., at Peters' Hall, for the purpose of considering the matter of the Graham murder.

The mass meeting was held at the time set, and after Justice Huson and the local officers were condemned in many heated denunciations the following resolution, drafted by a committee appointed for that purpose, was unanimously passed:

Resolved: That the action of one W. O. Huson, Justice of the peace at the City of Phoenix, in relegating to himself the powers of judge and jury in the recent preliminary examination of John Rhodes, accused of the murder of Tom Graham, is hereby condemned as an unwarranted assumption of power. That it is the opinion of the meeting that the evidence presented at said examination was in the minds of all honest men sufficient to bind the accused over to await the action of the grand jury.[6]

Nothing ever came of this resolution, and in a short time it seems to have been forgotten as interest centered in the legal battle waged to send Edwin Tewksbury to the gallows. If Rhodes had been the only person accused, it is probable that further action would have followed.

I have been unable to learn much of John Rhodes's activities during the fighting in Pleasant Valley but it is certain that he was connected with the Tewksburys from the beginning. The story is told that on one occasion he shot a finger off a hand of Jeff LaForce, a Graham fighter, but I never heard the details of this encounter. Through his connection with the Tewksburys he became acquainted with John Tewksbury's widow whom he later married.

Although John Rhodes quietly disappeared after his release at Phoenix, he spent the remainder of his life in Arizona. He has been dead these many years, but he is still remembered by old-timers as one of the best cowhands in the territory, and several years after the murder of Tom Graham he was foreman of a cattle ranch near Mammoth, on the San Pedro River, where I met him in 1903. Rhodes was a jovial man, popular among his neighbors at that time and respected by all, not the type you would pick for a killer; and it was always hard for me to believe that he had any connection with the Graham murder. He was the winner of a fine Winchester rifle that I raffled off at Mammoth. After the close of the vendetta he was noted as a good citizen in every way. He finally died of consumption. Some years ago I heard that his wife and daughter were keeping a boarding-house in Phoenix.

Mr. William MacLeod Raine, the author, informs me that one of the cowboys he saw in the

Tucson rodeo in 1929 was John Rhodes. Upon making inquiry, Mr. Raine learned that he was the stepson of the John Rhodes of vendetta notoriety and the real son of John Tewksbury, who was murdered with William Jacobs during the attack on the Tewksbury ranch in Pleasant Valley. This man of today was the infant in the Tewksbury cabin whose crying broke the silence of that September day more than sixty years ago when his mother flirted with death from some reckless cowboy's bullet as she bravely drove the hogs from the body of his murdered father. I have followed this further and learned that the boy took the name of his stepfather and at present lives on a ranch near Mammoth.

CHAPTER XX

EDWIN TEWKSBURY'S
FIGHT FOR LIFE

THE LONG BATTLE TO
save Edwin Tewksbury
from the gallows was
more thrilling and desperate than any gun fight
during the years of the vendetta. The war in
Pleasant Valley had cost money, and what little
the Tewksburys had at the beginning was soon
exhausted by the constant demands for food
and ammunition; but when Ed Tewksbury went
on trial for the murder of Tom Graham, money
came from some unknown source,[1] and the best
legal talent in the territory was retained in his
defense. Law is expensive; but after a long-
drawn-out battle through the courts he won,
because of the fact that he had expert lawyers
who saved him by a legal technicality from the
verdict of guilty at the first trial.

This is one of the most famous cases in the
criminal history of Arizona. After being
granted a change of venue, he was convicted of
murder once and was then granted a new trial.
The second jury disagreed, and two and a half
years after his arrest he was released on bail,
never to be tried again. His actions in prison
were certainly not those of a guilty man. Twice
in Phoenix he had opportunities to escape, but
refused them; and again in Tucson he rejected

an invitation to join with other prisoners in a break for liberty.

After the discharge of John Rhodes the case against Edwin Tewksbury was transferred on August 18, 1892, to the justice court of Phoenix precinct; and after a preliminary hearing on the twenty-ninth before Harry L. Wharton, justice of the peace, he was held for trial in the county court on practically the same testimony as that presented against Rhodes. In addition to the identification by the three children, W. J. White identified Ed Tewksbury as a man he had seen in Bowen's saloon in Tempe on the morning of the murder.

White was at the bar waiting for a drink; but just as the bartender set it down a man rushed in, seized the glass, and drank it. When White remonstrated, the stranger said: "I'm in a big hurry."

The man rushed out without paying, but no one interfered with him. The bartender explained that he was a ranchman just getting over a spree, and gave White another drink. When asked by Justice Wharton if he could identify the man, White pointed at Ed Tewksbury.

The next grand jury, of which Charles Pendergast was foreman, found a true bill against Ed Tewksbury on September 7; and on De-

cember 5 he was arraigned before Judge H. C.
Gooding in the district court of Maricopa County. In those times the mills of justice ground
even slower than today, and the action of the
law was impeded by many demurrers and pleas
in abatement entered by Messrs. Baker and
Campbell,[2] counsel for the defense. The hearings
made necessary by these technicalities required
time; and it was more than sixteen months after
the murder of Tom Graham before Ed Tewksbury was finally brought to trial.[3]

After every other means had failed to secure
a release or further stay, a motion for a change
of venue was filed. This interesting document,
signed before a notary public by Edwin Tewksbury with his rather shaky signature, is still on
file among the old, nearly forgotten records in
Phoenix courthouse. Allegations of bias and
prejudice against the defendent, supported by
affidavits, state that it would be impossible for
him to obtain a fair trial in Maricopa County.
The brief description of the attempt on John
Rhodes's life at the preliminary hearing is one
of the most important parts of the petition from
a historical point of view:

That one John Rhodes was jointly charged with the
affiant with the killing of said Graham, and at his
preliminary examination in open court, the widow of
said Graham attempted to kill said Rhodes by shooting

him in the back, and only failed in so doing because of the entanglement of the hammer of the pistol in the cloth with which it was wrapped.

In order to show the intense public feeling against the defendant, this affidavit is supported by newspaper clippings describing the mass meeting held by the citizens of Tempe on August 27, 1892.

The court of Maricopa County had fixed May 10, 1893, as the date for the trial; but this motion resulted in further delay. The district attorney opposed a change of venue, but it was finally granted after a long hearing, and on July 10 the case was transferred to the district court of Pima County. In view of the bitter feeling in Maricopa County it would have been almost impossible to have found a jury that would not have been prejudiced.

I am indebted to Mr. Louis R. Kempf, former county attorney of Pima County, for the court records of the two trials of Edwin Tewksbury, held at Tucson, and of his final release on bail more than two and a half years after the murder of Tom Graham. This was after the second jury disagreed.

The first trial opened on December 14, 1893, before Judge J. D. Bethune, with Messrs. Street and Cox as prosecuting counsel, and on the twenty-first the case was submitted to the jury.

At the second trial the territory was represented by M. H. Williams, W. M. Lovell, and Frank H. Hereford; but the reason for this change is not known. Tewksbury was defended, first by Baker and Campbell and subsequently by Fitch and Campbell, Barnes and Martin, and Thomas D. Satterwhite. It is doubtful if such an array of eminent legal talent on both sides was ever present in one case in all the history of Arizona. That long-drawn-out battle through the courts to save the clan leader's life was more expensive than all the gun fighting of the Pleasant Valley days; but the money was furnished by some mysterious hand, known only to Ed Tewksbury and his attorneys; and they all kept the secret well.

Over seventy-five witnesses were called by both sides during the seven days of the trial. Ed Cummings, his sister, Molly, and the Gregg girl, the three children who actually witnessed the shooting of Tom Graham, were the principal witnesses for the prosecution. Although he was only a boy at the time, Ed Cummings recalled vividly the events of that trial as he told me the story a third of a century later. His version of the killing has already been given in a previous chapter.

The defense was an alibi. Ed Tewksbury's testimony that on August 2, 1892, the day of the murder, he was in Tonto Basin, was corroborated by A. J. Stencel, a cowboy from the Winslow country, who stated that on that date he met the clan leader on the Reno road far from Tempe. The defense contention that the distance was too great for him to have traveled was attacked by the prosecution on the ground that he could have covered it on a fast horse.

The testimony was closed, and arguments started on December 20; and the next day the fate of Edwin Tewksbury, popularly known as "the last man," was placed in the hands of twelve of his peers. That the alibi made a deep impression is shown by the fact that the jury was out for two days before reaching an agreement; but the identification by the three children and the dying statement made by Tom Graham to his wife influenced the majority.

It was on the twenty-third that Judge Bethune was notified by a tipstaff that the jury had agreed; and the courtroom scene of more than fifty years ago in old Tucson was so vividly described to me by one who had been present that I could almost see it myself. An air of suppressed excitement filled the crowded room as the twelve men filed solemnly in. Men and women who had patiently waited for this moment for more than two days scarcely breathed as they strained their ears to hear every word. The scraping of the jurors' feet sounded almost like the tread of an army in the intense silence.

As he stood with his counsel facing the twelve men who held his life in their hands, Ed Tewksbury's eyes were riveted upon their faces as though he would read their minds and end the terrible nerve-breaking suspense.

"Gentlemen of the jury, have you agreed upon a verdict?" the court asked when they had taken their places in the box.

"We have," replied M. McKenna, the foreman, and he handed the clerk a slip of paper from which he read in a clear voice that sounded the knell to all the hopes of the Tewksbury leader:

We, the jury, duly impanelled in the above entitled cause, upon our oaths, do find the defendant guilty of murder and recommend him to the mercy of the court.
(Signed) M.McKenna, Foreman.[4]

The last of the Tewksburys had fought too many desperate battles against overwhelming odds to give up even in the face of a verdict of guilty of murder. His lawyers, past masters of their profession, immediately set in motion the ponderous machinery of legal technicalities that eventually saved Edwin Tewksbury from the gallows or at least from a long term in the penitentiary at Yuma. The recommendation for mercy, which was evidently placed in the verdict by the minority who believed in the alibi, would probably have resulted in a prison sentence. A motion for a new trial, filed on the ground that the defendant was not present in person at the time his plea in abatement was presented to and determined by the court, and for the further reason that no plea had ever been entered on record by the defendant, was finally granted on March 4, 1894. These reasons were, of course, only technicalities and had nothing to do with the merits of the case; but they were enough in the eyes of the law.

But another year passed before this motion and the ensuing arguments were disposed of by the court; and it was not until January 2, 1895, that Edwin Tewksbury was again placed on trial for the murder of Tom Graham, this time before Judge Richard E. Sloan. Thirty-four witnesses were called by the prosecution and forty-one by the defense. The evidence was practically the same as at the first trial, but one more day was required, and it was January 10 before the prisoner's fate was again in the hands of a jury. Just how long that body deliberated does not appear on the record; but the defense had raised at least a reasonable doubt in the minds of some of the jurors, for seven were in favor of an acquittal; and they were finally dis-

charged by the court when it was found that
they could not agree.

A motion to release the defendant on bail was
presented immediately. This was supported by
the following affidavit which is given here for
the additional historical light it throws on this
famous case:

In the District Court of the First Judicial District of
the Territory of Arizona in and for Pima County.
The Territory of Arizona
        against
Ed. Tewksbury, Defendant.
Territory of Arizona:
            SS:—
    County of Pima:
    Ed. Tewksbury being duly sworn on oath states;
that he is the defendant in the above entitled action;
that as soon as he was informed by public rumors in
Tonto Basin, Gila County, Arizona, that he was
charged with the offense for which he has been indicted he went to the officer, riding many miles and
gave himself up to the officer, on either the 5th or
6th of August, A. D., 1892. He states that since that
time he has been in custody upon said charge; that he
has been held in jail at Phoenix and in the jail at
Tucson; that during the time he was in jail at Phoenix
on two occasions he had opportunities to escape from
said jail and did not do so; that on other occasions
three prisoners in the jail with him sought to induce
him to endeavor to escape with them and in every case
he declined; that during the time he was in jail at
Tucson he was approached by prisoners who were
planning to escape and he declined to take part with
them, but informed the officers of the fact. He states
that he has been tried twice for the offense of which
he stands indicted; that at the trial just had he is

informed that seven of the twelve jurors found him
not guilty and persisted in that finding, and by reason
of their persistence there was a mistrial of said cause.
That the trials of said cause heretofore and upon
this time have not been delayed by his seeking.

That he is informed and believes that the condition
of the business of the court is now such that he cannot
be tried again before some time in February, and if
not then for perhaps a month or two later.

He therefore asks the court to be submitted to bail
in such sum as the court may deem proper.

He urges to the court that bail is allowed to every
person charged with crime except where the punish-
ment may be capital and then only when the proof is
evident and the presumption great, and that the failure
of the last trial of the jury to find a verdict of guilty
that particularly when a majority of the jury found
that he was not guilty is satisfactory evidence of the
fact that in this case the proof is not evident nor is
the presumption great.

And further the affiant saith not.

(Signed) Ed Tewksbury.

Subscribed and sworn to before me this 11th day
of January, 1895.

(Signed) John H. Martin,
Notary Public, Pima County, Arizona.[5]

This motion was denied at that time; but on
February 6, 1895, the Tewksbury leader was
admitted to bail. No matter whether he was
innocent or guilty of participation in the murder of Tom Graham he had paid the feud penalty
with two and one half years of his life in prison;
and during the inaction of his confinement he
contracted the disease that caused his death nine
years later.

After the passing of another year, the prosecution, evidently believing that a conviction would now be impossible, filed a motion to dismiss the charge. When this was granted on March 12, 1896, the curtain fell on the last act of the bitterest blood feud in the history of the old West—a story that has become a legend of old Arizona's cattleland. The fruitless battle of three and a half years to convict the last Tewksbury of the murder of the last of the Grahams had cost Maricopa County twenty thousand dollars. The price of the defense was never made public.

While the killing of Tom Graham is generally believed to have been the last of the sanguinary Pleasant Valley war, a young cowboy named Horace Philly was murdered in Reno Pass a short time later. It was reported at the time that he had been waylaid by the "Apache Kid," a notorious renegade Apache from the San Carlos agency; but Philly had worked on the Graham ranch during the stormy days of the vendetta, and some old-timers have expressed the opinion that he might have been another victim of the feud. No reason has ever been advanced for his murder in connection with the vendetta; and so it will ever remain another mystery of those fighting days of old Arizona.

Recently A. Lloyd Ozanne reported to me that

a young cowboy named Roach, with a friend, started for Pleasant Valley sometime during the war to find work. They were killed near Reno Pass, and it was reported that they were victims of the vendetta. This was evidently another instance of the fate of strangers who ventured into the feud district.

CHAPTER XXI

JIM ROBERTS, THE "LAST MAN"

JIM ROBERTS, a member of the Tewksbury faction and the last known survivor of all of those who took an active part on either side, was the real "last man" of the Pleasant Valley war, and his sudden death at Clarkdale on January 8, 1934, marked the passing of the last of that coterie of fighting men who made Arizona famous as the last frontier. A deputy sheriff and constable for more than fifty years, he was one of the very few old-time peace officers of the Southwest who survived the hectic frontier times to die at the age of seventy-five years of natural causes. When the Pleasant Valley war broke out in the spring of 1887 he espoused the Tewksbury cause for personal reasons which will be given later, and was rated as the very best fighting man of that clan. That age did not impair the deadly accuracy of his gun hand is proved by his killing of the outlaw Willard J. Forrester in a spectacular bank robbery at Clarkdale in 1928. Just how many men he killed during his long career as a member of the vendetta clan and later as a peace officer cannot be stated; Jim often said that he did not know. He always refused to talk for publication; but he had related many of the events of his life, especially during the Pleasant Valley war, to his son, William H. Roberts, of Clarkdale, to whom I am indebted for much information on this old-time fighter.

James Franklin Roberts was born at Beaver, Missouri, in 1858. It has been said with truth that Missouri and Kentucky supplied more pioneers for the settlement of the West than any other section. During the ninteenth century, the young men of those states were born with the wanderlust and love of adventure strong in their blood. Their fathers and mothers before them were the pioneers who had claimed the "Dark and Bloody Ground" and the Missouri country west of the great river from the Indians; and it was little wonder that the sons of such parents should turn their faces westward in search of a new land that would satisfy adventurous youth.

This was Jim Roberts' inheritance, a heritage that would not be denied; and so at the age of eighteen he turned his face westward in search of a new frontier. The great West was then in the making. The Sioux of the northern plains were still on the warpath, but the hostiles under Sitting Bull had fled to Canada after Custer's defeat, and much of the fighting spirit had been taken out of the Comanches, Cheyennes, and Kiowas, for the buffalo had been practically exterminated from the southern plains country. The line that marked the division between civilization and the raw frontier had moved farther towards the Pacific; and it is little wonder that this boy with a heritage of pioneering forefathers should drift westward until he found a land to his liking; a land raw and rough enough for any adventurous lad of the 1870's. And he found it in Arizona, the last frontier.

After wandering about the territory for a year or two, he finally unsaddled his horse near the head of Tonto Creek in what was later known as Pleasant Valley. This was the heart of the wildest section of a wild, remote land; and in this lonely spot he built a cabin. From his ancestors he had inherited a love for fine horses, and he quickly saw the possibilities of producing a hardy strain by crossing the tough, wiry range mares with blooded stock. With patience he saved his money until he had enough to purchase a purebred stallion. It was a beautiful animal with arched neck, deep broad chest, and long flowing mane and tail, and it is little wonder that every cowboy, rustler, and stockman in central Arizona longed to drop a rope over its proud head.

Jim Roberts became noted for his good horses, and as more ranchmen located in the valley his stock began to disappear, for be it remembered that this spot so far removed from the forces of law and order was the last haven on a fading frontier for men wanted in other sections. Jim paid little attention to the few head of horses that disappeared now and then, for that was to be expected in the stock business; but when his prized stud was missing he "saw red"; that was an entirely different matter, and he would make somebody pay dearly.

He charged the Grahams with the theft, but whether they were actually guilty or whether it was Andy Cooper's gang will never be certainly known. Jim was not a man to mince words, and his accusation strained the relations with the three brothers almost, but not quite, to the breaking point. There had already been an open rupture between the Grahams and Tewksburys, and events that finally led to hostilities were rapidly crystallizing. Matters became worse; accusations flew thick and fast over the range, but still Jim Roberts took no part in the feud that was gathering in dark, threatening clouds on the horizon of this peaceful land—not until he returned one evening to find his little cabin home a pile of smouldering ashes. Then his rage knew no bounds. He openly declared war against the Grahams; and thus the Tewksburys gained their most valuable fighting man.

After hostilities closed in 1888, Jim Roberts

returned to his ranch; but like many others on both sides the vendetta had cost him his last dollar, and he must look elsewhere for a new start. Senator William A. Clark, the Montana copper king, had recently leased the mines of the United Verde Copper Company and had launched an extensive development program.[1] This created plenty of work and excitement, and men from all sections of Arizona were rushing to the Jerome district. Jim Roberts joined in the rush because he had nothing better in sight, and he soon landed at the booming camp of Congress City.

His reputation as a first-class fighting man in the Pleasant Valley war had spread over the land, and when the noted William O. (Buckey) O'Neill[2] was elected sheriff, he appointed Jim Roberts as a deputy, beginning December 18, 1889.[3] This was the start of a long career as a frontier peace officer—a career that was only terminated by death forty-four years later. Jim served under O'Neill so well that on January 12, 1891, he was appointed by James R. Lowery,[4] the next sheriff. On December 8, 1892, he was elected constable of Jerome precinct,[5] and for eleven years he filled that office. On April 4, 1904, after the expiration of his last term as constable, he was elected town marshal of Jerome, the last of Arizona's hectic mining camps of the Wild West era.[6] Lawlessness was slowly strangling the town in a death grip; bad men from all sections of Arizona were openly defying the law. Similar conditions had existed in times past in practically every new mining camp and cow town west of the Mississippi. This problem had always been solved in the same way, by securing a man of iron nerve whose gun hand was a shade quicker than any other in the district. The businessmen of Jerome took the matter in hand, and cast their eyes about for a town marshal who would measure up to these specifications. No one was looking for the job. Even in Arizona.where there were plenty of good gunmen still left, there were no applicants; but finally someone suggested Jim Roberts, whose record as a first-class fighting man in the Pleasant Valley war and during fourteen years as a peace officer was still fresh, and Jim agreed to accept.

Jim Roberts faced a man-sized job when he became marshal of Jerome in April, 1904. It was a desperate fight in the beginning, for he had to kill several bad men before the tough element was made to understand that this officer with the lightning draw intended to enforce law and order even if he had to wipe them all out; and thereafter Jerome was a very peaceful mining camp.

After the cleanup Jim moved to the near-by camp of Clarkdale,[7] where he spent the remainder of his life as a special officer for the United Verde Copper Company, acting under a deputy sheriff's commission. It is related that on one occasion he trailed a Mexican into the Mingus Mountains, where he shot it out with the fugitive, threw his body across his saddle, and brought him in.

Jim's most notable exploit in recent years was the killing of Willard J. Forrester, Oklahoma outlaw, and the capture of Earl Nelson, his partner, while the bandits were attempting to escape with fifty thousand dollars taken in the spectacular holdup of the Clarkdale branch of the Bank of Arizona on June 21, 1928. During a rather hectic career in the Middle West, Forrester and Nelson met at Wichita, Kansas, in 1926, and agreed to try their luck together. Gradually working westward, they finally landed at Prescott in the early part of 1928. Both secured employment in Clarkdale, Forrester as driver of the stage to the hospital while Nelson worked at the Plaza Annex garage for a time.

They decided to make one big raid that would be remembered for years, and then leave the country. They were looking for big game, and after a check on the town they decided that the Bank of Arizona was their best bet. The fact that the Arizona of other days had a reputation for quick-shooting men meant little or nothing to them. Arizona had gone modern, and deadly gun fighters were in the far-distant past. If this pair of young bandits had ever heard of old Jim's past reputation, they evidently believed that his hand had lost its cunning with age, for he was then seventy years old, a relic of the past, so they believed. But in this they made their one great mistake.

Plans were made with care; and on the morning of June 21 they loaded their automobile with the accessories necessary for a first-class modern holdup. This included forty-seven cans of roofing nails to scatter over the road to block pursuit by automobiles; ginger, cayenne pepper, and oil of peppermint to rub on the soles of their shoes for the benefit of any dogs that might be put on their trail; a well-equipped arsenal for two, consisting of riot gun, four revolvers, a shotgun and a rifle, and several days' food supply.

For more than a week they had watched the bank and so timed their arrival at eleven o'clock in the morning as that seemed to be the hour when there were few customers. David O. Saunders, the manager, and R. G. Southard, the teller, with thirteen customers were quickly covered, and while Nelson held them under his threatening gun Forrester scooped fifty thousand dollars into a sack. Then he demanded twenty thousand more he believed was in the bank, but Saunders convinced him that it had been checked out the day before. When the bandits herded their fifteen prisoners into the vault, Saunders explained that this would mean a slaughter if they were locked in, for they would all die before the steel door could be opened. Moved by this plea, the outlaws only closed the auxiliary door, and then leaped into their automobile.

Seizing a gun in the vault, Saunders rushed out and opened fire, but he only shot twice, for the street was alive with townspeople.

Old Jim Roberts was walking leisurely along the sidewalk that morning. Years had passed since the aged deputy had been stirred into action by real lawlessness; yet he was on the job that morning just as he had been every morning for nearly forty years. Looking about the busy street he compared Clarkdale to the good old days of thirty years and more gone when the Arizona mining camps had "a man for breakfast" very frequently.

"Ah! those were the days," he mused. "A man has no use to pack a gun nowadays." But the habits of a lifetime are hard to break, and old Jim still carried his six-gun of rather ancient vintage on his hip, just as he had done for forty years and more, even though he had no use for it in these peaceful times.

Suddenly two men carrying a sack rushed from the bank, leaped into an automobile, and started down the street at terrific speed. Old Jim knew at once that something unusual was on foot. He was positive of this when a man ran from the bank and fired two shots at the machine, for long years as a peace officer on a wild frontier had taught Jim Roberts many things. Something was radically wrong. Life in an Arizona mining camp nowadays had its moments of trouble.

Instantly the aged deputy sprang into action with all the agility of youth. With a swift motion that would have done credit to an Arizona "gun slinger" of fifty years past, a Colt six-shooter of the old single action frontier vintage suddenly appeared in his hand as if by magic. Smoke flamed from the muzzle with a roar, and Willard Forrester, bank robber, suddenly slumped over the wheel with a forty-five lead slug in his brain. Old Jim Roberts' gun hand had lost none of its deadliness in spite of seventy years.

The automobile careened wildly across the sidewalk and crashed into the stone wall of a new school building, the guy wire from a telephone pole ripping off the top in the mad dash. Nelson leaped out, his gun spitting lead at the deputy; but old Jim had been under fire too many times to let this bother him in the least, and with the agility of a man forty years younger he ran in pursuit of the outlaw. The chase was short, not more than two hundred yards; and when the bandit's gun was empty, he surrendered, for a man with the ability to shoot the driver of a moving automobile through the head was not to be trifled with.

Earl Nelson was subsequently sent to the state penitentiary at Florence for a term of forty years to keep him out of further trouble, but his career of crime was not over, for he later staged a spectacular escape, and was only recaptured after a desperate chase almost across the state. It is believed that he has several thousand dollars loot from another bank robbery concealed in the Stoneman Lake country, and scores of treasure hunters have moved hundreds of tons of earth and rock in a fruitless search.

After a wild life of more than fifty adventurous years, Jim Roberts finally passed out with his "boots on," at the age of seventy-five years; but heart disease was the cause, and not a bullet from the gun of some fellow a shade quicker on the draw. "Uncle Jim," as he was affectionately known in his later years, was on duty when death called. It was about eleven o'clock Monday night, January 8, 1934, that he received the summons, and an hour later he was found lying on the ground in the rear of the Clarkdale drugstore. He was rushed to the Jerome hospital when a faint flicker of life was detected, but he died on the way. Three days later he was buried in the cemetery at Clarkdale, leaving a widow and two sons, William H. Roberts, of Clarkdale, and Hugh K. Roberts, of Jerome. And so old Jim Roberts, the "last man" of the Pleasant Valley vendetta of bloody memory, passed out over the long trail to join comrades and enemies in the land beyond the grave.

CHAPTER XXII

RECESSIONAL OF VENDETTA DAYS — WITH THE DISMISSAL of the murder charges against Edwin Tewksbury the Pleasant Valley war came to an end; but for many a year it was the main topic of conversation wherever rangemen gathered, and to this day old-timers entertain the younger generation with thrilling stories of old Arizona's cattleland. The fighting had been so fierce and the personal feelings so bitter that most of the participants were glad enough to forget. Few of them would even discuss it. "Let the dead past remain dead" was their motto. But stories of these desperate gun-fighting days, when men shot each other on sight and the law of the land was defied by both sides, have been told around Arizona campfires until they have become legends. It is doubtful if as much range fiction was ever invented on any other episode of Western history; and even to this day some new story comes to light. But an air of mystery still hovers like a cloud over many of the events of this strange and bloody vendetta, for most of those who took an active part carried their secrets to the grave.

Of the many men who fought in this bitter

feud of nearly half a century ago none are living. All those who survived the war have passed over the last trail to join old comrades and enemies on the Eternal Range beyond the Last Divide. But before they died some did talk in confidence, and from their stories that have come to me in one way and another I have written this account of that bitter range war of the old West.

Edwin Tewksbury, known for years as the "last man" and the hero of Zane Grey's thrilling feud romance *To The Last Man*, is generally believed to have been the last survivor of the principal families engaged. However, three families took an active part—the Tewksbury, the Graham, and the Blevins; and John Blevins was the "last man" of these three. It will be remembered that the disappearance of his father, Mart Blevins, was the indirect cause of the fight at the Middleton ranch; and four of Mart's five sons were killed during August and September, 1887. But old Jim Roberts was the real "last man" of the Pleasant Valley war, for he outlived all other survivors.

The fate of George Graham, whom I have mentioned frequently, was never known. Not long before Jim Roberts died, he told his son, in answer to an inquiry from me, that he last heard of this man in Phoenix after the war.

The mystery surrounding George Graham's identity has never been solved, and not much is known of his connection with the vendetta.

After Commodore Owens was forced to release John Blevins, they met several times but never spoke. John eventually dropped out of sight, going to southern Arizona, and many of his old friends on the northern range believed him dead until he attended the Fourth-of-July celebration at Flagstaff in 1926. The wound received in the fight with Owens troubled him to the day of his death. He was fatally injured in an automobile accident while riding with his granddaughter. The machine plunged over an embankment near Phoenix, and he died in the hospital two days later.

After his release from jail in Tucson, Edwin Tewksbury returned to Pleasant Valley; but the memories that it held were not pleasant. Although his father had remained there until his death, which occurred while the son was in prison awaiting trial, the ranch was neglected, and the small number of cattle and horses he had owned at the time of Tom Graham's murder had received no attention. Mavericks ran the range and only a few head now bore the Tewksbury brand. It was a land of bitter memories for Ed Tewksbury, and so he sold what little he had left and located at Globe. He spent the remainder of his life there as a peace officer, alternating as constable of Globe and deputy sheriff of Gila County.[1] That he was a good officer goes without saying, for the reputation of his quick and deadly gun hand was enough to make any bad man hesitate before starting trouble.

The last of the Tewksburys did not live long to enjoy his liberty, for he died at Globe on April 4, 1904, a victim of quick consumption, the seeds of which were sown during his imprisonment. I was riding the Arizona cattle range myself at the time, and I well remember the many stories of the Pleasant Valley war that were revived around campfires and in the press by the passing of this noted warrior of vendetta days.

Besides his widow Mrs. Brawley Tewksbury,[2] who is still living at Globe, he was survived by the following children: Elvira Elena, aged nine years; Edwin Frank, aged seven; James Hendry, aged five; and George Wilson, aged four. James survived his father just twenty years, dying at Globe June 30, 1924. Of the other three, George resides at San Diego, California.

Shortly after the fight at the Middleton ranch in which he was desperately wounded, Thomas Tucker, the Hash Knife cowboy, drifted away in search of further adventures; and in the latter 1890's we find him serving as undersheriff at Santa Fe, New Mexico, during the administration of Sheriff Cunningham. After leaving Arizona, Tucker returned to his native state of Texas, where Cunningham found him about· 1895 while looking for a fearless deputy to help exterminate numerous bad men in that section of New Mexico. That Tom Tucker was a man with a reputation we well know; and during the two years that he served under Sheriff Cunningham in old Santa Fe he killed several men who disputed his ability to arrest them. He finally lost his badge in a change of administration.

His reputation as a fighting man meant nothing to a twenty-two-year-old cowboy who rode into Santa Fe in the early spring of 1898 to enlist in the Rough Rider company then being recruited at that place. While sitting in the plaza of the ancient capital of the conquistadores one day enjoying the war excitement, he became involved in a quarrel with this youth, and, according to the story related to me by an eyewitness, the fearless Tom Tucker received a severe beating at the hands of this young Rough Rider. It was the opinion of my informant that the old fighter lost his nerve when his deputy's star was removed; but in all probability it was just another case of youth against an older man; and then Tucker's reputation as a fighter was made with a six-shooter, not his fists. He disappeared from Santa Fe shortly after this affair; and in 1929 he died in Texas at an advanced age.

The death of Charley Duchet marked the passing of one of the last gun fighters of the old West, from the wild days of Dodge City on the Kansas plains to bloody Pleasant Valley in the heart of the last frontier. He died with his "boots off" at Phoenix in 1925 at an advanced age. The caliber of this old-time Westerner is best shown by a duel he once fought with another man in a dark room, both stripped naked and armed with bowie knives. Duchet was victorious; but he was marked for life by a long scar down his face, and both hands and arms were badly cut.[3]

After Tom Graham's death Duchet disappeared; and it was generally reported that he was living in Los Angeles. As a matter of fact, he changed his name and tried to lose his identity; but he never left Arizona. About 1918 Ed Cummings, who remembered him at Graham's, near Tempe, met the old fighter at a lonely desert ranch, and recognized him immediately. Duchet at first denied his identity, but when he learned the name of his visitor, he admitted that he was Charley Duchet.

"But remember, when you leave here, that

Branding a Yearling in Old Arizona

George Smith, Ed Rogers, and Jim Hoy

Charley Duchet is dead." He explained that he did not care for the publicity that he attracted under his real name.

During the conversation between the two at that time, Duchet told the story of how he had once "killed" Ed Tewksbury and then met him a week later. This occurred after the war had developed into a bushwhacking game. One day when Duchet was concealed on a hillside watching a trail he heard someone approaching, and presently Ed Tewksbury, mounted on a mule, rode around a point of rocks. Duchet fired and Tewksbury fell into the dust of the trail; and when the former climbed down, he found a bullet hole apparently through his victim's head.

A week later Duchet met Tewksbury riding the same mule. Each man placed his hand on his six-shooter, but neither attempted to draw; and as they passed close enough to rub elbows each turned in the saddle and watched the other until a safe distance separated them. Duchet always believed that he had killed another man; but there could have been no mistake, for he knew both Ed Tewksbury and his mule well. If this incident ever actually occurred the bullet probably grazed the head, producing a temporary concussion.

Their conversation naturally drifted to the vendetta, and Duchet corroborated the opinion of others that a stranger who ventured into Pleasant Valley in those days was in more danger than a native. He must be a courageous man the feudists reasoned, and he was immediately marked for death by both sides.

Tom Pickett, Hash Knife cowboy, took part in two of the most sanguinary range wars in the history of the old West. A gunman with a wide reputation long before he drifted to Arizona, he received his early training under no less a teacher than Billy the Kid in the bloody Lincoln County war in New Mexico; and a hard, bitter school it was, so filled with hatreds and murder that even General Lee Wallace, governor of the territory, was powerless to stop the carnage. Pickett was one of the men with Billy the Kid and Tom O'Folliard that fated night of December 18, 1880, when the latter was killed at old Fort Sumner by Sheriff Pat Garrett. And after the fight at Stinking Spring three days later Garrett and his posse captured the Kid and his gang. Tom Pickett was one of the prisoners. When the Kid was taken to jail at Santa Fe, Pickett was left at Las Vegas, as there was no warrant for him, and he was subsequently released.

Walter Noble Burns in *The Saga of Billy the Kid*, states that Tom Pickett afterwards reformed and settled in New Mexico, where he became a respected citizen and died years later. This is a mistake. Pickett may have remained in New Mexico for a time after the Kid's death; but in 1885 we find him riding for the Hash Knife out of Holbrook. That the Tom Pickett of the Arizona days was the same Tom Pickett who rode with Billy the Kid there is not the slightest doubt, for three men who knew him intimately at Holbrook in the 1880's have assured me that he is the same man. The first was that well-known old-time cattleman, William Rhodan, of Flagstaff, who was well acquainted with Tom Pickett when they were both young cowboys on the northern Arizona cattle range in the 1880's. The second was Will C. Barnes, while the third man has lived in Holbrook for more than half a century; but he requested that his name be withheld.

About 1885 or 1886 Tom Pickett married Kate Kelly,[4] whose mother conducted a boarding-house at Holbrook for railroad section hands in the early days.

A wound received in the leg while fighting with Billy the Kid in New Mexico never healed, and this finally forced Pickett to give up range riding. Aggravated in later years by his increasing weight of over two hundred pounds, this old wound of forty-five years' standing finally endangered his life when gangrene set in, and his leg was amputated in 1925.

Like many other old range riders he turned to gambling; and we next find him in the last gold rush to the Nevada deserts during the first years of the century as proprietor of a gambling hall at Carson City and later at Goldfield. After the gold fever subsided he served for several years as a deputy United States marshal during the Wilson administration. This old fighter of pioneer days in the Southwest was still living in Nevada when I last heard from him in 1929; and occasionally he visited Globe and the scenes of his early adventures in central Arizona.

The disappearance of Mart Blevins remains a mystery that will probably never be solved. A skeleton discovered near the Houdon ranch some years later was believed to be his remains, but there was never any satisfactory proof. About 1894 J. F. Ketcherside, foreman of Newton and Vosberg's Flying V outfit of vendetta days, found a well-preserved human skull[5] in a hollow tree on one of the tributaries of upper Cherry Creek; and an old rifle, later identified as one carried by Mart Blevins, was leaning against the tree. Ketcherside and his men patiently searched for other bones, but nothing more was ever found. How the skull came to be in the cavity has never been explained. About twenty years ago another skull was discovered near the old Houdon ranch; and at first it was believed to be that of an Indian, but a closer examination showed that several teeth were filled with gold. It was never identified; and it is the general opinion that it was another victim of the war.

The Aztec Land and Cattle Company, known as the Hash Knife, was organized about 1885 by Eastern capitalists; and in its heyday this was the largest of all the cow outfits of old Arizona. With headquarters near the Mormon settlement of Saint Joseph, west of Holbrook, its cattle ranged over a thousand hills from the Little Colorado River far south into Tonto Basin. A rare photograph of the personnel of the original outfit, taken at the headquarters near Saint Joseph in 1886, was furnished me by Will C. Barnes. Some of those old Hash Knife cowboys were men with records who had fled to the safety of the last frontier in Arizona because the arm of the law could not reach that far west in those days. In this original outfit of 1886 were Henry Kinsley, Roxy, George Smith, Peck, Tom Pickett, Buck Lancaster, Don McDonald, I. M. Higgins, Billy Wilson, E. I. Simpson, Ames, Warren, and Vinal.

Henry Kinsley, a young man just out from the East, was secretary of the company, and in later years he was cashier of a Los Angeles bank. Vinal was a surveyor employed by the company to establish the lines of its land grants.

Tom Pickett's picturesque career has already been related; but George Smith, Buck Lancaster, Roxy and Peck, four more of the original outfit who supported the Grahams and the cattle interests, drifted away and finally vanished in the land of forgotten men.

McNeal, another Hash Knife cowboy who fought in the Pleasant Valley war, afterwards followed the outlaw trail through Arizona and Utah; and for a long period he outwitted the officers of both states. Once when the sheriff from Flagstaff thought that he had him trapped in a cabin, he only found a poem written on a scrap of paper nailed on the wall; but McNeal was finally captured and sent to the penitentiary for a long term. After his release several years ago he returned to northern Arizona, and in 1926 was living in Holbrook.

Pete Pemberton, another old-time Hash Knife cowboy, was still living in Winslow in 1929.

John T. Jones, the first range foreman of the Aztec Land and Cattle Company, was succeeded some years after its organization by Burton C. Mossman, who later became the most noted outlaw hunter in the Southwest. The equal of his swift, deadly gun hand and cool nerve could not be found in all Arizona, and this was at the time when quick-shooting gunmen were the order of the day. He remained with the company until it failed; and during those years he was the Hash Knife foreman he drove the rustlers from the northern range. When the Arizona Rangers were organized in 1901, Burton Mossman was chosen as the first captain. With a fearlessness seldom equaled in Western history, he carried the law into the desert and mesquite so thoroughly that he won the admiration and respect of all honest men; and today the name of Burton Mossman stands high among the fearless officers of old Arizona.

It was about 1900 that the Aztec Land and Cattle Company failed, and Barney Styles, of Holbrook, in partnership with Babbitt Brothers, of Flagstaff, bought the remnant of what had once been the largest cow outfit in all Arizona. The Hash Knife brand was continued with Styles as manager until the latter's death in 1909, when Charles Wyrick, of Winslow, purchased his interest. Wyrick and Babbitt Brothers still run a few cattle on the old range under this once famous brand.

James Stinson, one of the original settlers of Pleasant Valley and the man who claimed that his cattle were the real cause of the bad blood between the Grahams and Tewksburys, died at Kline, Colorado, January 8, 1932, at the age of ninety-four years. After leaving the valley, he settled near Tempe; but he was always in the vanguard of civilization, and when the Salt River Valley became too crowded for elbow room he moved to Colorado, where he spent the remainder of his life. He and his wife celebrated their golden wedding anniversary during the winter of 1930 and 1931 with their daughter, Mrs. Rachel Lamb, at Phoenix. He was one of the few remaining pioneers of the days when Victorio, Geronimo, and Natchez made life interesting for the settlers of old Arizona.

A few relics of those bloody days of the vendetta are still pointed out to the stranger in Pleasant Valley. The little boot hill graveyard on the old Graham ranch, which contains the graves of William and John Graham, Charles Blevins, Harry Middleton, and Al Rose, was donated several years ago by Miss Ola Young as a community burying ground for the settlers of Pleasant Valley. John Paine and Hampton Blevins, victims of the first fight, lie in unmarked graves somewhere near the site of the Middleton ranch house; John Tewksbury and William Jacobs are buried near the old Tewksbury cabin. Andy Cooper, Mose Roberts, and young Sam Houston Blevins, who were killed by Sheriff Owens, lie in the graveyard at Holbrook. According to Will C. Barnes,[6] the lone

grave of Billy Wilson, the wandering prospector who was lynched with Jim Stott and Jim
Scott that fateful August morning of 1888, is
the only one left to point out to the wilderness
traveler passing that way; but if Sam Brown is
correct all three victims still sleep there beneath
the whispering pines of the Mogollons.

A large stone chimney, standing like a sentinel over memories of a bloody past, marks the
site of John Tewksbury's ranch house, which
was besieged by Graham forces under Andy
Cooper on September 2, 1887. It was there
that Mrs. John Tewksbury defied the Graham
fighting men to shoot a woman while she buried
the bodies of her husband and William Jacobs
to save them from the ravenous swine. The
cabin was moved farther down the creek years
ago and is now occupied by a family named
Chapman; but the chimney was left. Some
distance in front of the site of this historic house
are the two graves where John Tewksbury and
William Jacobs still sleep the years away. A
Frank Tewksbury, one of the younger generation who did not figure in the feud, is said to be
buried somewhere near by.

John D. Tewksbury, father of the fighting
Tewksbury brothers, died a natural death at his
ranch about 1893[7], and, under a walnut tree
near by, his grave may still be seen, marked by

a post that was once part of a floor beam in a cliff dwelling. Few people knew the location of his grave until his son, Walter, the last of his family, returned after an absence of thirty-six years. The ranch is now owned by Henry Pullin, and the old log cabin that was once the home of the elder Tewksbury looks just the same today as when it was first built. There are two other graves beside that of the father; one is that of a young man from Colorado who died of ptomaine poisoning caused by eating stale oat meal found in a deserted cabin. The other is that of someone whose identity is unknown today.

S. W. Young, who took over Tom Graham's cattle on shares when the latter left the valley in 1889, was the father of Miss Ola Young, already mentioned. Miss Young afterwards homesteaded the Graham ranch and she still lives there after more than sixty years. In 1890, when a post office was established to serve the settlers of Pleasant Valley, the name was changed to Young. Located in a lean-to just six by six feet, and attached to the residence, this was known for forty years as the smallest post office in the United States. In connection with the postal service Miss Young conducted a miniature store, until recently the only one in Pleasant Valley; and possibly a greater tonnage of merchandise per square foot of floor space has passed through that little building than through any other mercantile establishment in the country. For forty years it supplied the settlers in an area as large as many an Eastern state.

In spite of the many stories to the contrary, the Graham ranch in Pleasant Valley was never attacked by Tewksbury forces. When a boy, Ed Cummings heard Mrs. Graham tell how her attention was attracted one night by a noise outside of the cabin, and when she looked up a face disappeared from the window. Leaping to her feet she blew out the candle, and the remainder of the night was spent on guard, ready to give their enemies a warm reception. They learned later that Tewksbury men had surrounded the house, believing that Graham and his wife were alone; but there was never a time when there was not a large force of fighting men at the ranch.

Mrs. Graham, the last participant in this bloody vendetta of nearly half a century ago, is still living in California. Her daughter, Mrs. Estelle C. Converse, who was an infant when Tom Graham was killed, lives on a cattle ranch near Santa Paula, California. By a strange coincidence Mrs. Converse, the only child of the fighting Grahams, visited her father's old ranch in Pleasant Valley in 1929, the same year that Walter Tewksbury, the last member of that family, returned to renew old memories in the land of the vendetta. Both visits were tinged with much sadness.

A strange case of mistaken identity was brought to my attention through a photograph of Mrs. Tom Graham, published with my article on the Pleasant Valley war in the October, 1927, issue of *Travel* Magazine. Dr. F. P. Watson, of Freeport, Texas, who lived in Winslow, Arizona, in the early 1880's, declared that this was an exact likeness of a woman named Kittie Mc-Carthy, whom he had known forty-three years before as the wife of Tom Pickett. Dr. Watson was well acquainted with both Pickett and his wife, and he informed me that the latter was the widow of Billy the Kid. Later I made careful inquiry among some old-timers in New Mexico who had known the Kid, but could find none who had ever heard of Kittie McCarthy. They all agreed that the Kid's amorettes were Mexican, without exception. This woman died just before Dr. Watson left Winslow in 1884. The photograph in question was furnished by Miss Ola Young, who is positive that it is correct; but not satisfied with this I made inquiry among people who were personally acquainted with Mrs. Tom Graham forty years and more ago, and established beyond all doubt that this is her likeness.

Part of the log cabin on Tom Graham's old

ranch, rendezvous of the fighting Grahams and their gun-slinging henchmen, and the ruins of a corral near by are preserved by Miss Young as relics of those bloody days of old Arizona.

Not far from the old Graham cabin the big stone building that was Perkins' store during the war is still standing. It is now owned by Jesse G. Ellison, a brother-in-law of Hon. George W. P. Hunt, Arizona's first governor after admission to statehood. Built before the Pleasant Valley war broke out, it was intended to be used as a fort during Indian raids, which occurred very frequently in those days, and a number of loopholes may still be traced in the heavy stone wall although they have been filled in with stone and mortar for many a year. Its massive construction made it capable of withstanding a siege of almost any duration, for nothing short of artillery could have reduced its heavy walls. The shooting of Charles Blevins and John Graham by Sheriff Mulvenon's posse was the only killing that occurred at Perkins' store, but it was a frequent rendezvous for numbers of the Graham faction. It is now conducted as a hotel, and is the only place in the valley where the chance traveler may secure shelter for the night.

The house built by Al and Ed Rose, and the cabin at the Houdon ranch, where Al Rose was killed, are other interesting relics still standing. Hon. George W. P. Hunt married Duett Ellison, daughter of an old settler in Pleasant Valley, and for several years they lived at what was Middleton's ranch in the days of the vendetta. James Tewksbury's place was located within sight of Graham's, but the building was torn down years ago; and the original cabin at the old Canyon Creek ranch, later known as Ramer's, where Mart Blevins and his sons lived, has entirely disappeared.

Major Frederick R. Burnham, one of America's best-known soldiers of fortune, who is now living in Los Angeles, California, was an adventure-seeking boy in Arizona during the early days of the feud. In Pleasant Valley when hostilities broke out in 1887, he was drawn into the conflict in spite of himself when partisan feeling became very tense, and was marked for death. But he remained neutral and through the aid of friends managed to get out of the feud district after several months and after he had had a number of narrow escapes. In his book, *Scouting on Two Continents*, he tells the story briefly so as to protect the friends who aided him in his hour of need.

After a series of thrilling adventures as a frontier peace officer in the West, Major Burnham entered the service of Cecil Rhodes in

South Africa, where he won further fame as a scout during the Matabele and Zulu wars, and for distinguished scouting service in the Boer War he was decorated by order of the king of England.

Billy Bacon afterwards related to Edwin B. Hill, now of Ysleta, Texas,[8] the story of his escape from death at the hands of the Tewksburys. With the help of a boy he had driven a herd of horses to Colorado and on their way back home he took the short cut through Pleasant Valley. This was during 1887 when the feud was raging, but Billy decided to take a chance, for he was well acquainted with John D. Tewksbury, Sr. and believed that the old man would help him out of a pinch.

One evening they rode into the Tewksbury camp and were immediately made prisoners. Suspicious of all strangers, the Tewksbury brothers decided after questioning them closely that the safest course would be to kill them as Graham partisans.

Finally Billy persuaded them to send for their father. "He knows me and he knows we're all right," he told the brothers.

It was a long wait, for the Tewksbury ranch was fifteen miles away, but at last the old man came riding in, mad clear through.

"I know this man," he told his sons. "He's

Billy Bacon. I'll vouch for him, and if Billy says the boy's all right, he's all right, too. Now we Tewksburys have enough on our hands without killing strangers. You boys remember that."

The Tewksburys built a fire and prepared to spend the night, but old John was too cautious to remain. Taking Billy and the boy he rode about half a mile away and camped without a fire.

"Billy, if the Grahams jump the boys we are far enough away," he said in explanation.

Billy Bacon spent a sleepless night, expecting to hear the crack of guns at the Tewksbury camp. But the night passed quietly, and the next morning when he was ready to leave, old John warned him: "Billy, it's bad business. Don't come this way again. We will all be killed in time, and I don't want to see my friends killed, too."

Needless to say Billy Bacon gave Pleasant Valley a wide berth after that experience.

Many neutrals left Pleasant Valley during the feud and were anxious to sell their homes very cheap. Several months after this adventure old John Tewksbury went to Bacon's ranch and told him of a good homestead in Pleasant Valley, located between the Tewksbury and Graham ranches, with excellent grazing, that could be purchased very cheap as the owner had been driven out by the vendetta. The old man advised Billy to buy.

"We won't bother you and the Grahams won't either," John Tewksbury promised.

It was a tempting prospect, but after talking it over with his wife she advised him to stay out of the valley, for she believed that the Grahams would accuse him of siding with the Tewksburys and the latter would declare that he was a Graham partisan.

When Billy told John his decision the old man said after a few minutes reflection: "She's right, Billy. I sure would like to have you there, but after all it ain't safe. Stay out of it."

It was one day in the early fall of 1929 that a tall man, whose breadth of shoulders revealed the power and strength that comes from a lifetime spent in the open, stepped from an automobile as it stopped under the branches of a spreading walnut tree in Pleasant Valley, and, pointing to a post scarred by the passing storms of many years, quietly said: "This is the place. We buried father right there just before we left the valley; and there is the grave of brother John."

Like a ghost out of the lurid past, Walter Tewksbury, the last of his family, had returned to the land of his youth, a land that held a father's and a brother's bones and many bitter memories. As he stood there in the clear October sunlight of a glorious Arizona day, gazing sadly, wistfully at the graves he had not seen for more than a third of a century, childhood memories that had lain dormant these many years were suddenly awakened: memories of a bloody past, of a cruel vendetta marked with terrible factional bitterness, ambuscades and thrilling gun fights and cold-blooded murder passed in review. He was only a boy of seven when the blood feud that had claimed the life of his half brother John in its death toll had swept the land; and memories of those terrible years when death followed chance meetings of fighting men of opposing factions had been seared on his youthful mind in letters of fire and blood.

Thirty-six years had passed since the family left the valley after the father's death; and the few old settlers remaining found it hard to recognize in this man of fifty years the boy they had known long ago. Little Walter Tewksbury, the half brother of the last of the fighting Tewksburys, was only a memory; and this man, big and powerful, with movements that spoke of quick action when necessary, reminded them of the fighting men they had known nearly half a century before. In spite of the inevitable changes of an advancing civilization, he knew every foot of the valley, and as he wandered here and there he pointed out many old landmarks. Walter Tewksbury had returned after all those years to care for the long-neglected graves of his father and other relatives on the lonely Tewksbury ranch.

The Double Butte schoolhouse near Tempe, where Tom Graham was shot from ambush, was abandoned years ago. Later it was purchased by a moving picture company and destroyed by an explosion of dynamite in filming a picture. The spot is now marked by a large hole. The old Graham ranch near by was owned until recently by Byron Carr.

To the Last Man, by Zane Grey, and *The Man Killers*, by Dane Coolidge, are two interesting novels based on the Pleasant Valley war. While neither story follows the feud in detail, both authors have woven some of the important events into exciting romances of the old Arizona cow country.

Time makes many changes, even in Pleasant Valley, once buried in the heart of the most remote and inaccessible section of Arizona. The land where Tom Graham's cattle once roamed and where the Tewksburys and Grahams fought to the death is now crossed by barbed wire fences, and settlers' homes may be seen on every side. The cattle have been pushed back into the hills, but a few head are still found here and there.

The automobile has brought the West of "way back beyond" nearer to the outside, and this little-known corner of the last frontier is now only a matter of hours from the largest towns where it was formerly a hard trip of days. Several years ago Gila County built a modern highway from Globe to this isolated section of Arizona's old cattleland. This road is now in course of construction across the Mogollons to Holbrook, while a new highway is being planned from Payson to the old Graham ranch at Young. The mail that was carried by stagecoach and on horseback between Globe and Young for thirty-five years, is now transported in a Ford; and a filling station, that ever-present vanguard of modern civilization, is one of the latest additions to this last frontier stronghold.

The spirit of days long dead when Pleasant Valley was the heart of the old Arizona cow country is revived each year in a rodeo held at the historic Graham ranch, for every Western community must have its rodeo. It is part of the atmosphere, a memory of days that will never come again. Three days and three nights are devoted to old-time frontier sports and dancing.

A larger store building has replaced the miniature post office where Miss Ola Young handed out mail to the settlers of the valley for forty years; and after serving its time and generation, the little frame shack, like other things of the olden days, has gone down the road to oblivion. With it the charm and quaintness of yesteryear is slowly but surely passing from the valley. A large orchard project is under way, and within a few more years Arizona's dark and bloody ground, christened with the lifeblood of its first settlers who dared the wrath of their Apache neighbors, and where the Graham and Tewksbury fighting men fought and died long years ago, will have completely passed into the land of memories.

One day in the summer of 1946 Mrs. Estelle C. Converse, Tom Graham's daughter, in company with her mother, again visited the old Graham ranch in Pleasant Valley. This woman, in her middle seventies, was the same Anne Graham who, fifty-four years before, during the preliminary hearing before Justice of the Peace Huson, had suddenly pressed her husband's six-shooter against John Rhodes's back and pulled the trigger. Contrary to statements of old-timers who remember the war, she told Miss Young that this was her first visit to Pleasant Valley. After her marriage to Tom Graham, her father refused to allow her to go to the valley on account of the danger, for the feud was still going on in all its fury.

On a day in mid-September, 1947, another visitor came to the Graham ranch. He was Samuel Graham, a brother of young Billy Graham and a half brother of Tom and John Graham. He had taken no part in the war, for he was not in Arizona at that time. For many years he has lived at Greeley, Colorado.

CHAPTER XXIII

THE VENDETTA'S TOLL

REPORTS OF THE number of men killed in the Graham-Tewksbury feud vary from seventeen to fifty, according to the source of information. The latter figure is greatly exaggerated and the former is a little below the actual number. The exact number of men who lost their lives in this sanguinary vendetta of the old Arizona cow country will never be definitely known. Strangers who went into the valley, adventurers lured by tales of the fighting, disappeared, and their fate was never known; but one thing is certain: they found the trouble they were looking for—some in unknown and forgotten graves in a lonely wilderness.

A total of seventeen men are known positively to have died a violent death during the years of the feud, while seven unknowns are reported to have been killed and three others were lynched. It is doubtful if the murder of Horace Philly had any connection with the vendetta, but as this is unsolved his name has been added to the list, making a total of twenty-eight.

An analysis of the manner in which the victims died is rather interesting. Of the four Tewksbury partisans, one was the Navajo sheepherder, while two others were John

Tewksbury and William Jacobs. These three were the only members of the Tewksbury forces known to have been killed in the vendetta. The actual manner in which George A. Newton, the fourth of this clan, met his death remains a mystery.

It is rather significant that in the toll of twelve Graham men only seven are known to have been killed in battle with Tewksbury forces or by assassination, while five were shot by officers of the law. If the stories of the shooting of the unknown cowboy by Jim Tewksbury and the assassination of Elliott are true, the total of Graham casualties is fourteen. The killing of six unknowns reported by Charles Perkins, the lynching of Stott, Scott, and Wilson, and the murder of Horace Philly with the four deaths on the Tewksbury side make a total of twenty-eight during the years of the vendetta. The three Graham brothers were killed to the last man, while only one Tewksbury and one of the Blevins boys survived.

The following list of men known to have been killed, or who died of natural causes during the Pleasant Valley war, is compiled from records in my possession:

MEMBERS OF THE TEWKSBURY FACTION

February, 1887. A Navajo Indian sheep-herder for Daggs Brothers was shot from ambush. The identity of the killer has never been established. He was the first victim.

September 2, 1887. John Tewksbury and William Jacobs were killed by Graham men in a field about a mile from the Tewksbury ranch house. The cattlemen then besieged the cabin, refusing to grant a burial truce when the swine started to devour the bodies. Driven by desperation, Mrs. John Tewksbury defied the enemy while she buried her husband and his comrade. The Graham forces then continued the siege until Justice of the Peace John Meadows arrived. According to his own statement made two days later in Holbrook, Andy Cooper himself killed both men.

December 4, 1888. James Tewksbury, one of the three brothers engaged in the vendetta, died at Prescott of quick consumption following an attack of measles. For years stories have been told that he was killed in the war.

September, 1891. George A. Newton, one of the owners of Newton and Vosberg's Flying V cattle ranch on Cherry Creek, disappeared while on his way from Globe to his ranch in Pleasant Valley. It was reported that he was shot from his horse while crossing Salt River at the Pinal Creek ford; but this was never verified. His body was never recovered, and the mystery of his death remains unsolved. He was the only cattleman known to have joined the Tewksburys.

MEMBERS OF THE GRAHAM FACTION

July, 1887. Mart (Old Man) Blevins, father of Andy Cooper and the four Blevins brothers, rode away from his ranch on Canyon Creek one morning late in July, and was never seen again. His fate remains a mystery to this day. Sam Brown claims that he was killed by Navajo Indians who trailed stolen horses to his ranch; but others acquainted with the facts inform me that this is not correct. Human bones found in later years are believed to have been his.

August 10, 1887. John Paine and Hampton Blevins were killed in the first pitched battle of the war when a party of eight cowboys, apparently searching for Mart Blevins, were attacked by a Tewksbury force at the Middleton ranch. Paine and Blevins were buried near the ranch house by Charles E. Perkins, storekeeper in Pleasant Valley, and John Meadows, justice of the peace at Payson. The exact location of their graves is unknown.

August, 1887. An unknown cowboy is reported to have been shot in the thigh one night by

Jim Tewksbury, while the latter was creeping back from a spring with canteens filled with water. The wounded man bled to death. While this story cannot be verified from an authentic source, it has been told so many years that it has become one of the legends of old Arizona, and is believed to be true. According to this old story, Tewksbury fired backwards over his shoulder, a method of shooting in which he was an expert. This incident is supposed to have occurred when the Tewksburys were besieged in a mountain stronghold after the killing of Paine and Blevins.

August 17, 1887. William Graham, aged twenty-two, the youngest of the fighting Grahams was shot and mortally wounded by James D. Houck, a deputy sheriff and a Tewksbury partisan, while riding along the Payson trail about three and a half miles from Graham's ranch. Billy Graham managed to reach home and died there the next day. His was the first grave in the little boot hill cemetery on the Graham ranch, which later held five victims of the vendetta.

September 4, 1887. Andy Cooper, whose real name was Andy Blevins, aged twenty-five, was killed by Commodore Owens, sheriff of Apache County, at the Blevins home in Holbrook, while resisting arrest. He was a son of Mart Blevins and was known as a rustler and a dangerous gunman. Buried in Holbrook.

September 4, 1887. Mose Roberts, a brother-in-law of the Blevins boys, was killed by Sheriff Owens at the Blevins home. He was known as a member of Cooper's gang of rustlers. Buried in Holbrook.

September 4, 1887. Sam Houston Blevins, aged sixteen, son of Mart Blevins, was killed by Sheriff Owens at the Blevins home. Buried in Holbrook. This was the most noted gun fight in all Arizona's frontier history. Although exposed to the fire of the men in the house, Sheriff Owens killed three and wounded John Blevins.

September 17, 1887. Harry Middleton, a wandering cowboy fighting for the Grahams, was mortally wounded in a battle with the Tewksburys on Cherry Creek, and died at the Graham ranch two days later. Little is known of Middleton. He was just a foot-loose cowboy, believed to have come from Texas, and was not related to the Middletons who settled in the valley at an early date. His was the second grave in the boot hill cemetery on the Graham ranch. Joseph Underwood, sometimes called Ellingwood, was wounded at the same time. The story is told that these casualties occurred during a raid by Graham forces on the Tewksbury camp in the early morning. Jim Tewksbury and Jim Roberts are reported to have done most of the shooting on the Tewksbury side.

September 21, 1887. John Graham and Charles Blevins, the latter a son of Mart Blevins and a brother of Andy Cooper, were shot to death by Sheriff William Mulvenon's posse in an ambush at Perkins' store within sight of the Graham ranch. Blevins was killed instantly, but Graham did not die until later in the day. Both were buried in the boot hill cemetery on the Graham ranch. Charles Blevins was the fourth of the Blevins brothers killed during the vendetta.

November, 1887. Al Rose, prominent Graham fighter, was shot from ambush while hunting horses in the early morning near the Houdon ranch on Spring Creek. Edwin Tewksbury afterward told that Glenn Reynolds, of Globe, fired the shot. Rose was the fifth victim of Tewksbury vengeance buried in the boot hill graveyard on the Graham ranch.

August 2, 1892. Thomas H. Graham, the last of the three brothers, was shot from ambush by two men near the Double Butte schoolhouse while hauling grain from his ranch in the Salt River Valley to Tempe. He was buried in Phoenix. Before he died that same day Graham accused Edwin Tewksbury and John Rhodes with his murder, and both were arrested. Rhodes was released at a preliminary hearing before Justice of the Peace W. O. Huson; but Edwin Tewksbury's two trials dragged through several years. A change of venue took the case to Tucson, where he was convicted of murder in the first degree, but on a technical error the verdict was set aside and a new trial granted. At this second trial the jury disagreed, and he was later released on bail. This killing marked the end of the vendetta, for no more Grahams were left to carry on.

1892. Horace Philly was shot in Reno Pass shortly after the murder of Tom Graham. It was reported at the time that he was killed by the Apache Kid, a notorious Apache renegade from San Carlos; but from the fact that he had worked for Tom Graham during the war some expressed the opinion that he might have been another victim of the vendetta.

OTHERS REPORTED KILLED

Late in 1887 or sometime in 1888 a man named Elliot was shot to death while riding a lonely trail in Pleasant Valley, and was buried by Charles Perkins and two other men. His connection with the vendetta is not known.

Six unknown men were reported killed along lonely trails during the bushwhacking late in

1887 and 1888, according to the statement of Charles Perkins. This is undoubtedly correct.

August 4, 1888. James Scott, James Stott, and Billy Wilson were summarily lynched by a self-appointed vigilance committee, reported to have been led by James D. Houck, a Tewksbury partisan. This occurred at the Stott ranch near Bear Spring in Phoenix Park, Mogollon Mountains sixty miles south of Holbrook. While this lynching was the result of a private grudge and had no connection with the vendetta, it was one of those acts of lawlessness that grew out of the war. None of the victims took any part in the feud, but Houck afterwards declared that they had wounded Jacob Lauffer, a Tewksbury partisan.

THE WOUNDED

1886 (exact date not known). John Gilliland, range foreman for James Stinson, was shot in the leg by Edwin Tewksbury during an argument over rustling in which Gilliland is said to have accused the Tewksburys of knowing something of Stinson's missing stock.

August 9, 1887. Tom Tucker was desperately wounded through the right lung in the fight at the Middleton ranch, while Robert Glasspie was shot in the hip, and Robert Carrington received a flesh wound. All three recovered. They were members of the party of cowboys searching for Mart Blevins.

September 4, 1887. John Blevins was wounded by Sheriff Owens at the Blevins home in Holbrook. This was the same fight in which Andy Cooper, Mose Roberts, and young Sam Houston Blevins were killed. John Blevins was fatally injured many years later in an automobile accident near Phoenix.

September 17, 1887. Joseph Underwood (or Ellingwood) was wounded in the same fight in which Harry Middleton was killed during the raid on the Tewksbury camp on Cherry Creek. He subsequently recovered, but took no further part in the war.

August 4, 1888. Jacob Lauffer, a Tewksbury partisan, was fired upon from ambush at his ranch in Pleasant Valley, and one arm was broken. Shots were fired at two other men named Cody and Coleman while they were on their way to Lauffer's ranch that same day, and Cody's horse was wounded. The men were not injured.

NOTES

CHAPTER I   [1]Even Walter Tewksbury, the
                             last of that family, claims that
the Grahams had a record in Texas. However, Walter Tewksbury was a half brother of John, James, and Edwin, and
was only seven years of age when the war broke out. That
some of the men who were intimately acquainted with the
Grahams in Arizona knew little of their past history is shown by
the fact that as late as 1930 James Stinson, during a visit to
Phoenix, declared that they were Canadians; and both Tom and
John Graham had worked for Stinson in the early days of
Pleasant Valley. In those times the men of Arizona told
nothing of their past, and it was not good frontier etiquette
to ask a man where he was from. His past life was his own
affair.

[2]Children of Samuel Graham by his second wife. At their
request their names were withheld

[3]All this is well established by letters written by Tom Graham
to his relatives in Iowa. These are still in the possession of his
family. That both John and Tom Graham were in California in
1882 is shown by two photographs submitted to the author. That
of John Graham was taken by Reiman, 26 Montgomery Street,
opposite Lick House, San Francisco, and on May 24, 1882 (shown
by date and name written on back), he sent it to his old home.
Tom Graham's photograph was taken by Worthington & Company, Red Bluff, California, in 1882. The first letter received
from the brothers after they went to Arizona was sent from Globe
in 1882.

[4]Will C. Barnes says that she undoubtedly belonged to either
the Digger or Pitt River Indians. See *Arizona Historical Review*,
October, 1931, p. 13.

[5]Although there are no records of such a marriage, I am
convinced that John D. Tewksbury, Sr., married this Indian
woman, and remained true to her until her death.

[6]Charles Perkins, who kept a store in Pleasant Valley
during the war, knew the Tewksburys well. He claims that
John and James were full brothers, while Edwin was only a
half brother. He describes the latter as of a different tempera-
ment, character, and habits, and as more of a man in every

way. See Will C. Barnes in *The Arizona Historical Review*, October, 1931, p. 14. This may be true, in which event John and James were sons of the Indian wife, and Edwin was the son of a second wife who evidently died before John D. Tewksbury, Sr., arrived in Arizona. However, Edwin Tewksbury's general appearance and character gave rise to the opinion that he had Indian blood in his veins.

[7]Some claim that he married Lydia Shultes before he went to Globe, and this may be correct. Neither Walter nor Parker Tewksbury were born in Pleasant Valley, and in the summer of 1887 Walter was seven years of age. If the father married this woman at Globe, he must have arrived there about 1879 or 1880.

[8]She also bore him a daughter, but her name is not known today, and none of the old residents can say what became of her. A daughter by the Indian wife was living in Globe in 1888 as shown by the old newspaper report that her brother James Tewksbury died at her home there. I am informed that she died in the Salt River Valley.

[9]Joseph Fish, in an old manuscript now in possession of the Arizona State Historian at Phoenix, states that James Stinson received cattle to the value of eleven thousand dollars in payment for his Snowflake ranch. Fifty years later Stinson said that he received twelve hundred cows in payment.

[10]The remains of this cabin are still standing on the old Graham Ranch, now owned by Miss Ola Young. Neither of the brothers filed a homestead entry on this claim. In those days and even for many years later, cattlemen simply built a cabin and claimed by the right of occupation. Miss Young later filed a homestead entry on the Graham ranch after her father, S. W. Young, took over Tom Graham's cattle on the shares when the last of the Grahams left the valley in 1889.

[11]In the summer of 1887 George F. Wilson was a boy in his teens. He took no part in the vendetta, but is generally believed to have been present during the fight at his ranch on August 10, 1887. He was still living in Globe in 1936.

[12]Some old-timers, among them Will C. Barnes, claim that Andy Cooper was a stepson of Mart Blevins. Since the first edition appeared a descendant of John Blevins has informed me that Andy Blevins, alias Andy Cooper, was a son of Mart and Mary Blevins and a full brother of John, Charles, Hampton,

and Sam Houston Blevins. Another authority, E. D. Tussey, states that Andy Blevins did not commit a murder in Texas, but that he left the Lone-Star State because he was wanted for horse stealing. Years later, Mrs. John Blevins said that she never knew a man more gentle around children or pets, and that he had a very pleasing personality.

[13]See Chapter XXII.

[14]See account of Tom Pickett in Chapter XXII and Note 4 of that chapter.

[15]After several years of fruitless work in that wilderness of central Arizona the inroads of rustlers upon his herd had become so great that James Stinson sold his cattle for twenty-five dollars a head. He then moved to Mesa in the Salt River Valley before hostilities broke out in the summer of 1887 and was not involved in any way, though some claim that he took a prominent part on the side of the cattlemen. This probably grew out of the fact that his Cherry Creek ranch was in the very heart of the feud country.

[16]Stinson was badly mistaken in regard to the nationality of the Grahams. As already stated they were natives of Iowa. Stinson may also have been mistaken in some other details.

[17]This charge that the Grahams and Tewksburys were engaged in rustling Stinson's cattle is made by Joseph Fish in his manuscript.

[18]William Graham was always referred to as the full brother of Tom and John, and it is not generally known in Arizona even today that he was only a half brother. It is also generally reported that he did not arrive in Pleasant Valley until 1886 or 1887. However, John Graham wrote to his father from Globe telling of the safe arrival of the two youths. This, according to information furnished the author by relatives, was about 1884 but it must have been before that, for the old court records of 1882 and 1883 at Saint Johns contain his name.

[19]Since I secured this record in September, 1924, from Mr. Levi S. Udell, the old court minutes have disappeared. When Mr. Dodd L. Greer, later county attorney of Apache County, in June, 1931, tried to locate this old record it could not be found. Someone had evidently "borrowed" it in the meantime, and the only record of the cases against either the Grahams

or Tewksburys in Apache County is found in the minutes of the Clerk of Courts. However, this does not show the charge.

20Joseph Fish, in his manuscript already referred to, gives the name of George as one of the Graham brothers. He mentions Tom, William, John, and George.

21From the territorial court records, June Term, A. D. 1884, furnished the author by the late Judge C. P. Hicks, of Prescott, and also by Mr. F. C. Bauer, deputy recorder of Prescott.

22In a letter dated July 15, 1931, received by the author from George W. Tewksbury, the youngest son of Edwin Tewksbury, it is intimated that cattle and sheep were not the real cause of the trouble. I was never able to learn just what Mr. Tewksbury meant by his statement. His letter was written at Globe, but when I wrote him again, he had evidently left there, for my letter was returned "unclaimed."

23This information on George Graham is contained in letters received by me and now in my possession from Messrs. Ruiz, Brown, and Evon Z. Vogt, of Gallup, New Mexico. The latter interviewed Messrs. Closson and Murray for me.

24There is a possibility that this George Graham was a a member of a Graham family that lived in Texas. This family consisted of several brothers, who ran afoul of numerous sheriffs and the Texas rangers, and one or two of them left the state. Then again this George Graham may have been a name assumed by some Texan wanted at home, and this may be the reason that Walter Tewksbury and some others in Arizona today believe that the Graham brothers of Pleasant Valley were from Texas.

25See the Joseph Fish manuscript in *The Arizona Historical Review*, October, 1931, p. 10.

26The old brand records in the courthouse at Phoenix show the following entries:

Thomas and John Graham: JT on the left hip, date Mar. 25, 1884, location Pleasant Valley, Ariz. The ear mark is smooth Crop off the left ear and a crop and half under bit on the right ear. Brand is made thus: JT

Thomas H. Graham: Brand made thus: ⁻E.

Mar. 25, 1884, location Pleasant Valley, Ariz., the earmark is Smooth Crop off left ear and a crop & slit
in right ear.

So much for the brand records and their bearing on the
cause of trouble. However, this does not prove the rustling
charge against either the Grahams or Tewksburys.

[27]See Note 22, p. 324.

CHAPTER II

[1]John C. Gilliland died at his home in Phoenix, January 2,
1937. Fish says that the foreman went to the Graham ranch,
accompanied by a boy, and was shot there; but this is a mistake, for Edwin Tewksbury himself told the story afterwards,
and regarded it as a very amusing incident. He stated that he
did not want to hurt Gilliland, which was probably his reason
for running, for Ed Tewksbury was never lacking in courage.
See Will C. Barnes in *The Arizona Historical Review*, January,
1932, p. 36. This affair disproves to some extent the story that
the Tewksburys and Grahams had been engaged in rustling
Stinson's cattle in partnership, and that the recording of the
alleged partnership brand by Tom Graham in 1884 was the real
cause of the bad feeling between them.

After the first edition appeared, E. D. Tussey, a teacher of
history at the Phoenix High School, informed me that he had
read Gilliland's own account of this fight, which was taken down
by the latter's nephew as the old man dictated it long afterward.
According to this version, Gilliland had caught the Grahams and
Tewksburys rustling Stinson's cattle, and he claimed that they
knew that he "knew too much." 'Lisha, John Gilliland's cousin
from Texas, was visiting him and wanted to hunt turkeys. They
went to the Tewksbury ranch house to ask for permission.
There they found Ed and Jim Tewksbury and John Graham. A
fight took place and both Gilliland and 'Lisha were wounded;
but he did not say what started the trouble. However, Gilliland
declared that he was later tried at Prescott on a charge of assault
with intent to kill and was acquitted. This may be partly correct; but in those days in Arizona, and for many years afterward, when a man wanted to hunt turkeys or any other game he
did not ask permission of anyone; and there was plenty of good
turkey hunting all through the Mogollons. The Tewksbury
ranch, or land owned by them, was hardly large enough for much

game, as that was in the days of the open range. In all probability they went to the house looking for Stinson's cattle or horses, as already related.

[2]There were several brothers in this firm, which started in the sheep business at Flagstaff in 1879, and they were very successful until they became involved in the vendetta. Although taking no active part in hostilities, they had more to do with the Pleasant Valley war than any other individuals, for it was undoutedly their money that financed the Tewksburys. In a letter written from Claremont, California, to the Arizona Pioneers' Historical Society of Tucson, dated May 29, 1926, P. P. Daggs declared that the Pleasant Valley war had cost him ninety thousand dollars. His statement in this letter that the enemy "are still sleeping with their boots on" shows the feeling that still existed after the passing of forty years—a feeling justified in view of that loss of ninety thousand dollars. Mr. Daggs has since joined his enemies on the last trail.

[3]Founded by John W. Young, a son of Brigham Young and one of the Mormon pioneers of northern Arizona, the Arizona Cattle Company in its day was one of the largest cow outfits in all Arizona. Young purchased thousands of head of cattle from all sections of the Southwest and turned them loose on the range in the vicinity of Flagstaff. The home ranch was located at Fort Rickerson in the Fort Valley at the foot of the San Francisco Mountains, nine miles north of Flagstaff.

The history of this famous outfit is interesting. In 1880 John W. Young and Ammon W. Tenney were granted grading contracts for the Atlantic and Pacific Railroad (now the Santa Fe) through western New Mexico and for one hundred miles in eastern Arizona, and also to furnish fifty thousand ties. Young established a tie camp in what was later Fort Valley. Navajo and Apache Indians were constantly harassing the construction gangs, and when reports reached Young that a big raid was planned on the headquarters camp in the Fort Valley he built a fort of double length ties set on end in a trench on three sides of a square. On the fourth side was a one-story log building about seventy-five feet long, with a powder magazine at one end. Young named this place Fort Moroni in honor of the Mormon angel.

The railroad reached Flagstaff the next year. This marked the real beginning of the cattle business in northern Arizona, and as soon as his grading contracts with the railroad were completed Young embarked in the cattle business on a large scale and with other Mormons he organized the Mormon Cattle Company. In 1883 he became associated with some eastern capitalists, and the Arizona Cattle Company was formed, with the brand A One Bar (A 1). This was Arizona's first big cow outfit. As danger from Indian raids was no longer a menace, the stockade was cut down to fence height, several new building were erected, and the name was changed to Fort Rickerson in honor of Charles L. Rickerson, of New York City, the first treasurer of the company, and its last president. But the ranch was known among the cowboys as "The Fort" until it disappeared before the homesteaders thirty-seven years later.

The other officers of the new company were: John C. de la Vergne, president; Henry R. Von der Horst, vice president; Ellis Wainwright, managing director, and H. W. Guernsey, secretary. Wainwright, who resided in St. Louis, held his position from the beginning until the end sixteen years later. Charles Goren was the first general manager, with headquarters at Fort Rickerson, but he only remained until the fall of 1885 when he was succeeded by Captain B. B. Bullwinkle, of Chicago, a picturesque character in the history of the Arizona cattle business.

The company purchased from the Atlantic and Pacific Railroad one hundred and thirty-two thousand acres of the finest timber and grazing land in northern Arizona, but its cattle ranged over an area of eight hundred seventy-five square miles, from Clarks Fork to the Grand Canyon and from the Little Colorado River to Ash Fork. Over a million dollars were invested in land, cattle, and horses, and for years it had more than fourteen thousand head of cattle on the range.

The fame of Fort Rickerson as a cattle ranch spread far and wide. The Fort Valley where the ranch was located became noted as a roundup ground, and probably more cattle have been bunched there than at any other spot in all Arizona. From the days of John W. Young in the early 1880's down into the years of the present century, long after the A One had passed out of existence and when the C O Bar was the largest outfit in northern Arizona, this was the roundup ground; but like almost everything else of the old West, it has vanished before the homesteader, and when I last visited the place it was so crossed by fences and covered with fields of grain that I could scarcely recognize it as the old roundup ground of former years.

Young severed his connection with the company about 1885,

and hurriedly left the territory forever because of a warrant charging polygamy.

Few of those old-time cattlemen of northern Arizona are better remembered today than Captain B. B. Bullwinkle, who became field manager of the Arizona Cattle Company in the early fall of 1885. A lover of fast horses, he imported some of the best stock to be found in Kentucky, and erected a large barn with a dozen box stalls. When I last saw the valley in 1926, this building was all that was left of what was once the most famous cattle ranch in the old Southwest.

Those thoroughbreds had no match for speed in all Arizona, and each time the captain rode to Flagstaff he tried to break his previous record.

In 1888 Captain Bullwinkle met a tragic death. While on his way to keep an appointment with the Hash Knife foreman in Flagstaff, his horse stumbled and fell just outside of the town. Its rider was thrown violently, and his neck was broken.

Frank Livermore, a practical stockman of the old school, became field manager after Bullwinkle's death, and he remained in charge until the company went out of business in 1899.

William Thomas, a Texas cowman with a past, who was still living at Globe in 1926, was the first range foreman; but in the early 1890's he was succeeded by Jack Diamond, who remained as the A One range boss until the company failed.

In addition to Fort Rickerson and Cedar Ranch the company established winter camps at Squaw Tank and Tappan Spring, the latter place once having been headquarters for a notorious band of rustlers.

The company prospered for some ten years under Livermore's management; but the end was inevitable. With the advent of more cattlemen and sheep the range became overstocked. In 1899 the A One management closed out its holdings, and during that summer the last big roundup took place under the direction of Jack Diamond. Ten thousand head of cattle were gathered and shipped from Flagstaff to eastern markets.

In November, 1899, the company sold its timber and grazing land to William F. Baker, of Manistee, Michigan, as trustee for the Manistee Lumber Company, for $140,000. This concern was later consolidated with the Saginaw Lumber Company, which cut the best part of the timber, and during the next few years, Flagstaff enjoyed a boom as a lumber camp as well as a cow town.

In the early 1880's when Fort Rickerson was still Fort Moroni, Lot Smith, a Mormon pioneer who had settled at Tuba

City on the Painted Desert, established his famous Circle S ranch at Mormon Dairy, twenty-five miles south of Flagstaff. He was also a lover of fine horses, and crossed Kentucky stallions with range mares. As a result the horses with the Circle S strain were noted for speed and endurance for many a year. Old-time cowboys still talk of the days when Smith rode from Tuba City to Fort Moroni, and then to Mormon Dairy on the same horse the next morning, a total distance of one hundred and thirty miles.

Lot Smith's reputation as a killer is second to none in all Arizona, even to this day; and yet when the matter is sifted down, it is impossible to find the name of one man he is supposed to have slain. For years this reputation was the talk of the range; but as a matter of history he never killed; in fact, his record shows that he had a respect for human life. Perhaps a little ruthless in gaining his ends, this pioneer lived in a hard, lawless land at a time when each man was compelled to make his own laws. He finally had trouble with the Navajos when he cut their sheep off from water at the Tuba City springs, and on June 20, 1892, when he started to kill Indian sheep in his alfalfa field, he was shot to death from ambush.

In 1886 four brothers from Cincinnati named William, Charles, David, and George Babbitt opened a mercantile establishment at Flagstaff and embarked in the cattle business under the C O Bar (C O) brand. During more than forty years following, William Babbitt was the range manager. In 1899 Babbitt brothers purchased Fort Rickerson and Cedar Ranch from the Arizona Cattle Company and removed their home ranch from Clark Valley to the fort; but it was abandoned in 1904 after a summer ranch was established at the old Buckler place, far up on the western slope of the San Francisco Mountains. Babbitts gradually absorbed many other outfits, both large and small, until they became the largest cattlemen in northern Arizona, if not the entire territory.

After the abandonment of Fort Rickerson it was only used as an occasional roundup camp until the historic building was completely razed in 1920 by the C O Bar foreman, without orders from the owners and much to their disapproval.

[4]The exact date is not known, but from the fact that the Indian herder was killed early in February, 1887, it must have been in the late fall of 1886.

[5]The approximate date of the Indian's death is established by an item found in the old *Silver Belt* of February 12, 1887,

a weekly newspaper then published in Globe. The item states that the killing occurred about ten days before. It also gives the information that the herder was a Ute Indian; but old-timers agree that he was a Navajo. This is probably correct, for that section of Arizona was far removed from the Ute country. Some also claim that this herder was a Mexican, but this is evidently a mistake. *The Silver Belt* gives the additional information that the killer was trailed to a house in the vicinity, but it does not state the name of the place. The trailers, fearing an ambush, did not approach the cabin. The name of the man who killed the Indian, who was the first to die in this feud, was never known.

Hoofs and Horns, a stock paper published by Buckey O'Neill at Prescott, under date of February 10, 1887, also relates the story of the killing, and adds that the herder's head had been severed from the body. The Joseph Fish manuscript states that at one time James Stinson offered a reward of $500 for the head of any man who brought sheep into the valley. Will C. Barnes (see *The Arizona Historical Review*, October, 1931, p. 32) says that this may account for the story in *Hoofs and Horns*, but he was unable to verify Fish's statement from any other source. Personally, I never heard this; and Stinson indignantly denied it.

⁶This tree was about five miles west of Rock House in Rock House Canyon. Mr. Ketcherside, who was still living in Phoenix in 1931, believed that the skull was that of Mart Blevins. See Barnes in *The Arizona Historical Review*, Oct-ber, 1931, p. 34.

CHAPTER III

¹Joseph Fish gives the name of Thomas Covington, alias Edward Clark, as one of the party. Nothing more is known of him.

²See Barnes in *The Arizona Historical Review*, January, 1932, p. 25.

³Located about two miles southeast of Taylor, and about four miles from Snowflake, Navajo County, Arizona. On a bluff near by, which overlooks Pinedale Creek, a tributary of the Little Colorado River, is the famous Four Mile ruin, the largest and most important of the prehistoric ruins in that section. This was excavated for the first time in 1897 by Dr. Jesse Walter Fewkes, of the Bureau of American Ethnology.

⁴Statement to the author by W. H. Roberts, of Clarkdale, Arizona, a son of James F. Roberts.

⁵Years later James F. Roberts, who was in the cabin that day, told his son W. H. Roberts that John Paine acted as spokesman for the cowboys, while the others tried to find out how many men were in the ranch house. Roberts told his son that twelve men were in the party, six remaining on a hill above, while the others rode to the cabin with Paine in the lead. According to this version, Paine threw a rock at the door instead of calling. The Tewksbury force, composed of the Tewksbury brothers, James Roberts, Joseph Boyer, William Jacobs, and a man named Tucker, had stopped at the ranch to get something to eat. Roberts must have been mistaken in this name of Tucker, for the only man of that name known to have taken part in the vendetta was Tom Tucker, who was with the cowboys. Roberts stated that when Jim Tewksbury opened the door a little, he told Paine, in answer to the cowboy's inquiry for a meal, that they were not running a boardinghouse. Paine then asked for George Newton, and Jim told him that he was branding calves at Red Tanks, a short distance away.

⁶Statement of James F. Roberts made years later.

⁷I have also heard another version to the effect that Tucker, after a desperate ride of a day and a half reached Al Rose's cabin, nine miles from the Middleton ranch and within sight of the Graham place. Reports of some details are so conflicting that this may be correct.

⁸Joe T. McKinney, who is still living in Arizona, served as undersheriff of Apache County in 1887 while Commodore Owens was sheriff. James D. Houck, an open Tewksbury partisan and the man who killed William Graham, was also an undersheriff at this same time. McKinney's duties took him into Pleasant Valley several times during the summer of 1887. He seems to have been friendly with members of the Tewksbury faction, and his statements may be a little prejudiced in their behalf. See *Reminiscences*, by Joe T. McKinney, in *The Arizona Historical Review* for April, July, and October, 1932. According to Edwin Tewksbury's statement to McKinney, there were seven in the Middleton cabin that day.

There is considerable reason for doubting this version of Tucker's escape, although it may contain some elements of truth. I never heard from any other source that his horse fell, and if it had fallen on the gun as claimed, it would have been almost impossible for Tucker, with a bullet through his lungs, to have turned the animal over. Then it is very doubtful if any sane man would have stopped to secure his rifle under such circumstances when bullets from seven Winchesters were kicking up dust all around him. It must also be remembered that some of the best rifle shots in Arizona were behind those Winchesters; and they were men who would not miss such a good target, especially Jim Tewksbury. McKinney is now dead.

9James F. Roberts, the "last man" of the Pleasant Valley war, died at Clarkdale, Arizona, January 8, 1934. (See Chapter XXI). His son W. H. Roberts informed me that his father told him that he and Joseph Boyer took part in the fight at the Middleton cabin. See Notes 4 and 5 of Chapter III. On December 3, 1887, the grand jury at Prescott indicted Edwin and James Tewksbury, Joseph Boyer, James Roberts, George Newton, Jacob Lauffer, and George Wagner for the murder of Hampton Blevins. This does not indicate that all these men were present, for it is a well-established fact that George Newton was not there; but the others may have been.

10I have never been able to learn the real reason that induced George A. Newton, a cattleman, to join the Tewksburys in the vendetta. See account of George Newton in Chapter XVI and accompanying notes.

11William Middleton, one of the first settlers in Pleasant Valley, located on what is now known as Wilson Creek, named for a later settler of the place. The spot where his cabin stood is a short distance below the old Ellison ranch. After the fight with Apaches in 1881, Middleton sold his cattle to J. J. Vosberg and George A. Newton, owners of the Flying V brand.

12Old newspaper accounts give two spellings of Robert M. Glasspie's name, using Gillespie more than Glasspie. Robert M. Glasspie died June 29, 1946, at his home at Coolidge, Arizona, aged eighty-five years. James Peterson, of Mesa, Arizona, who was reared on a ranch in the Mogollons and who knew many of the incidents of the war, informed me under date of April 5, 1948, that Tom Tucker and Bob Glasspie recuperated at the "Red" Holcom ranch instead of at the cabin of Robert Sigsby. I am not prepared to say which report is correct, but at this late date it makes little difference.

CHAPTER IV

[1] See James Roberts' statement in Chapter III regarding the appearance of a band of Apache Indians.

[2] This tends to contradict Charles Perkins' story that he and John Meadows buried the bodies. McKinney recalls that a man named McFadden, William Voris, and Richard Williams were in this burial party. A few miles farther on, McKinney was overtaken by Louis Parker and a man named Bonner, who were watching for Tewksbury men.

[3] John W. Francis, who has been dead for a number of years, afterwards became one of the largest sheep owners in northern Arizona. John W. Weatherford was always a progressive citizen. At the beginning of the century he erected the present Weatherford Hotel in Flagstaff, and was its proprietor for more than thirty years. In more recent times he built the present theater in Flagstaff, and in 1926 the automobile highway up the San Francisco peaks, the highest in the Southwest, was completed through his efforts and money. I have known him for many years, and when I last heard from him in January, 1933, he was living in Phoenix, where he had been very ill for several months.

Barnes states that Mulvenon's posse consisted of only five men. Heretofore the names of Mulvenon, Francis, Odell, and Weatherford have been given, and Weatherford informed me that the fifth member was Fletcher Fairchild; but the Sheriff undoubtedly had deputies with him from Prescott. In his letter to me Weatherford gives the name of only four men from Flagstaff (Francis, Odell, Fairchild, and Weatherford) who met Mulvenon's outfit at Payson. All of the members of this posse on the first invasion of Pleasant Valley have been dead for many years with the exception of John W. Weatherford. He told me that they remained in the valley about ten days.

[4] I am not certain whether Cooper and his men remained with the posse that night or not, but I doubt it.

[5] I am informed by residents of Pleasant Valley and others acquainted with the facts, who knew the country in the days of the feud, that this battle took place at the old Middleton ranch, not at Newton's.

[6] From information secured from court records furnished by Mr. F. C. Bauer, of Prescott, Arizona.

[7]From information secured from court records furnished by the late Judge C. P. Hicks, of Prescott. Before this date, December 3, 1887, John Tewksbury and William Jacobs had been killed in the attack on the Tewksbury ranch on September 2, 1887.

CHAPTER V

[1]The age of William Graham was given to me by a close relative still living in the Middle West. This same party (who does not wish the name to be made public) informed me that William had been in Arizona about five years before his death.

[2]It is not generally known that Louis Parker was a nephew of the Graham brothers. He was a son of a daughter of Samuel Graham by his first wife. A close relative in the Middle West informed me that young Parker never returned to his home in Iowa. After hostilities ceased in 1888 he left Pleasant Valley, and finally settled at Las Cruces, New Mexico, where he was married. His wife died a few years later, leaving him with three small children. He also died within a few years, and was buried in Las Cruces. Miss Naomi Parker, a sister, still lives at Las Cruces. It would appear from this that she went there to care for his children after the death of his wife.

[3]Will C. Barnes relates that some years after the war Houck, while drinking, told him the story of the shooting of William Graham. Houck declared that while he was in the valley with a warrant for the arrest of Jim Stott on a charge of horse stealing he met young Graham on the trail. "We both drew at sight of one another, but I shot first and got him," Houck declared. See Barnes in *The Arizona Historical Review*, January, 1932, p. 23.
This story of the warrant for Jim Stott is as bad as the one for John Graham, for Stott's ranch was far removed from Pleasant Valley, and it is a known fact that he carefully avoided the feud district during the trouble in 1887.

[4]This statement comes from a close relative in the Middle West. It was undoubtedly made by Tom Graham to his father when the latter visited his son in Arizona in the fall of 1887.

[5]See Barnes in *The Arizona Historical Review*, January, 1932, pp. 24 and 38.

[6]A cowboy "riding the chuck line" is one out of work who goes from ranch to ranch or from one cow camp to another and lives off the proprietors. He usually does enough work to pay for his board.

[7]See Chapter IX and Note 4 of that Chapter, and Chapter X.

CHAPTER VI

[1]In a letter from a Graham relative it is stated that after the killing of Billy Graham both Tom and John declared that they would not stand for such acts.

[2]Will C. Barnes says that John Tewksbury and William Jacobs were shot from an adjacent hillside and lay in plain view of the house. See *The Arizona Historical Review*, January, 1932, p. 30.

Joe T. McKinney says that they were killed in the morning while out looking for horses. See *The Arizona Historical Review*, July, 1932, p. 145.

[3]The story that hogs were allowed to eat the bodies has become one of the legends of the war. Some deny that such a thing took place, but the evidence of those who remember the killing shows that it actually occurred. Will C. Barnes (see *The Arizona Historical Review*, January, 1932, p. 30) casts doubt upon the story; but he quotes Charles Perkins, who claimed to have helped John Meadows bury the bodies. Perkins says in this connection: "It was not possible to move them. They were badly torn by the hogs, and decomposition had gone so far that burying them was a most disagreeable task. All we did was to dig two very shallow graves and roll the swollen, mutilated bodies into them with our shovels."

Joe T. McKinney, a member of Sheriff Mulvenon's second posse, denies that the bodies were touched by hogs. See *The Arizona Historical Review*, July, 1932, p. 145. However, McKinney did not reach the valley until some days after the killing. He further says that Mrs. Tewksbury went to the scene of the killing and when she asked for the bodies of her husband and William Jacobs, Tom Graham replied: "No, the hogs have got to eat them."

In support of the story that swine were allowed to devour the bodies, McKinney himself says that when Mulvenon's posse arrested the Tewksburys at their ranch on September 21 (see Chapter X), he heard Jim Tewksbury say: "No damned man

can kill a brother of mine and stand guard over him for the
hogs to eat him and live within a mile and a half of me." See
The Arizona Historical Review, October, 1932, p. 202.

Forty-five years after the fight at the Tewksbury ranch, Jim
Roberts told his son that hogs did not eat the bodies. However,
he also stated that John Tewksbury and William Jacobs were
killed at the Newton ranch in the same fight in which John
Paine and Hampton Blevins were slain. According to his
version, Tewksbury and Jacobs had gone to the pasture to catch
horses so that all could escape. Time had evidently confused
the two fights in old Jim's head, for there is absolutely no doubt
that Tewksbury and Jacobs were killed at the Tewksbury ranch
on September 2. The records of the two battles cannot be disputed in this respect.

In a letter dated January 7, 1933, John W. Weatherford
informed me that he "understood that the hogs partially ate
the bodies before Mrs. Tewksbury got to them." Mr. Weatherford was a member of Sheriff Mulvenon's first posse.

[4]While Charles Perkins and some others deny that Mrs.
Tewksbury buried the bodies, the preponderance of evidence
shows that she carried out this service for her husband and
his comrade. I first heard the story years ago from men who
clearly remembered incidents of the war, and later from residents of the valley who were acquainted with the facts. In this
connection I refer to John W. Weatherford's statement in his
letter quoted in Note 3 of this chapter in which he said that he
"understood that the hogs partially ate the bodies before Mrs.
Tewksbury got to them." According to information I have
received John Meadows exhumed the bodies for the inquest
which he held on the spot.

[5]Will C. Barnes (see *The Arizona Historical Review*, January, 1932, p. 30) says that the Graham forces kept the
Tewksbury ranch under siege for several days, but my information is that the attack was made in the early morning and that
Meadows arrived that evening. This is possible, even considering the distance of twenty-five miles from Payson to Tewksbury's. The men of old Arizona were hard riders and covered
long distances in a day. Had the siege extended into the night,
the besiegers would undoubtedly have set fire to the cabin.
Another point to prove that the siege could not have lasted
for more than one day is the fact that Andy Cooper was in
Holbrook in the early morning of September 4, and told the
story of the part he had taken in the killing.

Charles Perkins (see *The Arizona Historical Review*, January, 1932, p. 30) gives the impression that John Meadows rode into the valley alone. This is hardly probable: for although Meadows had the courage, he well knew that he would be unable to stop the fighting if alone; and he would have no trouble in gathering men at Payson for such an adventure.

[6]The records of John Meadows as justice of the peace were destroyed by a fire at Payson a number of years ago.

CHAPTER VII

[1]While this fight was not directly connected with the events in Pleasant Valley, all of the participants had taken part. Every member of Cooper's gang had fought for the Grahams, and even Sheriff Owens once led a posse into the valley. Therefore this fight had a relationship to the war, and should properly be included.

[2]From a statement made to me by Sam Brown, who was still living in Gallup, New Mexico, in 1931. In the 1880's he was a prominent resident of Holbrook, and a member of the coroner's jury that exonerated Sheriff Owens.

[3]For a diagram and description of the location of the buildings in 1887 I am indebted to Mr. W. H. Clark, secretary of the Holbrook Chamber of Commerce. These buildings may have been razed in recent years.

[4]Some of the old-timers claim that Andy Cooper was a full brother of the Blevins boys, but changed his name to Cooper after going to Arizona because of the warrant in Texas. In that case Mrs. Blevins was his mother and not his stepmother.

[5]A descendant of the Blevins claims that Mrs. Gladden had gone to Texas before the fight at Holbrook. However, a verbatim transcript of the testimony taken at the coroner's inquest shows that Mrs. Gladden testified that she was in the house.

CHAPTER VIII

[1]The *Coconino Sun* was mistaken in the name of the boy. Instead of Hewston Blevans it should have been Sam Houston Blevins. The inquest referred to was not in his death, but in the killing of Andy Cooper. The old records fail to show that any inquest was held in the death of Sam Houston Blevins or Mose Roberts.

2Picketwire was the name given to the Purgatoire River by the early American frontiersman and cowboys. This is the same stream as El Río de Las Animas Perdidas (the River of Lost Souls) of the Spanish conquistadores. The French-Canadian trappers called it the "Purgatoire," but this was corrupted to "Picketwire" by the American mountain men, and by that name it was known among all of the cow outfits in that section during the last forty years of the nineteenth century. Among the Cheyennes it was known as "Difficult River to Cross," because of the perpendicular banks and deep canyons at its source. The Las Animas or Purgatoire River flows into the Arkansas from the south about fifteen miles below the site of Bent's Old Fort, and east of the present Las Animas, Colorado. This city takes its name from the stream.

CHAPTER IX

1This man's name appears in some of the newspaper accounts of that time as Joseph Ellingwood; but his real name seems to have been Underwood. This is the same man that Perkins claims was with Billy Graham when he was mortally wounded.

2See Barnes in *The Arizona Historical Review*, January, 1932, p. 29.

3See *The Arizona Historical Review*, July, 1933, p. 144.

4His complete recovery and arrival at Globe is noted in *The Silver Belt* of January 14, 1888.

CHAPTER X

1At that time the territorial capital was at Prescott. This town was the first capital of Arizona Territory, but in 1867 it was moved to Tucson, where it remained until 1877; then it was taken back to Prescott. On February 4, 1889, the capital was permanently located at Phoenix.

2See *The Arizona Historical Review*, October, 1932, p. 199. McKinney claims that Jim Houck joined his posse, but my information is that Houck met Mulvenon at Payson. Houck probably met McKinney while the latter was trailing the train robbers, and then went to Payson.

[3]The Saint Johns *Herald* for September, 29, 1887, states that Blevins was hit seven times with rifle bullets and Graham twice.

[4]An attempt was afterwards made to indict Sheriff Mulvenon for the killing of John Graham and Charles Blevins, but this move failed.

[5]When Tom Graham was arrested at Phoenix in October, 1887, he voluntarily surrendered to Sheriff Mulvenon. See Chapter XI.

[6]This was the Mexican named Miguel Apocada. Leslie E. Gregory, on July 2, 1946, informed me that Al Rose and Miguel Apocada were tried before Justice of the Peace Meadows at Payson for arson in connection with the burning of the Newton ranch house a few days after the fight there on August 10, 1887; but the case was dismissed after a jury trial. Gregory related that a lawyer still lived at Globe at that time (1946), aged eighty-eight, who claimed that he bought the jurymen off for five dollars each, and that he received eight hundred dollars for the defense of Rose and Apocada. This lawyer did not mind telling the story in his later years.

[7]Sheriff Mulvenon's two invasions of Pleasant Valley cost Yavapai County $3,168.78.

CHAPTER XI

[1]Bond for the release of the Tewksbury brothers and their comrades, who were taken by Sheriff Mulvenon to Prescott, was not arranged until nearly the middle of October. This is shown by an item in *The Silver Belt* of October 18, 1887, which also states that George A. Newton had returned to Globe.

[2]From the records in Phoenix of the marriage license issued to Thomas H. Graham and Anne Melton.

[3]This information and the statement in the preceding paragraph are not gossip, but were told to me by a close relative of Tom Graham's still living in the Middle West.

[4]Gathered from items that appeared in the Phoenix *Herald* of October 13, 15, and 18, 1887, and *The Silver Belt* of October 18 and 22, 1887.

CHAPTER XII

¹Judge Charles P. Hicks, one of Arizona's pioneers, died at Prescott on December 24, 1929.

²I am of the opinion that only one person now living knows the reason for Newton's action. That is George W. Tewksbury (see Note 22 of Chapter I), and he will not talk. The evidence shows that something more than sheep and possibly something else besides cattle rustling was back of the personal hatreds.

³From the old court records at Prescott; information furnished by the late C. P. Hicks.

⁴This is the first time that this information has been brought out. Heretofore it has not been generally known that there was an indictment against James Tewksbury at Saint Johns.

⁵At this time Tom Graham was thirty-four years of age.

⁶It is impossible to account for this claim to relationship by this man if his real name was George. At that time (1888) Tom Graham was the only member of the family left alive in Arizona. See Notes 23 and 24 of Chapter I.

CHAPTER XIII

¹The -Prescott *Courier* of November 7, 1887, reports his murder by masked men.

²Joseph Fish says that he was hit eleven times, but this is probably somewhat exaggerated.

³This story of the killing of Al Rose was related to me by an old resident of Pleasant Valley.

⁴See Joe T. McKinney in *The Arizona Historical Review*, July, 1932, p. 144.

⁵On November 2, 1889, Sheriff Glenn Reynolds, of Gila County, started with nine prisoners (eight Apache Indians and one Mexican) for the penitentiary at Yuma. When the party reached a long hill four miles southeast of Riverside, near the present Kelvin on the Gila River, Reynolds with one deputy, William H. (Hunkeydory) Holmes, started to walk up the hill with their prisoners. Suddenly the Indians turned on the officers, killing both. They then shot Eugene Middleton, the stage

driver, who was following slowly, and left him for dead with a bullet wound in his cheek. One of the Indians who escaped was the notorious Apache Kid, whom Jack (Walapai) Clark claimed he killed about 1893 or 1894 near Camp Condon in the Santa Catalina Mountains, north of Tucson.

[6]According to Sam Brown, the lynching of Stott, Scott, and Wilson took place about three months before the shooting of Jacob Lauffer. This may be correct. The statement that the lynching was after the attempt to murder Lauffer originated with the tale Jim Houck told when he was in Flagstaff about the middle of August, 1888. The Flagstaff *Champion* of August 18 carried the story of the wounding of Lauffer and the lynching of Stott, Scott, and Wilson in retaliation; but Houck may have lied about the date of the lynching to cover his part in the affair. On the other hand it is more than probable that the date of the lynching was confused in Mr. Brown's memory after the passing of so many years. See Chapter XV.

[7]See Will C. Barnes in *The Arizona Historical Review*, January, 1932, p. 35.

[8]See Will C. Barnes in *The Arizona Historical Review*, January 1932, p. 35.

[9]See Will C. Barnes in *The Arizona Historical Review*, October, 1931, pp. 14-15.

I am of the opinion that the *Herald* made a mistake in the name of the town where James Tewksbury died. My information that he died in Prescott comes from a letter written April 16, 1931, by James E. Owens, of Globe, undersheriff of Gila County, to Dodd L. Greer, county attorney, of Saint Johns. Mr. Owens says: "Your letter of April 6th received in reference to James Tewksbury. Through good authority we find that Mr. Tewksbury died in Prescott, Arizona, in the year 1888 with quick consumption brought on by measles." Other information contained in this same letter leads to the conclusion that Mr. Owens knew what he was talking about. We would probably call this disease cancer of the lungs today.

CHAPTER XIV

[1]*Life of Tom Horn, Government Scout and Interpreter, Written by Himself*... (Denver, [1904]), pp. 249-50.

[2]See the account of the killing of Al Rose in Chapter XIII and the accompanying notes.

[3]See Note 5 of Chapter XIII.

[4]In 1931 Walter Tewksbury told Sidney Kartus, at that time secretary to the Arizona State Historian, that Tom Horn positively took an active part in the war. Letter from Mr. Kartus to the author.

CHAPTER XV

[1]The details of the lynching were related to me by Sam Brown, who was still living at Gallup, New Mexico, in 1931, and also by Will C. Barnes.

[2]Remember that it was a band of Daggs Brothers' sheep driven over the rim of the Mogollons into Pleasant Valley the year before that opened the old sore between the Tewksburys and Grahams. In connection with the lynching of Stott, Scott, and Wilson it is well to remember that if Sam Brown had had any partisan feeling in the vendetta, it would have been on the Tewksbury side, for he was a sheep owner and associated with Daggs Brothers. Jim Houck was also a sheep owner.

[3]Blotched brands are brands that have been "worked over" into another brand, and placed on stolen horses and cattle by rustlers.

[4]Tom Horn gives this man's name as "Big Jeff," but Horn is unreliable. (See *Life of Tom Horn*. pp. 249-50.) In reporting the lynching of these three men the Flagstaff *Champion* of August 18, 1888, gave his name as Jeff Wilson. This information, however, was given to the *Champion* by Jim Houck. Sam Brown is certain that the name was Billy Wilson.

[5]Sam Brown gave the date as May 6; but from what I have learned from other sources I think that he was mistaken in the month. Will C. Barnes gives the date of the lynching as August 12, but this is not correct. See *The Arizona Historical Review*, January, 1932, p. 39. The date of the lynching was August 11, 1888.

[6]It is well to remember in this connection that in September, 1887, Sheriff Mulvenon had only been able to gather twenty men for his second invasion of Pleasant Valley.

[7]When relating this Sam Brown stated that the reason suspicion was directed upon Houck was on account of his actions and stories he told of the lynching—stories that those acquainted with the facts felt could not be true. The account in the Flagstaff *Champion* is an example.

[8]Mr. Burt, treasurer of the Hyde Park Savings Bank, is a man of standing in his community. He informs me that Stott's sister is still living at Wellesley, Massachusetts.

[9]F. A. Ames, a native of New England and a relative of Governor Ames of Massachusetts, was employed by the Aztec Land and Cattle Company, and was well acquainted with James W. Stott in Arizona.

[10]James Stott, the father, was a native of England, but came to this country when a young man and married Hannah Burt, a member of an old New England family. Twenty-seven years before his death he lost his right arm and left hand in saving the life of a fellow worker whom he had sent to repair a water wheel. This man was not injured.

[11]From a letter written by F. A. Ames to James Stott, the father, from Boston, December 8, 1888, a copy of which is before me.

[12]This is the same location mentioned in the previous account in this chapter.

[13]Quoted from Ames's letter. The charges mentioned probably refer to the story of buying horses with blotched brands as told by Sam Brown. There is no evidence today that this charge was true.

[14]This sister is still living.

[15]See Note 13 of this chapter.

[16]It was August 16 that Mr. and Mrs. Stott received a telegram announcing their son's death. When they went to the ranch in Arizona they found that everything of value had been removed, his horses were gone, and they never recovered a cent of the money invested in property or stock.

Anna Burt Taylor, of Fontana, California, a cousin of James W. Stott, recalls some details of the murder and the visit of his parents to Arizona. She gives the following recollections of the affair: "As I understood it a number of men came at night and strung Jamie and a man who had stopped for the night on his way from the mail, both to a tree, hanging them both till they were dead. It was said that their excuse was that Jamie was accused of horse stealing. Aunt Hannah (Stott's mother) said that she went into town where records of horses were kept, which I suppose was Holbrook, and was told that Jamie's records of his horses were the most accurate they had. Every horse's record was accounted for in detail. Aunt Hannah said that she was sure she talked with some of the men who committed the murder and she told them a curse would follow them for what they had done. We saw Jamie, of course, when we went to North Billerica and he seemed like a big husky boy as I remember. I never heard a word against his character. They said he was venturesome; apt to be on top of the woolen mill and other risky places."

Walter Carleton Burt, of North Attleboro, Massachusetts, another cousin, recalls the visit of Stott's parents to Arizona after the murder. After their return they went to his fathers' store at 154 State Street, Boston, where he was bookkeeper, and he heard their story. His aunt told of talking personally to a man who admitted to her that he was one of the mob that hanged her son. When she heard this admission she declared that she would bring him to justice if it was the last thing she ever did, but he answered defiantly: "Try and do it. I wanted that land and place and I intend to get it and I will." Mrs. Stott found later that nothing could be done. This was Arizona in 1888.

George Frank Burt, now an instructor in the Auburn High School, Auburn, Rhode Island, recalls that Stott had a companion with him who was spared by the lynchers. This was probably Clymer, the "lunger." Stott's sister who is still living says that this man's name was Mott Clymer instead of Floyd Clymer. This helps to corroborate Sam Brown's story in which he says that the "lunger" brought the news of the lynching to Holbrook.

17This description of the opening of the graves was written by Fred A. Turley of Sundown Ranch, Alpine, Arizona, to Leslie E. Gregory on March 12, 1946. Mr. Turley was present at the scene.

CHAPTER XVI

1In spite of all my efforts I have been unable to learn the real reason that induced George Newton to join the Tewksburys. In his letter to me on July 15, 1931, George W. Tewksbury hints at it in this statement: "As for George Newton when you find out the real reason for this feud you will know that cattle and sheep had very little bearing on this part." I have never been able to learn just what he meant by referring to Newton.

That personal reasons influenced Newton is plainly stated in a letter from Hinson Thomas, of Globe, to Mrs. George F. Kitt, secretary of the Arizona Pioneers' Historical Society of Tucson, in 1931. His letter in part follows: "Have just succeeded in meeting B. F. Crawford, one of our early cattlemen, and who was here during the Pleasant Valley war, and he tells me that in the beginning the Tewksburys and Grahams were (with Newton) good friends, and when they became enemies, the two factions—Newton went with the Tewksburys on personal grounds."

[2]See Note 11 of Chapter III. Hon. James H. McClintock, of Phoenix, former Arizona State Historian, informed me several years ago that when he lived in Globe in 1881 and 1882 he was well acquainted with George Newton; but he was unable to explain the reason Newton joined the Tewksburys.

[3]A package of mail Newton was taking to his men and neighbors was found. A letter to his foreman James Ketcherside was blurred by water but still legible. See Barnes in *The Arizona Historical Review,* January 1932, p. 40.

CHAPTER XVII

[1]According to family records, Tom Graham owned about seven hundred head of cattle at this time.

[2]Will C. Barnes (see *The Arizona Historical Review,* October, 1931), says that Graham turned his cattle over to William Young. This is an error, for Miss Ola Young, the daughter of the man who took Tom Graham's ranch and cattle, informed me that her father was S. W. Young.

[3]This mustache was grown after Tom Graham went to Arizona. The photograph taken in California and sent back to his father in Iowa shows a good-looking young man in his twenties with smooth face.

[4]Now Mrs. Estelle C. Converse, of Santa Paula, California. See Chapter XXII.

[5]In spite of reports still current that Tom Graham returned to Pleasant Valley frequently after he settled near Tempe, I am informed by one who lived in the valley that this was his first visit after he left in 1889.

[6]An account of this meeting was published in the Phoenix *Herald.* See Barnes in *The Arizona Historical Review,* October, 1931, pp. 21-22. My account of Tom Graham's return to Pleasant Valley was given to me by a party who was on the Graham ranch or rather the Young ranch, at that time, but whose name is withheld by request.

[7]Colcord was still living in Arizona in 1946.

[8]Tom Graham purchased his ranch near Tempe on April 28, 1890, and his widow sold it to Byron Carr on September 30, 1898, according to information furnished in 1944 by A. Lloyd Ozanne of Phoenix.

CHAPTER XVIII

[1]It is generally believed in Arizona today that Ed Tewksbury fired the shot, and this may be true as it would have been an easy matter for Ed Cummings, not being acquainted with the men prior to the shooting, to have made a mistake in identification.

Both J. F. Ketcherside and Charles Perkins, who were well acquainted with John Rhodes, informed Will C. Barnes that Rhodes told them several times that Ed Tewksbury fired the shot that killed Tom Graham. Both Ketcherside and Perkins were of the opinion that Rhodes was not of the killer type, and that he never looked for trouble but always avoided it. See Barnes in *The Arizona Historical Review,* October 1931, p. 27-28.

From what I learned of John Rhodes while living in southern Arizona in 1903 and 1904 it is hard to believe that he would willingly have committed murder; but, on the other hand, he certainly knew Ed Tewksbury's intentions when he accompanied him to the ambush that morning, and the fact that he was with his brother-in-law shows that he was a party to the killing, even if he himself did not fire the shot; and Ed Cumming's story may be correct.

[2]Measurements and comparisions made by John Labarge and Bone Lewis of the tracks of a horse found near the scene

of the shooting proved that they were made by Rhodes's animal. Even the worn shoes could be traced in the tracks of both.

[3]Details of the manner in which Ed Tewksbury was taken to Phoenix appeared in the Tempe *News* of August 20, 1892.

CHAPTER XIX

[1]Will C. Barnes says that the hearing only lasted for three days, and that Rhodes was released on August 9. See *The Arizona Historical Review*, October, 1931, p. 25.

However, Mr. Johnson informed me that it was ten days. Corroboration of this is found in the account of the decision of Justice of the Peace Huson which appeared in the Phoenix *Gazette* of August 20. This is proof that the hearing must have just terminated a day or two before.

[2]Some claim that Mrs. Graham had the weapon in a handbag; others say it was concealed in a cloth.

[3]See Barnes in *The Arizona Historical Review*, October, 1931, p. 25.

[4]See Chapter XX.

[5]Will C. Barnes says that Rhodes was later indicted with Edwin Tewksbury, and was confined in the jail at Phoenix without bail until acquitted. See *The Arizona Historical Review*, October, 1931, p. 26.

However, Mr. Johnson was unable to find any record of this indictment and acquittal. As a matter of fact, Edwin Tewksbury was never tried in the courts of Maricopa County for the very good reason that he secured a change of venue to Tucson. If Rhodes had been indicted with him, he would also have been granted a change of venue in view of the intense public feeling; and John Rhodes was never tried at Tucson. Therefore we must accept the court records as the best evidence that Rhodes was never tried after his release by Justice Huson.

[6]Barnes states (see *The Arizona Historical Review*, October, 1931, p. 26) that Rhodes's hearing was held at Tempe. However, this resolution states plainly that it was at Phoenix.

CHAPTER XX

[1]While the source of the money for Edwin Tewksbury's defense was never disclosed, it is generally believed that it came from Daggs Brothers, who are also reported to have financed the Tewksbury faction during the fighting in Pleasant Valley in 1887. However, this is only a supposition, as there is no proof that they gave any financial support after their sheep were driven out of the valley.

P. P. Daggs afterwards went to California, where he died a few years ago. In 1926 Mrs. George F. Kitt, secretary of the Arizona Pioneers' Historical Society of Tucson, wrote to him with a request to write some of his memories of the Pleasant Valley war for the society. She received the following reply:

Claremont, California, May 29, 1926.
My Dear Madam:

Your kind favor reached me here. Fifty-eight years and writing history. I have failed in most everything else, so I must be a historian. I know you would not be unkind enough to lure me into anything for which I would be captured and shot at sunrise. I have one consolation: the enemy will not do it. They are all "sleeping with their boots on."

I ought to know something about the "Tonto Basin War." It cost me ninety thousand dollars. General Sherman once said "War is hell." He was right. Two years more and I will write the history of Dear Old Arizona—if I don't forget it.

Yours sincerely,
P. P. Daggs.

From this it appears that he wanted to forget the events that had cost him a fortune; but the old sore still rankled. The fact that he admitted the feud had cost him ninety thousand dollars gives some color to the rumors that he financed Edwin Tewksbury's defense.

[2]Joseph Campbell defended John Rhodes at his preliminary hearing.

[3]Will C. Barnes (see *The Arizona Historical Review*, October, 1931, p. 18) says that Ed Tewksbury was first tried in the district court in Phoenix late in 1893; but, as I have just stated this is not correct. However, the prevailing belief that

Tewksbury was first tried at Phoenix probably grows out of the preliminary hearing.

[4]The verdict is taken verbatim from the old court records at Tucson, a copy of which was furnished me by Louis R. Kempf.

[5]This petition is taken verbatim from the court records at Tucson, a copy of which was furnished by Mr. Kempf.

CHAPTER XXI

[1]Copper was first discovered in the Jerome district in 1877 by Al Sieber, Arizona's noted scout of the Apache wars, who staked out the Verde claim in the Black Hills section; and that same year John Dougherty and Captain J. D. Boyd located claims where Jerome now stands. These were followed by others, and by 1882 several mines were in operation on a small scale, Sieber's old Verde being owned by the Verde Queen Company. However, none were on a paying basis when F. F. Thomas appeared on the scene, but he saw the possibilities of the district and purchased the Wade Hampton from John and Angus McKinnon for twenty thousand dollars and leased eleven other claims. George A. Treadwell, a noted mining expert, became interested in the property with Thomas, and in 1883 the now famous United Verde Copper Company was organized with James A. McDonald as president and Eugene Jerome, after whom the town was named, as secretary and treasurer. The mine was very rich in copper, but the reduction methods of that time prohibited much profit. This is shown by the fact that during the first year the company realized a total production of seven hundred and seventy-nine thousand dollars worth of copper and only paid sixty-two thousand dollars in dividends. Others who attempted to operate the property experienced similar trouble; and finally, in February, 1888, Senator William A. Clark, the Montana copper king who had already amassed a huge fortune from the "mountain of copper" at Butte, secured a lease on the property. After his expert, J. L. Giroux, had completed his examination in January, 1889, Clark purchased the controlling interest in the company. This marked the beginning of boom days for Jerome, the richest copper district in all Arizona, and among the most productive in the United States. Clark's money soon put the mines on a paying basis. A narrow gauge railroad was built, and a larger and improved

smelter was erected. In later years a broad gauge replaced the narrow gauge of early days; and in 1915 a new reduction plant was completed in the valley, and the town of Clarkdale was founded.

²William O. (Buckey) O'Neill, Captain of Troop A, Rough Riders, was killed in action during the battle of San Juan Hill, Cuba, July 1, 1898. He was shot through the head.

³Copy of the appointment and oath of James Roberts as deputy sheriff of Yavapai County, Arizona Territory, December 18, 1889:

Territory of Arizona,
County of Yavapai,
Office of the Sheriff.

Know all men by these presents, that I, the undersigned Sheriff of the County of Yavapai, Territory of Arizona, do hereby appoint James Roberts, of Congress City, in said County, a Deputy Sheriff in and for said County.

In witness whereof I have hereunto set my hand this twelfth day of December, A.D., 1889.

Wm. O. O'Neill,
Sheriff of Yavapai County, Arizona.

Territory of Arizona,
County of Yavapai.

I, James Roberts, do solemnly swear that I will support the constitution of the United States, and the laws of the Territory of Arizona; that I will true faith and allegiance bear to the same, and defend them against all enemies whatsoever, and that I will faithfully and impartially discharge the duties of the office of Deputy Sheriff in and for the County of Yavapai to the best of my ability. So help me God.

James Roberts.

Subscribed and sworn to before me this 18 day of December, 1889.

W. H. Kirkland, J. P.

⁴Copy of the appointment of James Roberts as Deputy Sheriff of Yavapai County, Arizona Territory, January 12, 1891.

County of Yavapai,
Territory of Arizona, ss.

Know all men by these presents: That I the undersigned Sheriff of the County of Yavapai in the Territory of Arizona, do hereby appoint James Roberts of Congress Precinct in said County, a Deputy Sheriff in and for said County.

In witness Whereof I have hereunto set my hand and seal this 12th day of January, 1891.

James R. Lowry   (Seal).
Sheriff of Yavapai County.

I hereby certify the above to be a full true and correct copy of the appointment of James Roberts as a Deputy Sheriff of Yavapai County, Arizona.

J. R. Lowry,
Sheriff.
By H. H. Carter,
Under Sheriff.

[5]Certificate of the election of James Roberts as constable of Jerome precinct, November 8, 1892:

Territory of Arizona, County of Yavapai.

James Roberts

Having received the highest number of votes cast for office of Constable for Jerome Precinct of said Yavapai County at the election held on the eighth day of November, 1892, is hereby declared elected to said office.

Seal of the Su-   IN WITNESS WHEREOF I have
pervisors of   hereunto set my hand and the seal
Yavapai County   of the Board of Supervisors this 23
Prescott,   day of November 1892.
Arizona.   E. J. F. Horne,
Clerk of the Board of Supervisors,
Yavapai County, Arizona.

[6]Letter of appointment as town marshal of Jerome, Arizona, April 6, 1904:

Council Chamber
of the
Town of Jerome.

Office of the Clerk
and Treasurer.

Jerome, Arizona, April 6th, 1904.

Mr. J. F. Roberts,
        Jerome, Arizona.

Dear Sir:—

I beg to notify you that the election held in the Town of Jerome, Arizona, April 4th, 1904, that you were duly elected Town Marshal for the ensuing two years.

Yours very truly,
        R. A. Smith, Clerk.

[7]Named in honor of the late Senator William A. Clark, the Montana copper king and principal owner of the United Verde Copper Company.

CHAPTER XXII

[1]I have been unable to find out the dates of his service as constable and deputy sheriff; but he held at least one term as deputy in 1898 and 1899 under Sheriff Dan Williamson.

[2]I have not been able to find out the date of Edwin Tewksbury's marriage. The records of the ages of his children at the time of their father's death were furnished by George Tewksbury, a son.

[3]If this story is true it is sufficient proof of Duchet's boast that he was not afraid of any man that ever lived. Considerable mystery surrounds this strange character. There is little doubt that he was an old plainsman of the generation of the 1870's; but some of the old-timers who knew him in the days of the vendetta claim that he received that terrible scar on his face during a drunken fight in a saloon. This may be true; but there is no proof. It is certain, though, that he did keep bad feeling alive by talking too much.

Before he died Duchet made a statement to the attending physician, who wrote the story down. This manuscript is now in possession of the Arizona State Historian at Phoenix, who refuses to reveal its contents. In view of Duchet's known boastful character in connection with the vendetta, its historical value may be very doubtful. One thing is certain; for some reason not known a very warm friendship existed between him and Tom Graham.

[4]Dr. F. P. Watson, of Freeport, Texas, who lived in Winslow, Arizona, from 1884 to 1886, informed me that Tom

Pickett married Kittie McCarthy, who died about a year later. He stated that he knew Tom Pickett and Kittie McCarthy intimately.

[5]The story of the discovery of this skull and rifle was told to Will C. Barnes by Mr. Ketcherside, who was living in Phoenix in 1931. The exact location of the tree is described as about five miles due west of the Rock House in Rock House Canyon. See Barnes in *The Arizona Historical Review*, October, 1931, p. 34.

[6]Will C. Barnes informed me that the bodies of Stott and Scott were removed by relatives to their old homes; but Sam Brown declared they were never moved. See Chapter XV.

[7]This date is not certain.

[8]This was told by Bacon to Edwin B. Hill about twenty five years later. Mr. Hill was stationed at Granite Reef, Arizona at the time in government work. He returned to Arizona in 1946, and died at Tempe, April 6, 1949.

ACKNOWLEDGMENTS

MANY THANKS   I first rode the Arizona cattle range about fifteen years after the close of hostilities in Pleasant Valley, and stories of those gun-fighting days were campfire legends. Some were true; some were fictitious. Edwin Tewksbury was still living in Globe, and John Rhodes was foreman of a ranch down in the San Pedro country. A few of the older cowboys had either taken some part or had ridden during the latter 1880's for the Hash Knife and other cow outfits in Tonto Basin and adjoining territory, and many of the events of the war were related by them to me because of personal friendship. Where those old friends are now I do not know. Cowboys are ever wanderers, and during my last visit to Arizona I found, after an absence of years, that those old comrades of my cowboy days had drifted on to other ranges; some over the trail that leads to the last big roundup "where cowboys like dogies will stand"; others into the land of forgotten men for reasons best known to themselves. Other Arizona friends who lived during those times have furnished much additional information, but at their own request their names are withheld. Even today the hand of the feud is still felt.

However, I am indebted for much valuable information to Mr. Will C. Barnes, of Washington, D.C., a former deputy United States forester, now retired (died December 17, 1936), who was one of the pioneer cattlemen of the Mogollon Mountains; to Mr. William MacLeod Raine, the noted Western author, of Denver, Colorado; to the late C. P. Hicks, of Prescott, Arizona, for copies of the old Yavapai County court records and for personal recollections of both the Grahams and the Tewksburys; to Mr. F. C. Bauer, of Prescott, Arizona, deputy recorder of Yavapai County, for brand entries made by the Grahams and for old court records; to Mr. Levi S. Udell and Mr. Dodd L. Greer, of Saint Johns, Arizona, both former county attorneys of Apache County, for old court records of the cases against George and William Graham at Saint Johns in 1882 and 1883; to Mr. Edw. E. Johnson of Phoenix, Arizona, former assistant county attorney of Maricopa County, for copies of the court records of the preliminary hearings of Edwin Tewksbury and John Rhodes for the murder of Tom Graham; to Mr. Louis R. Kempf, of Tucson, Arizona, former county attorney of Pima County, for the court records of the trial of Edwin Tewksbury; to Mr. Edwin Cummings, of Grand Canyon, Arizona, for his story of the shooting of Tom Graham; to Mr. Sam Brown, and Mr. Alfred Ruiz, of Gallup, New Mexico; to Mrs. George F. Kitt, secretary of the Arizona Pioneers' Historical Society, of Tucson; to Mr. J. C. Kilburn, of Russellville, Oklahoma; to Mr. James C. Harvey, of Santa Fe, New Mexico; to Mr. William Rhodan and Mr. William Babbitt, old-time cattlemen of Flagstaff, Arizona; to Mr. Evon Z. Vogt, of Ramah, New Mexico, and to all my old comrades and others whose names are withheld, all of whom helped make this the most authentic account of the Pleasant Valley war yet written.

I am indebted to Mr. William H. Roberts, of Clarkdale, Arizona, son of "Uncle Jim" Roberts, member of the Tewksbury faction and the "last man" of the Pleasant Valley war, for many of the facts of his father's life. While old Jim would never talk for publication he related many incidents of the vendetta to his son, and this information has been of great assistance to me.

I also wish to make special acknowledgment to Mrs. Elizabeth Owens, of Seligman, and to Mr. W. H. Clark, of Holbrook, Arizona, for information on the life of Commodore Owens and his bloody battle with the Cooper-Blevins gang at Holbrook, which, added to what I already had, makès this a complete and true account of the most sanguinary gun fight of old Arizona. Mrs. Owens is the widow of that famous fighting sheriff of a past generation of fighting men.

BIBLIOGRAPHY

FOR REFERENCE   Barnes, Will C. "The Pleasant Valley War of 1887." Published in two parts in *The Arizona Historical Review*; Part I in Vol. IV, No. 3 (October, 1931), pp. 5-34; Part II, in Vol. IV, No. 4 (January, 1932), pp. 23-45.

Burnham, Fredrick Russell. *Scouting on Two Continents.* Garden City, N. Y.: Doubleday, Page & Company, 1926. Contains a slight mention of the Pleasant Valley war.

Fish, Joseph. "History of Arizona." Unpublished manuscript in possession of the Arizona State Historian, Phoenix, Arizona; written shortly after the fighting in Pleasant Valley was over.

Forrest, Earle R. "Red Years on the Arizona Frontier," *Travel*, XLIX (October, 1927), 22-26. Illustrated. (Reprinted by permission in *Arizona Peace Officer's Magazine*, Vol. I, Nos. 2-3, February-March, 1937.)

Gregory, Leslie E. "Arizona's Haunted Walls of Silence," *Arizona Highways* (Phoenix, Arizona), October, 1947. Finished by Earle R. Forrest after Mr. Gregory's death November 29, 1946.

Horn, Tom. *Life of Tom Horn, Government Scout and Interpreter, Written by Himself, together with His Letters and Statements by his friends; a Vindication.* Denver: for J. C. Coble by the Louthan Book Company [1904].

Lockwood, Frank C. *Pioneer Days in Arizona; from the Spanish Occupation to Statehood.* New York: The Macmillan Company, 1932. Pp. 286-87.

McClintock, James Harvey. *Arizona, the Youngest State.* Chicago, S. J. Clarke, 1916. Pp. 484-86.

McKinney, Joe T. "Reminiscences." Published in three parts in *The Arizona Historical Review*; Part I in Vol. V, No. 1 (April, 1932), pp. 33-54; Part II in Vol. V, No. 2 (July, 1932), pp. 141-45; Part III in Vol. V, No. 3 (October, 1932), pp. 198-204.

Raine, William MacLeod. *Famous Sheriffs and Western Outlaws.* Garden City, N. Y.: Doubleday, Doran & Company, Inc., 1929. Pp. 225-35.

———. "The War for the Range," *Frank Leslie's Popular Monthly*, February, 1903. Illustrated. This was the first account written of the Pleasant Valley War.

——— and Will C. Barnes. *Cattle*. Garden City, N.Y. Doubleday, Doran & Company, Inc., 1930. Pp. 255-58.

MAGAZINES

Arizona Highways; published monthly by the Arizona Highway Department, Phoenix, Arizona; see Leslie E. Gregory in October, 1947.

Arizona Historical Review; publ'shed quarterly by the Arizona State Historian, Phoenix, Arizona; ceased publication in January, 1933; see Will C. Barnes in October, 1931, and January, 1932; Joe T. McKinney in April, July, and October, 1932. Publication resumed by the University of Arizona and Arizona Pioneers' Historical Society, Tucson, Arizona.

Frank Leslie's Popular Monthly, New York; no longer published; see William MacLeod Raine in February, 1903.

Travel, New York; see Earle R. Forrest in October, 1927.

NEWSPAPERS

Arizona Silver Belt; formerly published at Globe, Arizona, by William O. (Buckey) O'Neill; files for 1887, 1888, and 1892.

Coconino Sun; published at Flagstaff, Arizona; files for 1887 and 1888; still published.

Flagstaff *Champion;* published at Flagstaff, Arizona; files for 1888; no longer published.

Hoofs and Horns; livestock paper founded at Prescott, Arizona, by William O. (Buckey) O'Neill; files for 1887, 1888, and 1892.

Phoenix *Gazette;* published at Phoenix, Arizona; see files for 1887, 1892, and 1893; still published.

Phoenix *Herald;* published at Phoenix, Arizona; files for 1887, 1888, and 1892; no longer published.

Prescott *Courier;* published at Prescott, Arizona; files for 1887, 1888, and 1892; still published.

Prescott *Journal-Miner;* published at Prescott, Arizona; files for 1887 and 1888; still published.

Saint Johns *Herald;* published at Saint Johns, Arizona; files for 1887 and 1888; still published.

Tempe *News;* published at Tempe, Arizona; files for 1892 and 1893; still published.

Tucson *Star*; published at Tucson, Arizona; files for 1892, 1893, and 1894; still published.

COURT RECORDS OF ARIZONA TERRITORY

See court records and minutes at Phoenix, Saint Johns, Prescott, and Tucson.

THE PRINCIPAL CHARACTERS

THE GRAHAM FAMILY Thomas H. Graham; the last of the Grahams and leader of the cattlemen; killed August 2, 1892, aged thirty-eight.

John Graham; brother of Tom; killed at Perkins' store by Sheriff Mulvenon's posse on September 21, 1887.

William (Billy) Graham; half brother of Tom and John; killed by Jim Houck on August 17, 1887.

Samuel Graham, of Boone, Iowa; father of the Graham brothers, but he took no part in the war; visited by Tom in Phoenix in October, 1887.

George Graham, the man of mystery. Most of the old-timers claim that he did not exist. However, Fish mentions him in his manuscript, and his name appears on the court records at Saint Johns in 1882 and 1883, and again in 1888. James F. Roberts remembered him in Phoenix after the war. He was not related to the Graham brothers. He was probably from Texas.

Louis Parker; nephew of the Graham brothers; died in later years at Las Cruces, New Mexico.

Anne Melton; married Thomas H. Graham on October 8, 1887. She was just seventeen at the time, and he was thirty-three.

THE BLEVINS FAMILY

Mart Blevins; father of the Blevins brothers, all of whom fought for the Grahams. Mart Blevins disappeared in July, 1887, and was never heard of again.

Andy Blevins, known in Arizona as Andy Cooper; son of Mart Blevins and leader of the Pleasant Valley rustlers; a danerous gun fighter; killed by Sheriff Owens at Holbrook on September 4, 1887.

Hampton Blevins; killed by Tewksbury forces at the Middleton ranch, August 10, 1887.

Charles Blevins; killed by Sheriff Mulvenon's posse at Perkins' store, September 21, 1887.

John Blevins; the only member of this family who survived the vendetta; wounded by Sheriff Owens in the fight at Holbrook, September 4, 1887. He did not serve a term in the penitentiary at Yuma as previously reported; he was killed in 1928 in an automobile accident near Phoenix.

Sam Houston Blevins; youngest of the family; killed by Sheriff Owens at Holbrook, September 4, 1887.

Mary Blevins; wife of Mart Blevins and mother of the five brothers.

Lela Blevins; only daughter of Mart Blevins.

Eva Blevins; wife of one of the Blevins brothers.

GRAHAM PARTISANS

Al Rose; early settler in Pleasant Valley and one of the best of the Graham fighters; killed from ambush at Houdon ranch on Spring Creek in November, 1888.

Ed Rose, his brother; early settler in Pleasant Valley.

Charley Duchet; an old-time frontiersman. The friendship between Tom Graham and this strange character was so strong that the Frenchman was one of the few who remained with his leader until the last. He died in Phoenix in 1925.

John Paine; Hash Knife cowboy; killed at the Middleton ranch, August 10, 1887; a fighting Texan.

Mose Roberts; a member of Andy Cooper's gang; killed by Sheriff Owens in the fight at Holbrook, September 4, 1887.

Thomas Tucker; Hash Knife cowboy; severely wounded at the Middleton ranch, August 10, 1887, went to New Mexico and served as undersheriff at Santa Fe; died years later in Texas.

Joseph Underwood; often referred to as Joe Ellenwood or Ellingwood; a wandering cowboy who fought for the Grahams; wounded in the leg in the attack on the Tewksbury camp on September 17, 1887; recovered.

Harry Middleton; cowboy for the Defiance Cattle Company at Navajo Springs; believed to have come from Texas; fatally wounded in the attack on the Tewksbury camp on September 17, 1887; died September 19.

Miguel Apocada; a Mexican vaquero who fought for the Grahams. He disappeared after his release by Justice of the
Peace John Meadows at the preliminary hearing following
Mulvenon's second invasion, and nothing more is known
of him.

Robert Glasspie; Hash Knife cowboy; wounded in the hip at the
Middleton ranch, August 10, 1887; recovered and spent the
rest of his life in Arizona; died at Coolidge, June 29, 1946,
aged eighty-five years.

Robert Carrington; sometimes called Thomas Carrington; cowboy, wounded in the fight at the Middleton ranch, August 10,
1887; recovered; nothing more known of him.

Tom Pickett; Hash Knife cowboy; with Billy the Kid during the
Lincoln County war in New Mexico; living in Nevada a
few years ago.

Buck Lancaster; Hash Knife cowboy; nothing more known
of him.

George Smith; Hash Knife cowboy; nothing more known of him.

———McNeal; Hash Knife cowboy; nothing more known of
him.

———Roxy; Hash Knife cowboy; nothing more known of him.

———Peck; Hash Knife cowboy; nothing more known of him.

Jeff LaForce, who lost a finger in a gun fight with John
Rhodes.

Horace Philly; a young cowboy who worked on the Graham
ranch during the vendetta; murdered by an unknown assassin in Reno Pass in 1892.

THE TEWKSBURY FAMILY

John D. Tewksbury, Sr., a native of Boston; father of the
three Tewksbury brothers. He took no part in the war and
died a natural death several years later.

John Tewksbury, Jr., a son of John D. Tewksbury, Sr. by his
Indian wife; killed at the Tewksbury ranch, September 2,
1887.

Edwin Tewksbury, a son of John D. Tewksbury, Sr. by his Indian wife; the last of the Tewksburys and the leader of that
faction. It is claimed that he was one of the men who killed
Thomas H. Graham, August 2, 1892. He was tried for murder, convicted once, and jury disagreed the second time.
He was later released and never brought to trial again;
died at Globe, April 4, 1904.

James D. Tewksbury, a son of John D. Tewksbury, Sr., by his
Indian wife; died in Prescott of quick consumption following measles.

Lydia Crigler Shultes Tewksbury; an Englishwoman with two
husbands to her credit when she married John D. Tewksbury, Sr.; mother of Walter and Parker Tewksbury, both of
whom were children during the war.

Mary Crigler Tewksbury; daughter of the second wife of John
D. Tewksbury, Sr., by her first husband. She married her
stepbrother, John Tewksbury, and drove the swine from his
body after he had been killed.

Walter Tewksbury; son of John D. Tewksbury, Sr. by his second wife; he took no part in the war; lived at Crown King,
Arizona; died several years ago.

Parker Tewksbury; son of John D. Tewksbury, Sr. by his second wife and a full brother of Walter Tewksbury; took no
part in the war.

TEWKSBURY PARTISANS

Daggs Brothers (P. P. and A. A.); owners of the sheep driven
into Pleasant Valley under the protection of the Tewksbury
guns. This act turned the feud into a sheep and cattle war.

James F. Roberts; the best gun fighter of them all. The last
survivor of all those who took an active part on either side
and known as "the last man of the Pleasant Valley war."
Died January 8, 1934, of heart trouble.

George A. Newton; a jeweler at Globe; in partnership with
J. J. Vosberg in the Flying V cattle ranch in Pleasant Valley. He became involved on the Tewksbury side and disappeared in September, 1891, while on his way from Globe
to Pleasant Valley. The mystery of his death has never
been satisfactorily solved, but it is generally believed that he
was drowned at the Pinal Creek ford of Salt River.

William Jacobs; a partner with the Tewksbury brothers in protecting the sheep driven by Daggs Brothers over the "dead line of the Mogollons"; killed with John Tewksbury during the attack on the Tewksbury ranch, September 2, 1887.

John Rhodes; married the widow of John Tewksbury; arrested with Edwin Tewksbury for the murder of Tom Graham, and released at the preliminary hearing after Mrs. Anne Graham attempted to shoot him with her husband's six-shooter.

Tom Horn; known to have been associated with the Tewksburys, but his part in the vendetta has never been clearly established; hanged at Cheyenne, Wyoming, November 20, 1903.

Jacob Lauffer; wounded by a Graham partisan, August 4, 1888.

George Blaine; indicted with the Tewksburys at Prescott in 1884 for cattle stealing.

William Richards; indicted with the Tewksburys at Prescott in 1884 for cattle stealing.

W. H. Bishop; indicted with the Tewksburys at Prescott in 1884 for cattle stealing; his fate is not known, but he either died from natural causes or was killed, for his widow remarried.

Joseph Boyer; in the Middleton cabin the day of the first fight, August 10, 1887.

Navajo Indian sheepherder; killed by an unknown assassin after the sheep were driven into the valley.

George Wagner.

William Colcord.

————Elliott; married the widow of W. H. Bishop, and he in turn was killed.

Cody and Coleman; little is known of either. They were fired upon from ambush on August 4, 1888, while on their way to Jacob Lauffer's ranch.

NEUTRALS

James Stinson; pioneer cattleman who drove the first herd into Pleasant Valley. Tradition says that a dispute over cattle stolen from him was the real cause of the vendetta. He left the valley before the war broke out in 1887.

Charles E. Perkins; storekeeper in Pleasant Valley. His store figured prominently as headquarters for the Grahams. He was still living in Phoenix in 1931.

James Stott; a remittance man from Massachusetts; owned a ranch in Phoenix Park, sixty miles south of Holbrook; hanged by unknown parties believed to have been led by James D. Houck on August 13, 1888.

James Scott; a young Texas cowboy riding for the Hash Knife; hanged with James Stott; took no part in the war.

William (Billy) Wilson; a wandering prospector traveling from Durango, Colorado, to Globe; stopped for the night at Stott's ranch and was hanged with Stott and Scott; he was a stranger in that section.

S. W. Young; took over Tom Graham's cattle and ranch on shares when the partisan leader left Pleasant Valley in 1889.

Ed Cummings, Molly Cummings, and a girl named Betty Gregg; the three children who witnessed the shooting of Tom Graham on August 2, 1892.

W. T. Cummings; father of the two Cummings children. Tom Graham died at his house.

Sam Brown; liveryman and sheep owner at Holbrook.

C. P. Hicks; clerk at the O K Corral and store, where the Grahams and Tewksburys camped together in Prescott; and a member of the grand jury that indicted the Tewksburys and members of their faction on December 3, 1887.

Mrs. Amanda Gladden; deserted by her husband, she was left in the wilderness with a large family. Mart Blevins watched over her, and when the sheep were driven into the valley he removed her to Canyon Creek Ranch. After his disappearance she accompanied the Blevins family to Holbrook.

Will C. Barnes; owner of the Esperanza Cattle Company with headquarters at the Long Tom ranch in the Mogollons; Died December 17, 1936.

James F. Ketcherside; foreman of Newton and Vosberg's Flying V cattle ranch on Cherry Creek, and worked for J. J. Vosberg for some years after Newton's death; not known to have taken any part in the war; now living in Phoenix.

John Gilliland; range foreman for James Stinson during 1886.

J. E. Simpson; Hash Knife foreman during 1887.

Ed Rogers; Hash Knife wagon boss in the summer of 1887.

Robert Sigsby, who took Tom Tucker into his cabin and dressed his wound.

William Middleton; who brought the first blooded cattle into Pleasant Valley and one of its first settlers; owned the Middleton ranch before the war; left the valley before the vendetta broke out.

Harry Middleton, his son; wounded by Apaches in the fight at the Middleton ranch, September 2, 1881; took no part in the feud.

Eugene Middleton, another son; took no part in the feud.

Henry Moody; killed by Apache Indians in the fight at the Middleton ranch, September 2, 1881.

George L. Turner, Jr.; killed by Apache Indians in the fight at the Middleton ranch, September 2, 1881.

———Haigler; owner of a ranch in Pleasant Valley.

J. W. Ellison; an early settler in Pleasant Valley.

Frank Wattron; druggist and a prominent citizen at Holbrook.

Rev. W. J. Melton, Baptist preacher; father of Mrs. Thomas H. Graham.

Mr. Parker, of Boone, Iowa; father of Louis Parker and a brother-in-law of the Grahams.

Mr. Wilson; a ranchman in Tonto Basin. Edwin Tewksbury was working for him when Tom Graham was murdered.

SHERIFFS

William Mulvenon, of Prescott; sheriff of Yavapai County; led two posses into Pleasant Valley in an effort to restore peace.

Commodore Perry Owens; sheriff of Apache County; killed Andy Cooper, Mose Roberts, and Sam Houston Blevins, and wounded John Blevins in the most thrilling gun fight in all

Arizona's frontier history, at Holbrook, September 4, 1887; died at Seligman, Arizona, May 10, 1919, with his "boots off"; buried at Flagstaff.

John Montgomery, of Phoenix; sheriff of Maricopa County.

———Findlay, of Tucson; sheriff of Pima County.

Glenn Reynolds, of Globe; sheriff of Gila County; reports indicate that he was a Tewksbury partisan; McKinney says that he killed Al Rose; killed by the Apache Kid.

DEPUTY SHERIFFS

John W. Francis, of Flagstaff; deputy sheriff of Yavapai County; accompanied Sheriff Mulvenon on both invasions of Pleasant Valley.

John W. Weatherford, of Flagstaff; deputy sheriff of Yavapai County; accompanied Sheriff Mulvenon as a deputy on the first invasion of Pleasant Valley.

E. F. Odell of Flagstaff; constable and deputy sheriff of Yavapai County; accompanied Sheriff Mulvenon on both invasions of Pleasant Valley.

Fletcher Fairchild, of Flagstaff; accompanied Sheriff Mulvenon as a deputy on the first invasion of Pleasant Valley.

———Jacobs, of Flagstaff; accompanied Sheriff Mulvenon on the second invasion of Pleasant Valley.

———Jacobs, a brother of the man just mentioned; accompanied Sheriff Mulvenon on the second invasion of Pleasant Valley.

George Bristow, of Prescott; deputy sheriff of Yavapai County; accompanied Sheriff Mulvenon on the second invasion of Pleasant Valley.

E. M. Tackett, of Prescott; deputy sheriff of Yavapai County; accompanied Sheriff Mulvenon on the second invasion of Pleasant Valley.

S. J. Sullivan, of Prescott; deputy sheriff of Yavapai County; accompanied Sheriff Mulvenon on the second invasion of Pleasant Valley.

James D. Houck, sheep owner; deputy sheriff of Apache County: but an avowed Tewksbury partisan.

Joe McKinney; deputy sheriff of Apache County; with Sheriff Mulvenon on the second invasion of Pleasant Valley; died in 1948, aged ninety years.

John Scarlett; deputy sheriff of Apache County; accompanied Sheriff Mulvenon on the second invasion of Pleasant Valley.

Lon Hawes; deputy sheriff of Apache County; accompanied Sheriff Mulvenon on the second invasion of Pleasant Valley.

Joe Herschey; deputy sheriff of Apache County; accompanied Sheriff Mulvenon on the second invasion of Pleasant Valley.

Osmer D. Flake; deputy sheriff of Apache County; accompanied Sheriff Mulvenon on the second invasion of Pleasant Valley.

Thomas Elder, of Phoenix; deputy sheriff of Maricopa County who arrested Edwin Tewksbury at the Wilson ranch.

Henry DeNure; deputy sheriff of Maricopa County who took Edwin Tewksbury from Tucson to Phoenix.

Henry Garfias, of Phoenix; deputy sheriff of Maricopa County who met DeNure and Tewksbury and helped lodge the prisoners in jail at Phoenix.

COURT JUDGES

James H. Wright; judge of the circuit court before whom John Blevins was convicted at Saint Johns in September, 1888, for his part in the fight with Sheriff Owens.

H. C. Gooding; judge of the district court of Maricopa County before whom Edwin Tewksbury was arraigned on December 5, 1892.

J. D. Bethune; judge of the district court of Pima County before whom Edwin Tewksbury was tried the first time for the murder of Tom Graham.

COURT OFFICERS

Frank Cox, of Phoenix; district attorney of Maricopa County, who prosecuted Rhodes at his preliminary and afterwards prosecuted Edwin Tewksbury.

Attorney Street; who aided Frank Cox in the prosecution at the first trial of Edwin Tewksbury.

M. H. Williams, W. H. Lovell, and Frank H. Hereford; attorneys who represented the Territory of Arizona during the second trial of Edwin Tewksbury.

Alfred Ruiz; clerk of the district court at Saint Johns in 1888; still living at Gallup, New Mexico.

Charles Pendergast; foreman of the grand jury that indicted Edwin Tewksbury for the murder of Tom Graham.

M. McKenna; foreman of the jury at the first trial of Edwin Tewksbury when he was found guilty of murder.

ATTORNEYS

Joseph Campbell; who defended John Rhodes at his preliminary hearing, and, with Attorney Baker, was one of the counsel for the defense of Edwin Tewksbury.

Fitch and Campbell, Barnes and Martin, and Thomas D. Satterwhite; who defended Edwin Tewksbury at his second trial.

JUSTICES OF THE PEACE

John Meadows, of Payson; before whom the prisoners captured by Sheriff Mulvenon during his second invasion of Pleasant Valley, were given a preliminary hearing. He also led a rescue party to the Tewksbury ranch on September 2, 1887, and raised the siege of the cattlemen.

W. O. Huson, of Phoenix; before whom John Rhodes was given a preliminary hearing for the murder of Tom Graham. Huson released Rhodes at this hearing.

Harry L. Wharton, of Phoenix; before whom Edwin Tewksbury was given a preliminary hearing for the murder of Tom Graham.

D. G. Harvey, of Holbrook; who held the inquest after Sheriff Owen's battle with the Cooper-Blevins gang.

MISS OLA YOUNG

Pioneer and Cattle Queen of Pleasant Valley

The life story of Miss Ola Young, who settled on the Graham Ranch in Pleasant Valley when her father took charge of Tom Graham's cattle "on the shares" in 1889, reads like a romance of the old West. She and her sister, Miss Betty Young, together with another sister, Mrs. Ed Gilliland, and a brother, William, have lived just about every phase of pioneer life in the old West, from traveling in a covered wagon to homesteading and running a cattle ranch.

It was in the 1880's that their pioneering father, S. W. Young, moved his family from the old home in Missouri to Texas. But Mr. Young did not like the country, and in 1888 he loaded his wife and children into a covered wagon, and headed west. Three months later, after an almost endless journey across plains and mountains and deserts, they reached central Arizona. It was a beautiful country, and they all liked it so well that they decided to homestead on Weber Creek, but they had scarcely started when an Indian scare drove them to Payson.

Then, in the spring of 1889, Mr. Young made an agreement with Tom Graham to run his cattle "on the shares," and the family moved to the Graham Ranch in the heart of the Pleasant Valley feud country. This has been the family home ever since. The war had made the valley range safe for cattle, if it accomplished nothing else, and Mr. Young prospered as a cattleman. His children, William, Ola, Katy, and Betty, rode the range and helped with the cattle. As the years passed brands were established for each of the children until they eventually had their own herds.

Other settlers came into the valley after the war, and when a school was established Miss Ola was the first teacher, and many an Arizonian of today learned his "readin' 'ritin' and 'rithmatic" under her tutelage. When a post office (the only one in Pleasant Valley) was established at the ranch in 1890 and named Young, Miss Ola was appointed postmistress, a position she held until she retired in 1939, after serving in that capacity longer than any other person in the United States; and she was so beloved that the people of Pleasant Valley gave her a great "Thank You" celebration, and presented her with a medal.

During those early years Pleasant Valley was the far frontier with the nearest supply points at Globe and Holbrook, each more than seventy-five miles away, and a store was added to the post office, the only one in the valley for many years.

When the mother died Miss Ola homesteaded the old Graham Ranch. William took up a homestead and married. Katy married Ed Gilliland.

Miss Ola Young is a real "cowman" of sixty years standing, and what she does not know about the business, well—"just isn't worth knowin'." The ranch contains one thousand acres of patented land and a large range on the National Forest; and since she retired as postmistress she and Miss Betty have devoted their entire time to their cattle—"cattle queens" of old Pleasant Valley of sanguinary memory.

APPENDIX

William Clay Colcord, the last man of Pleasant Valley War days, died May 16, 1961, in the Gila General Hospital at Globe, Arizona. He was ninety-four and had long outlived every man in any way connected with the feud. Bill Colcord, as he was known among his friends, took no part in the partisan trouble in the valley; he was one of the very few neutrals, perhaps the only one, who was respected by both sides and permitted to remain in the valley—and live. The reason for this was his widespread reputation for honesty, and for minding his own business, as Roscoe Willson, Phoenix newspaperman, explained in his obituary.

When Tom Graham and Charley Duchet returned to Pleasant Valley in 1892 for Graham's share of the cattle he had left with S. W. Young, it was Colcord who met them to ask, ". . . is it peace or war?" When assured by Tom that it was peace they shook hands, and while Graham gathered his cattle and drove them out of the valley, Colcord saw to it that they were not molested.

Colcord was born in Jefferson Parish, Louisiana, January 14, 1867, and came to Arizona in 1886 with his mother and brother, Harvey. Willson stated that another brother, Charles, was in charge of the famous A One outfit owned by the Arizona Cattle Company. In 1886 when Babbitt Brothers brought in their first cattle to Arizona and started the now famous C O Bar, young Colcord was one of their cowboys. This was at the same time that William Rhodan worked for this outfit, for I once heard him say that he was the Babbitt Brothers' first cowboy.

Colcord evidently did not work long for the C O Bar, for in the fall of 1886, he and his brother, Harvey, with their mother, started their own cattle ranch in Pleasant Valley. Later they owned ranches at Marsh Creek and Colcord Mountain, which was named for this family.

Jim Roberts, who figured prominently on the Tewksbury side and years later was a deputy sheriff and peace officer, was Colcord's nearest neighbor. During the feud both had horses stolen, and Roberts joined the Tewksburys; but Colcord remained neutral.

Memorial services for pioneer William Colcord were held in the Carr Mortuary at Tempe, on May 18, 1961. He was buried in the Double Butte Cemetery at Tempe.

Edwin Tewksbury's only daughter, Ella Elvira, named in memory of his sister, died May 31, 1961, in the Gila General Hospital, at the age of sixty-four. She was born in Globe on January 18, 1897, and in 1914 married Vicente Garcia, by whom she had four sons and a daughter. In 1925 she was granted a divorce on the grounds of nonsupport, and resumed her maiden name of Tewksbury. Her mother and two sons, Joseph and Vicente, survived. Interment was in the Globe Cemetery. This establishes the fact, which I have mentioned in the narrative, that the Tewksbury brothers did have a sister.

It seems rather a strange coincidence that on that same day of May 31, 1961, Mrs. Anne Graham Hagan, whose first husband was Tom Graham, died in Phoenix at the age of ninety-four. Born in Coffeeville, Mississippi, she came, when a young girl, to Arizona with her father, the Rev. W. J. Melton, a Baptist missionary. Ten years after Tom Graham's death she married an Englishman named Hagan, and they moved to California.

Estella Graham, the daughter of Tom Graham, who became Mrs. Estella Converse and then Mrs. Hill, moved to Phoenix after her second marriage, and about 1953 her mother returned to Arizona to make her home with her daughter, where she died. She was buried in Whittier, California.

What is probably the final chapter in the saga of Edwin Tewksbury and the Pleasant Valley War was written November 26, 1962, when his widow, Mrs. Braulia Rivera Tewksbury, died in the Gila General Hospital at the age of ninety-two. Funeral services were held at the Walker Mortuary at Globe. She was buried beside her husband whom she had survived for fifty-eight years, and she had outlived all of her family.

She was born in 1869 at Tehachapi, California, and married Edwin Tewksbury on March 18, 1897, at Dudleyville, near Globe. Three sons and one daughter were born to this union. James and George died more than twenty years before their mother. Edwin F. was accidentally killed September 18, 1956, in Cherry Creek, near the Andy Gump mine where he worked. While he was bathing he slipped and his head struck a rock. The death of Ella Elvira, the daughter, in 1961, has already been described.

After Ed Tewksbury's death the people of Globe held a community dance, and they turned the proceeds over to his widow and four children. Perhaps people today may think it strange that a dance would be held to raise money for this purpose; but Arizona was still the frontier in 1904, and the pioneers frequently held a dance to raise money for some worthy cause—for a church, a school, and, in one case I remember, to secure funds to build a fence around the village graveyard. A dance was just about the only means they had of raising money.

I wish to thank Jess G. Hayes, Mrs. Nora McKinney, and Mrs. Sara S. Gregory, widow of my old friend Leslie E. Gregory, all of Globe, and W. R. Ridgway, of Safford, for furnishing me with the information on these deaths that mark the end of an historic era in Old Arizona.

INDEX

Adamson, J. Q., on coroner's jury, 126
Ames, F. A., 293; letter to Stott's parents describing lynching of Stott, Scott, and Wilson, 205; meets Stott, 208; gives account of Stott's life in Arizona, 208-10; places blame for lynching on Houck, 209-11; did not know third man, 213
A One (A 1 Bar) Outfit. *See* Arizona Cattle Co.
Apache Indians, menace of, 24, 25; White Mountain reservation, 27, 38; war party at Middleton ranch after fight, 71-72, 73-75; attack Middleton's ranch, 74; defeat Carr at battle of Cibicu, 74; Perkins' store erected as fort during Apache wars, 147; Geronimo's surrender, 186
"Apache Kid," Sheriff Glenn Reynolds killed by, 187; n. 5, 340; reported killed by Jack Clark, n. 5, 340; Horace Philly killed by, 269
Apocada, Miguel, arrest of, 85, 150, 153; release of, 152, 170, n. 6, 339
Arizona Cattle Co. (A One Outfit), 48; history of, n. 3, 326
Arizona Daily Gazette, The, of Phoenix, account of hearing of John Rhodes, 249, 254
Arizona Rangers, Burton C. Mossman captain of, 295
Arizona Silver Belt, The, of Globe, 87; account of fight at Tewksbury ranch, 103-4, 105; account of killing of John Graham and Charles Blevins, 154
Armbruster blacksmith shop, 114, 121
Aztec Land and Cattle Co. (Hash Knife Outfit), 29; history of, 38-40, 293-95; Hash Knife cowboys in Pleasant Valley war, 37, 55; Hash Knife cowboys search for Mart Blevins, 60; Hash Knife cowboys in fight at Middleton ranch, 60-71; withdrawal from the war, 176; Gov. Talbot interested in, 207; F. A. Ames employed by, 208; new Hash Knife men had no interest in the war, 225; leaders approved action of their men, 225
Aztec Spring, 208

Babbitt Brothers, buy interest in Hash Knife, 295; owners of C O Bar Outfit, n. 3, 327, 329
Babbitt, William, n. 3, 329
Bacon, Billy, narrow escape of, 303-4
Bagley, Marion, 43
Bailey, George, present owner of Stott ranch, 215
Baker, A. C. (attorney), retained by Tom Graham, 160
Barnes, Will C., ranch in Mogollons,

36; denies story of Navajo raid on Blevins' ranch, 58; tells of Hash Knife cowboys who went in search of Mart Blevins, 60; tells of burial of Paine and Blevins, 77; version of raid on Tewksbury camp, 140-43; his story of Tom Graham's arrest at Saint Johns, 170, 171; quotes Phoenix *Herald* on Jim Tewksbury's death, 182; opinion of Tom Horn, 185; lynching of Stott, Scott, and Wilson not connected with feud, 193; version of lynching, 204; error in regard to removal of bodies, 215; quotes stories from newspapers on attempt to shoot John Rhodes, 252; knew Tom Pickett, 291
Bauer, F. C., n. 6, 333
Bear Spring, 36; Stott's ranch at, 195
Bethune, Judge J. D., presided at first trial of Edwin Tewksbury, 262
Big Dry Lake, 60, 67
Billy the Kid, 8, 39, 290-91
Bishop, W. H., settles in Pleasant Valley, 28; charged at Prescott with stealing cattle, 42; widow married Elliott, 179
Blaine, George: settles in Pleasant Valley, 28; charged at Prescott with stealing cattle, 42-43
Blevins, Andy. *See* Cooper, Andy
Blevins, Charles, 37; killing of, 148-49, 153, 317; grave of, 296
Blevins cottage, description of, 113; Owens' fight with Blevins gang at, 115-23, 128-32; still standing, 137
Blevins, Eva (Evelyn), 59, 115, 167; claimed Andy Cooper unarmed, 118, 122
Blevins, Hampton, 37; in search of father, 60; killed at Middleton ranch, 64, 94, 314; funeral of, 77; Tewksburys charged with murder of, 80, 85, 86, 169; grave of, 83, 296
Blevins, John, 37; warned Cooper of Owens arrival, 114; in fight with Owens, 115-18; wounded by Owens, 118, 121, 123, 129, 131, 320; testified at inquest, 125; trial of, 125-26; never served term, 126-28; "last man" of three families in war, 284; later life of, 285
Blevins, Mart, settles in Pleasant Valley, 28; disappearance of, 37, 57-59; 87, 94, 314; known as "Old Man" Blevins, 38, reported alive, 140; skeleton at Houdon's and skull on Cherry Creek, 292
Blevins, Mary, widow of Mart Blevins, 115, 118; claimed Andy Cooper unarmed, 118; her son died in her arms, 120; testified at inquest, 125
Blevins, Mesa, 167

INDEX

383

Ruiz, Alfred, clerk of courts at Saint Johns, 43; story of George Graham's arrest and release at Saint Johns, 171-74

Saint Johns, Grahams charged with stealing cattle, 42-45; account of fight at Middleton ranch in Saint Johns *Herald*, 69-71; record of Andy Cooper inquest unearthed at, 112, 124-25; trial of John Blevins at, 125-26; Grahams arrested at, 170; Graham and Tewksbury forces gather at, 170-74; James Tewksbury indicted at, 172

Saint Joseph, headquarters of Hash Knife, 293

San Carlos, Underwood's wound treated at, 142-43

Santa Fe (N. M.), Tom Tucker at, 287; Billy the Kid in jail at, 290

Satterwhite, Thomas D. (attorney), defended Edwin Tewksbury, 263

Saunders, David O., manager of Bank of Arizona, 278

Scarlett, John, deputy with McKinney, 145

Scott, James (Jim), 36; Hash Knife cowboy, 198; lynching of, 179, 193-219, 312, 319; grave of, 201, 205, 215, 218, 297; body not removed, 205, 215, 218; Burt's version of lynching, 205-15; Ames placed blame for lynching on Houck, 209-10

Scott, Robert, tells of Tom Horn's visit to Pleasant Valley and meeting him there later, 189-90

Second invasion of Pleasant Valley by Mulvenon, 106, 144-54

Sieber, Al (scout), 185; discovery of Jerome copper mine, n. 1, 349

Shultes, Lydia Crigler, n. 7 and 8, 322; second wife of John D. Tewksbury, Sr., 31

Sigsby, Robert, Tucker reaches cabin of, 66

Silver Belt, The, of Globe, notes Underwood's return from San Carlos, 143, n. 4, 338

Simpson, E. I., Hash Knife cowboy, 293

Simpson, J. E., Hash Knife foreman, 38

Skeleton, at Houdon's ranch, 292; believed to be Mart Blevins, 59

Skull, found on Cherry Creek, 292; at Houdon's ranch, 293

Sloan, Judge Richard E., second trial of Edwin Tewksbury before, 266

Smith, claimed to be son of James Tewksbury, 183

Smith, George, Hash Knife cowboy, 39, 293, 294

Smith, Lot, n. 3, 328, 329

Snowflake, Stinson's ranch at, 32

Sombrero Butte, 75

Southard, R. D., teller of Bank of Arizona, 278

Spring Creek crossing, 35

Star, The, of Tucson, account of Ed Tewksbury's arrival at Tucson, 244; account of John Rhodes' discharge, 253; editorial on John Rhodes' discharge, 255

Stencel, A. J., corroborated Edwin Tewksbury's alibi, 264

Stinson, James (Jim), n. 5, 330; settles in Pleasant Valley, 28, 32; employed the Grahams, 34, 45; story that he started the trouble an error, 40; his theory of cause of feud, 41; Tewksburys and other acquitted of stealing cattle from, 43; John Gilliland, range foreman for, 47; later life of, 295; not involved in the war, n. 15, 323

Stott, James, 205; sent money to son, 210; went to Arizona after son's murder, 214, n. 16, 343; sketch of, n. 10, 343

Stott, James W., n. 3, 342; lynching of, 179, 193-219, 312, 319; grave of, 201, 205, 214, 218, 297; body not removed, 205, 215, 218; Burt's version of lynching, 206-16; early life of, 206-8; in Texas, 207; in Arizona, 36, 208-11; murder was result of plan, 209; visited by mother and a sister, 211; Ames placed blame for lynching on Houck, 211-12; ranch now owned by George Bailey, 215; graves opened in 1942, 218

Sullivan, S. J., deputy on second invasion, 145

Styles, Barney, buys interest in Hash Knife, 295

Tackett, E. M., deputy on second invasion, 145

Taylor, Anna Burt, recollections of lynching of Stott, n. 16, 343

Tempe, Tom Graham and Anne Melton married at, 158; Tom Graham settles at, 229; drives cattle to, 233; P. P. and A. A. Daggs go to, 237-38; public sentiment over Tom Graham's murder, 243, 244, 245, 247; attempt to lynch Rhodes, 243, 244, 247; Justice Huson condemned at mass meeting, 256, 262; Edwin Tewksbury seen in, 260; James Stinson settles at, 296-97

Tewksbury brothers, not from Texas, 29; expert shots, 33, 50; charged with stealing cattle, 42; employed by Stinson, 45; Daggs Brothers make agreement for them to drive sheep into Pleasant Valley, 49; besieged in mountain stronghold, 77-79; refuse to surrender unless Grahams are arrested, 84-85;

320 ; found by Mulvenon at Graham ranch, 150

United Verde Copper Co., leased and developed by Senator Clark, 275 ; Jim Roberts a special officer for, 277 ; organization of, n. 1, 349

Unknown cowboy killed, 79, 312, 314 ; unknown men killed, six, 179, 318

Verdict against Edwin Tewksbury for murder, 265

Victims of the feud, five buried on Graham Ranch, 26

Vinal, ———, surveyor for Hash Knife, 293

Vogt, Evon Z., n. 23, 324

Vosberg, J. J. Newton's partner, 36, 59, 63, 220

Wagner, George, settles in Pleasant Valley, 29 ; charged with murder of Blevins, 86 ; arrested by Mulvenon, 151, 152 ; indicted at Prescott, 169 ; case dismissed, 170

Wallace, Lew (governor of N. M.), unable to stop Lincoln County war, 290

Warren, Hash Knife cowboy, 293

Watson, Dr. F. P., believed Anne Graham's photograph was Kittie McCarthy, 300, n. 4, 352

Wattron, Frank, helped elect Owens sheriff, 110 ; Cooper tells him he will never surrender, 113 ; testimony at inquest, 121, 124 ; corner Houck, 203

Weatherford, John W. (deputy sheriff), n. 3, 333 ; joins Mulvenon's posse for first invasion, 80 ; informs author of Tewksbury's agreement with Mulvenon on first invasion, 84 ; reported killed, 87 ; heard that hogs did eat bodies of John Tewksbury and William Jacobs, n. 3, 336

Wharton, Harry L. (justice of the peace), held Edwin Tewksbury for trial, 260

White, W. J., testified against Edwin Tewksbury, 260

Wilford, deserted on account of the feud, 212

Williams, M. H. (attorney), prosecuted Edwin Tewksbury, 263

Wilson, Billy, a wandering prospector, 197 ; lynching of, 179, 193-219, 312, 319 ; grave of, 201, 297 ; Burt's version of lynching of, 205-14 ; Ames placed blame for lynching on Houck, 211-12

Wilson, Billy, Hash Knife cowboy, 293

Wilson, George, owner of Middleton ranch, 37

Wilson, George F., n. 11, 322

Wilson, J. H., on coroner's jury, 125

Wilson ranch, Ed Tewksbury arrested at, 242-43, 244

Wright, Judge James H., trial of John Blevins before, 125-26

Wyrick, Charles, buys interest in Hash Knife, 295

Yaney, W. P., foreman of coroner's jury, 125

Young, John W., founder of Arizona Cattle Co., n. 3, 326

Young, Ola (Miss), states that no fight took place at Graham ranch, 180 ; her memories of Tom Graham, 229 ; present owner of Graham ranch, 298, n. 10, 322 ; her store and post office, 298, 308

Young ranch : postoffice at, 298 ; mail carried from Globe to, 308

Young, S. W.: takes Tom Graham's cattle on shares, 229 ; Graham's cattle increased, 231 ; helped Tom Graham gather his cattle, 232 ; father of Ola Young, 298

Yuma, John Blevins sentenced to penitentiary, but did not serve, 126 ; Finn Clanton sentenced to penitentiary at, 136

Zulick, Gov. C. Meyer, decides that sheriff must sweep through Pleasant Valley, 144